Queering Digital India

Technicities

Published
Lyotard and the Inhuman Condition: Reflections on Nihilism, Information and Art
Ashley Woodward

Critical Luxury Studies: Art, Design, Media
Edited by John Armitage and Joanne Roberts

Cold War Legacies: Systems, Theory, Aesthetics
Edited by John Beck and Ryan Bishop

Fashion and Materialism
Ulrich Lehmann

Queering Digital India: Activisms, Identities, Subjectivities
Edited by Rohit K. Dasgupta and Debanuj DasGupta

Forthcoming
Zero Degree Seeing: Barthes/Burgin and Political Aesthetics
Edited by Ryan Bishop and Sunil Manghani

www.edinburghuniversitypress.com/series/tech

Queering Digital India

Activisms, Identities, Subjectivities

Edited by Rohit K. Dasgupta and
Debanuj DasGupta

EDINBURGH
University Press

Edinburgh University Press is one of the leading university presses in the UK. We publish academic books and journals in our selected subject areas across the humanities and social sciences, combining cutting-edge scholarship with high editorial and production values to produce academic works of lasting importance. For more information visit our website: edinburghuniversitypress.com

Edinburgh University Press Ltd
The Tun – Holyrood Road
12 (2f) Jackson's Entry
Edinburgh EH8 8PJ

First published in hardback by Edinburgh University Press 2018

Typeset in 11/13 Adobe Sabon by
IDSUK (DataConnection) Ltd, and
printed and bound by CPI Group (UK) Ltd, Croydon, CR0 4YY

A CIP record for this book is available from the British Library

ISBN 978 1 4744 2117 1 (hardback)
ISBN 978 1 4744 5266 3 (paperback)
ISBN 978 1 4744 2118 8 (webready PDF)
ISBN 978 1 4744 2119 5 (epub)

Contents

List of Figures

Series Editors' Preface

Technological transformation has profound and frequently unforeseen influences on art, design and media. At times technology emancipates art and enriches the quality of design. Occasionally it causes acute individual and collective problems of mediated perception. Time after time technological change accomplishes both simultaneously. This new book series explores and reflects philosophically on what new and emerging *technicities* do to our everyday lives and increasingly immaterial technocultural conditions. Moving beyond traditional conceptions of the philosophy of technology and of techne, the series presents new philosophical thinking on how technology constantly alters the essential conditions of beauty, invention and communication. From novel understandings of the world of technicity to new interpretations of aesthetic value, graphics and information, Technicities focuses on the relationships between critical theory and representation, the arts, broadcasting, print, technological genealogies/histories, material culture and digital technologies and our philosophical views of the world of art, design and media.

The series foregrounds contemporary work in art, design and media while remaining inclusive, both in terms of philosophical perspectives on technology and interdisciplinary contributions. For a philosophy of technicities is crucial to extant debates over the artistic, inventive and informational aspects of technology. The books in the Technicities series concentrate on present-day and evolving technological advances but visual, design-led and mass-mediated questions are emphasised to further our knowledge of their often-combined means of digital transformation.

The editors of Technicities welcome proposals for monographs and well-considered edited collections that establish new paths of investigation.

John Armitage, Ryan Bishop and Joanne Roberts

Acknowledgements

The editors are grateful to many people for making this volume happen. We would like to first thank the series editors, Professor Joanne Roberts, Professor John Armitage and Professor Ryan Bishop, for commissioning this volume. We are grateful to the three anonymous peer reviewers whose comments and feedback have made this a much stronger volume. Some of the conversations and discussion which led to the creation of this volume started at the 3rd European Geographies of Sexualities Conference in Rome where we suggested a panel on 'Queering Digital India'. Thanks to the organisers (especially Cesare di Feliciantonio), participants and audience (especially Dr Gavin Brown and Dr Shaka McGlotten) for their thought provoking response and feedback.

We are grateful to several friends who have influenced, read sections of the draft and encouraged us to work on this volume and in this area (in no particular order): Tim Aldcroft, Radhika Gajjala, Paul Boyce, Aniruddha Dutta, Sharif Mowlabocus, Ruth Vanita, Niharika Banerjea, Rahul Rao, Jussi Parikka, Ed D'Souza, K. Moti Gokulsing, Kaustav Bakshi, Christopher Pullen, Sayantan Dasgupta, Sunil Gupta, Sara Davidmann, William Raban, Toby Miller, Sunil Gupta, Pawan Dhall, Anindya Hajra, Minakshi Sanyal, Subhagata Ghosh, Raina Roy, Deep Purkayastha, Basudeb Roy, Mejbul Haque, Subesh Poddar, Caroline Osella, Silvia Posocco, Bill Grantham, Graham Murdock, Anamaria Tamayo-Duque, Jo Tacchi, Seth Giddings, Daniel Ashton, Mary Thomas, Shannon Winnubst, Lynn Itagaki, Jennifer Suchland, Hugh Urban, Ken Foote, Manisha Desai, Kaciano Gadelha, Robert Kulpa, Ece Algan, Burce Celik, Shinjoung Yeo, Shamira Meghani, Kathe Browne, Leela Bakshi, Ila Nagar, Jaime Grant, Lipi Begum, Reina Lewis, Rittika Dasgupta, Jack Harrison Quintana, Bishnupriya Ghosh and Sri-Devi Thakillapati. We also remember the inimitable Agniva in our fond memories, who passed away while this book was in production. Sunil Gupta deserves a special mention for his photograph which has become our cover image. The image captures the changing tensions between the analogue past and the digital future of India. Sunil needs no introduction as a globally recognised South Asian queer artist but he is also a friend, ally and teacher.

The authors would also like to thank Cathy Sclund-Vials, Director of the Asian & Asian American Studies Institute at the University of Connecticut for generously providing us with a faculty research grant in order to support the indexing costs during the final production of this book. Rohit would also like to thank the Wellcome Trust (Grant number: 201329/Z/16/Z) for providing funding to carry out some of the research in this book.

We thank the EUP team, especially Ersev and Carol, for all their hard work on this volume. Finally, we would like to thank our respective institutions and colleagues for their support and understanding while we were working on this volume and our families both the chosen and the biological across the world who have nurtured and supported us through this and many other of our projects.

Chapter 1

Introduction: Queering Digital India

Rohit K. Dasgupta and Debanuj DasGupta

This book emerges out of the need for understanding the entanglements between digital technologies, nationalism, neoliberalism and sexual subjectivities in India. The present political conjuncture in India is marked by rise of the Hindu nationalist Bharatiya Janata Party (BJP). The economic policies of liberalisation, the welcoming of global capital and the establishment of technological hubs are interlaced with the promotion of an overtly Hindu, heterosexual, family-oriented vision of India. We will situate the emergence of digital technologies within this emergence of neoliberalisation, nationalistic visions of a digitally productive India and question how diverse Lesbian, Gay, Bisexual, Transgender, Koti, Hijra, Queer (LGBTKHQ) communities navigate the digital/national assemblage. In a word, the book is concerned with how a desire for an economically productive, Hindu India and desire for LGBTKHQ recognition inform each other. Queering is considered as a form of questioning dominant power-knowledge formations that work to construct normative ideas of gender, reproduction and the family. Recent scholars in queer theory have argued that queering (especially in the context of Asia), requires a geopolitical interrogation of the 'impersonal, structural, and systemic workings of power' (Liu 2015: 7). We take on diverse strands of queer theory in order to name the ways neoliberalism, nationalism, digital technologies and movements for queer rights converge with each other within present-day India. In this introduction, we will present key theoretical constructs that are being mobilised throughout the book by different authors. Our hope is to present a broad theoretical rubric for our readers, or a suggested road map for understanding how we approach sexuality politics, neoliberalism, Hindu nationalism and queer community formation in and through digital technologies. Queer signifies diverse kinds of desiring bodies, and regimes of truth that render certain kinds of desires as legible to the law, while some others as illegal or dangerous. Digital in this context indicates the various media networks through which desire circulates and takes on multiple meanings. Simultaneously, digital signifies the dominant desire (or a map) of the contested nation. Our introduction can be read as a genealogy of multiple desires, regimes of truth and how their emergence encodes itself in historically specific moments in India. After all, a truly specific understanding of bodies and desires require an understanding of the 'context of the interrelationship between historically specific bodies' (Butler 1987: 238).

The introduction is divided into five major sections in order to present the broad architecture of the edited collection. First, we present what we mean by sexuality politics and enumerate how sexuality is a form of truth-telling regime and biopolitical ordering of bodies. Secondly, we turn to discussing our notions about neoliberalism in India, one marked by the intensification of neoliberal rationalities in multiple domains of social relations including measures such as demonetisation, the push for a paperless economy, and intense political debates over the rights of diverse sexual minority communities. The idea of digital India is also deeply connected with neoliberal Indian nationalism, exemplified in government initiatives such as *India Shining* and *Digital India*. These two governmental guiding principles about a modern Indian nation exemplify the nation's desire for becoming a major player in the global economy. Glib marketing projects related to *India Shining* and *Digital India* signify a map of India that is territorially bound, yet offering flexible borders for the movement of (digital) capital. The idea that Bangalore (Bengaluru) is the Silicon Valley of India and cities such as Hyderabad, New Delhi and Gurgaon are connected with the global circulation of technological capital puts the 'digital' firmly at the centre of what we now imagine as the modern Indian nation state (see also Oza 2006; Legg and Roy 2013). If digital technologies remain inextricably linked to the imaginary of a modern Indian nation-state, then what kinds of sexual-national-digital formations are engendered through demands for state recognition launched by diverse sexual minorities? Who gets to be a part of digital India? What kinds of desires are legitimated through multiple digital formations? And how is the idea of India mapped in and through digital platforms?

In the third section, we outline what we mean by queer desires and how they play in and through digital space. We argue queerness (and queering) is a kind of optics through which certain kinds of transgressive desires are brought within the folds of *Digital*

India, while many others are relegated as dangerous and excluded from the gates of the Indian nation-state. Throughout the book we will present different apparatuses of power that seek to inform and regulate digital spaces and the use of digital technologies in order to discipline transgressive desires. What then are transgressive desires within the present Indian context? We argue that merely identifying oneself as LGBTKHQ does not constitute a transgression in the context of digital India. Multiple kinds of bodies, whose desire does not conform to the national normative desire of a digitally productive Hindu nation-state are rendered abject, and violently relegated to a slow death within present day India. Queering digital India requires interrogating apparatuses of power such as policing online hook-up sites, shutting down the Facebook accounts of Kashmiri activists, and how linguistic, regional and class divisions create contested maps of India on digital spaces. The juridical struggles related to the removal of anti-sodomy provisions in the Indian Penal Code as well as the rights of transgender persons are sites for the juridico-political construction of the rights-bearing homosexual and transgender subject. The rights-bearing homosexual and transgender citizen-subject comes to signify the normative move within present-day sexuality politics in India. The desire for state recognition for queer persons in India remains inextricably intertwined with the neoliberalisation of the Indian economy. The shift from a Nehruvian welfarist state toward an entrepreneurial state (exemplified through ideas such as *India Shining* and *Digital India*) reflects how the relationship between the state and individual has shifted in present-day India (also see Leitner et al. 2007). The good Indian citizen is a consumer citizen, one who is dividend earning and capable of furthering their own economic interest (Nagar and Dasgupta 2015). Many of the authors in this collection suggest that we need to situate the demand for state recognition of sexual minorities within this neoliberalising moment in India. In this section we will highlight how the idea of an economic man remains embedded within sexuality politics in India. Situating the juridico-political activism related to LGBTKHQ rights (Dasgupta 2015, 2017) within the desire to become a digitally productive entrepreneurial nation-state allows us to read how certain kinds of transgressive desires are being accommodated within neoliberal India. We will discuss how Hindu religious imaginaries and ideas about the economic man remain intertwined with the Supreme Court judgement related to the Section 377 and transgender rights in order to map out the move toward normative (Indian) society within certain sections of the LGBTKHQ community.

Our introduction suggests two ways of thinking about queering digital India: (1) queer as diverse forms of sex-gender presentations and how such presentations are sedimented as LGBTKHQ identities within digital spaces; (2) queering as a form of figuration through which certain non-normative bodies are being folded within the nation-state while many others are being relegated as failures, threatening to the nation-state and left to die (both real death and social death). We hope that an elaboration of the three broad concepts – (1) neoliberal-digital India; (2) queer identities and the formation of digital queer spaces; and (3) queer normativity and the formation of monstrous queer bodies – will help our readers situate the broad architecture of the book, and how each author plays with these concepts within their disciplinary frameworks and arguments.

In the fourth section we elaborate the three theoretical traditions that frame the choice of chapters, the major arguments and the broad theoretical contribution that our book wishes to fulfil. We discuss how French continental philosophy, postcolonial theory and Queer of Colour theory provide the bulwark of the book. Finally, we will provide a road map of the different chapters, and highlight how each chapter takes up questions of neoliberal nationalism, queer subjectivities, regulation of bodies and pleasures, and the potentials for undercutting neoliberal regulation and the disciplining of bodies. Thus the introduction is organized as a way of mapping the major concepts, theoretical traditions and chapter organisation for our readers. Let us now turn toward what we mean by queer(ing) and sexuality politics in the context of present-day India.

Sexuality as Operations of Biopower

Substantively speaking the book offers two major ways of conceiving queer and queering: first as a set of identificatory regimes through which certain kinds of non-heteronormative identities are sedimented into what gets broadly termed as LGBTKHQ identities in India; secondly, the book elaborates queering as technologies of power through which certain bodies are marked worthy of life and certain bodies are relegated to death within Indian neoliberalism. In doing so, the book doesn't intend to set up a binary between life and death. Instead, we situate the operations of multiple apparatuses of power that place bodies on a continuum between life and death. Sexuality is defined as the lynchpin for the operations of power through which bodies are remade as subjects of life within Indian neoliberal modernity. We will approach sexuality at the intersection of body, population and enterprise.

Following Michel Foucault, we argue that sexuality is an apparatus of biopower through which power is effected over life and death (Foucault 2003). In his *History of Sexuality Vol. I*, Foucault argues biopower as a modality for the governance of bodies based on their sexual behaviour and reproductive capacity. This form of governance produces population categories such as those at high-risk for HIV/ AIDS or those as infertile, impacting population growth and public health negatively. The operations of biopower seek to categorise human beings into a global mass based on vital bodily functions. Sexuality therefore is a dense point of exchange of power through which certain bodies emerge as worthy of rights while others are produced as dangerous contagions that need regulation and discipline. Foucault traces the emergence of biopower as a newer form of power, distinct from sovereign power during the eighteenth and nineteenth centuries. Biopower is interested in managing life and death globally. Building on Foucault's work recent scholars have developed ways of thinking how life is now contingent upon scientific discoveries such as HIV medications, vaccines and treatments for emerging diseases (Dasgupta and Dhall 2017; Sunder Rajan 2006). These scientific breakthroughs seek to enhance life, while certain kinds of bodies are marked as risky, dangerous and therefore sought for systematic regulation or death. We do not suggest that life and death operates as an agonistic binary within biopolitical operations, rather we are arguing that the in-between zones between life and death is rife with potentials for new kinds of social projects (see the chapters by DasGupta and Malik, as well as Rai's responses in the roundtable). Scholars such as Elizabeth Povinelli enumerate that bodies are not merely subjected to death (real or social), but rather are fretted out as 'failures' and abandoned within neoliberal notions of success and enterprise (Povinelli 2011). Thus throughout the book we have highlighted the works of authors who interrogate how different apparatuses of (sexual) regulation, discipline and violent killing are constitutive of the Indian nation-state. We have highlighted authors who interrogate how sexuality rights-based activism is formulated in and through digital spaces. In doing so, this book argues that both sovereign power (one that is based on juridical power, territoriality and ideas of autonomy) and biopower are parallel projects that work to construct a dominant form of Indian (sexual) nationalism. As mentioned in the beginning of the introduction, we situate the biopolitical as well as sovereign apparatuses for regulating sexual desire within the rise of Indian neoliberalism. In the following section we suggest that tracing the liberalisation of India and the development of ideas related to digital entrepreneurship need to be conducted through a longer genealogy of neoliberalism in India.

The (New) Neoliberal Digital India

Since the late 1980s the Indian economy has undergone liberalisation and focused on creating a public culture of consumption-based modernity (Ganguly-Scrase and Scrase 2009; Grewal 2005; Oza 2006; Legg and Roy 2013). The movement of Indian workers trained in information technology to information sector hubs such as the Silicon Valley in the US, London and Germany followed by the growth of digital sector hubs in India has enabled the sedimentation of digital capital in India (Ninan Thomas 2012). India remains the leader in software development and client services for the global IT sector, whereas China has emerged as a nodal point in hardware manufacturing. These regional divisions inform how different Indian government(s) over the past three decades have pursued different policies to attract digital capital to India. In this section we will highlight two major representations of modern India that seek to highlight the digital capacities of the Indian people. *India Shining*, launched between 2003 and 2004 by Atal Bihari Vajpayee, the then prime minister of India, sought to highlight the new economic optimism of India while *Digital India*, the latest governmental initiative related to modern India, was launched by the current prime minister Narendra Modi in 2015. 'Digital India' reconnects India with global hubs of technological capital such as the Silicon Valley and represents how the idea of digital excellence and digital literacy remains central to the imagination of modern India. Indeed, to be a good Indian citizen today means finding one's face reflected through the memes of digital India. Changing one's Facebook profile picture to that of one's face at the centre of the *Digital India* frame comes to signify how citizenship, nationalism and digital technology comes together to form a provisional assemblage represented through *Digital India*. Assembling digital India requires an understanding of how carnal and capital constitutes a specific spatio-temporal formation that sets multiple kinds of desires at a rhizomatic scale on digital space.

The concept of *India Shining* as a glib marketing programme launched in 2004 came on the heels of the genocide in Gujarat (2002) and the upcoming parliamentary elections. This came to signify a new India, one that was the leader in medical and information technology-related research. The marketing programme and the desire of becoming a global centre for the purveying of digital capital is not a new nation-building project. Projects such as *Mera Bharat Mahan* ('My India Is Great') was popularised by Rajiv Gandhi when he was prime minister between 1984 and 1989. His *Mera Bharat Mahan* represents two crucial breaks from Nehru's India; firstly, Rajiv Gandhi's era marks the liberalisation of the Indian economy (Oza 2006), and secondly, Rajiv Gandhi stressed the need for developing India as a leader in science and technology (especially biotechnology). The move to remove trade barriers and producing consumer goods along with the need for biotech innovation is syncretic to what scholars such as Kaushik Sunder Rajan term as 'biocapital' (Sunder Rajan 2006). Sunder Rajan's multi-sited ethnography in the San Francisco Bay area and New Delhi suggests that the global flow of biotechnological innovation is deeply connected with neoliberal entrepreneurship. Rajiv Gandhi's *Mera Bharat Mahan* pre-dates the period that was studied by Sunder Rajan. However, we argue that Rajiv Gandhi's *Mera Bharat Mahan* is a precursor of what Sunder Rajan calls 'technoscientific capitalism' (Sunder Rajan 2006: 114). Sunder Rajan argues that scientific innovation in the life sciences is seen as an excessive kind of value and ushers in a different kind of capitalism, one that is hyped to be providing unimaginable discoveries related to genomic structures, life-saving medications and breakthroughs in treating life-threatening diseases. Returning to Rajiv Gandhi's vision for a new India, one needs to remember that in 1986 Gandhi established the first Department of Biotechnology (DBT) as a part of the Ministry of Science and Technology. The opening of the DBT suggests that the desire of *Mera Bharat Mahan* ('My India Is Great') was to become a new technologically savvy India, one that broke from India as the land of ancient civilisations and spectacular architectures. *India Shining* continues this desire for a tech savvy India.

The image of *India Shining* (Figure 1.1) conjures a map of India that includes the disputed territories of Kashmir and North-Eastern states. This territorially bound India is open for foreign capital and is evidently tech savvy, exemplified by the capacity of Indians to work in medical and technological innovation. *India Shining* was highly contested in the general elections by the opposition, and as the Congress-led government came to power, the concept was replaced by *Bharat Nirman* ('Constructing India'). However, the idea of excellence in digital literacies, developing centres of excellence in IT education remained central to *Bharat Nirman*. While the *India Shining* campaign died out after the defeat of the Vajpayee-led BJP government in 2004, the idea continues to exist (digitally) as a Facebook page. The *India Shining* Facebook page showcases India's many technological innovations, patriotic songs and most notably updates about border security issues related to the disputed territory of Kashmir. One of the recent posts on the *India Shining* Facebook page includes a YouTube video link to a warning poem by an Indian soldier. The soldier warns Pakistan that Indian soldiers

Figure 1.1 *India Shining*

are not afraid of atomic wars, and throughout the poem the soldier is joined by other soldiers, and together they recite in chorus, 'Kashmir might happen, but Pakistan will not remain.' This post about the contested space of Kashmir between India and Pakistan on the *India Shining* Facebook page signifies how territoriality, technology and capital remains intertwined with ideas about digital India. The digitally excellent India requires spatial security from the risks of terrorist attacks. The new neoliberal (digital) India can flourish only when its borders are secured. In this way, territory-capital-digital remain inextricably intertwined with the desire for a new productive India. Digital technologies are not only effective tools for the Indian economy, bt rather are constitutive of the imagined neoliberal Indian nation-state.

The desire for a new digital India has been growing virally and taking on multiple formations. In July 2015 Prime Minister Narendra

Modi met with the owner of Facebook, Mark Zuckerberg, and spoke at a dinner addressing Indian IT sector leaders in the Silicon Valley which led to their formation of this campaign. *Digital India* seeks to connect rural India to high speed internet. Further, mobile applications such as e-Hospital and the e-Sign Framework promise to allow Indian citizens to register, sign and pay for hospitals and other important services through phone-based apps. *Digital India* not only promises access to high-speed broadband but rather is also an indication of India's leadership potential in technocapitalism. Mark Zuckerberg changed his profile picture on Facebook (Figure 1.2) to show his support for *Digital India*. The changing of the profile picture in support of *Digital India* circulated virally. Many Indians around the world changed their profile pictures in order to display their support for *Digital India*. Adopting the icon of *Digital India* to display one's face on Facebook comes to suggest how this idea takes hold on digital platforms, and gathers speed through viral diffusion. Indeed, showing one's face via the icon comes to exemplify the good Indian citizen, one who wishes to be a part of the modern Indian nation. The imagined digital India is discursively created and virally circulated on digital spaces. The digital, the digital platform and digital capital come to represent a new Indian map, one that is territorialised through the tri-colour of the Indian flag, but connected through a capillary-like (digital) network. You can be an

Figure 1.2 Zuckerberg and Modi change their Facebook profile pictures to support the *Digital India* campaign

Indian anywhere in the world yet remain connected via Facebook (and other social networks) to each other. *Digital India* comes to suggest a de-territorialised map of India (unlike the territorially bound map of *India Shining*), one that is multi-sited, multi-pronged and yet tethered through nodes, hubs and e-apps. Digital India is a provisional shape -shifting assemblage of neoliberal capital, desire for bio and technological excellence and digital nationalisms. Understanding how queer subjects navigate digital (Indian) space requires rethinking a territorially bound India, as an unbounded, virally circulating desire for capital-technology-nation(alism). In the next section, we outline how queer (and queering) is understood in the context of neoliberal digital India.

Another way of thinking about queer digital India leads us to understand how digital spaces are made and re-made through LGBTKHQ activism and desires. As some of our authors have argued, queer people in India, as in other parts of the world, are creating spaces and 'communities' using digital and social media. Many members of the LGBTKHQ community navigate their daily existence through their everyday interaction and presence on these sites (see the chapters by Rohit DasGupta, Khubchandani and Krishnan). Queer online spaces in India can be mapped as a vast terrain of digital sites that range from gay blogs (Gajjala and Mitra 2008), to listservs created specifically for queer people (Roy 2003) to social networking sites such as PlanetRomeo and more generic social networking spaces such as Facebook. Since 2010 with the proliferation of smart phones and mobile technology queer locative applications such as Grindr have also become popular, especially in the metropolitan cities such as Bangalore, Delhi, Mumbai and Kolkata, for those who can afford such hardware and data connection. Scholarly material focused on digital culture and queer identity in India is scant and at this time we have found only a handful of sources who have written on them, Roy's (2003) work on South Asian queer lists and queer websites in the 1990s being one of the earliest examples. Gajjala and Mitra (2008) and Mitra (2010) have undertaken research into queer Indian blogging, and finally Shahani (2008) has published an ethnographic study on the GayBombay community. It is important to comment that most of these sites are North American and European in origin. Our research indicates that Grindr was started by an Israeli entrepreneur residing in the US and is now a global phenomenon. Grindr has now initiated a global LGBT human rights project online titled 'Grindr for Equality'. These formations take on local meanings within a global virtual network. While power inequalities such as ownership and management concentrated in North America mark digital spaces, we engage with digital technologies and platforms not as a monolithic terrain but rather as a vast landscape of multiple power relations and contestations.

While selecting submissions for the book, we wanted to highlight the utopian potentials of digital spaces providing safe community spaces for LGBTKHQ communities in India as well as gesturing toward the regional, ethnic, religious, class and linguistic conflicts that inform the formation of queer digital communities. In doing so, we agree with Rheingold, Swiss and Hermann who argue that digital spaces hold the potential for bringing in virtual communities. However, as the chapters by Rohit DasGupta, Singh and Nagar will suggest, the formation of virtual communities is marked by exclusions and contestations. Such a layered conceptualisation of digital spaces resonates with the works of Gajjala, Rybas and Altman (2008), who suggest that digital space is not 'a' place, but rather a locus around which modes of social interaction, commercial interests and other discursive and imaginative practices coalesce.

Thus as we (dis)assemble Queer digital India, we knit together a range of scholarship that addresses how queer bodies and desires rhizomatically circulate through digital spaces in order to affect multiple digital-capital-carnal formations. Any discussion on digital queer spaces in India also needs to be contextualised and understood through its complex entanglement with nationalism and even a form of digital nationalism (see Kuntsman 2008). Scholars such as Puar (2005, 2013) have argued that there needs to be a shift from thinking about queer as an identity to queering as an optics through which certain transgressive bodies are folded into the life of the nation, while many others are created as bodies marked for death. In the next section we discuss these entanglements and proffer new ways of thinking about queerness.

LGBTKHQ Normativity and Monstrous Queers

We situate the proliferation of digital technologies within a multiplicity of sexual cultures in India. We argue that the Supreme Court judgements and the antecedent mobilisation of LGBTKHQ activists demanding inclusion within the nation is a slow move toward national normativity. The BJP and its ideological front RSS has made statements against Section 377, and yet strangely accommodates Hijra and transgender bodies through claims to Hindu mythology (the Supreme Court judgement related to transgender and gender identity refers to Hijras and transgender existence in ancient India by mentioning Hindu mythologies, as well as Islamic cultural practices). This is truly a queer conjuncture. The chapters in this book seek to disentangle these multiple assemblages as they relate to digital platforms. Queering within this context is referred to as a modality through which certain bodies are now emerging as sexual monsters as opposed to the good rights-bearing sexual subject (Banerjea and Dasgupta 2013; Nagar and Dasgupta 2015; Dasgupta and DasGupta forthcoming). The movement for Kashmiriyat, policing of online sexual spaces, and the bodies of young men who are marked as gendered failures and potential rapists, are arguably queer figurations. This book challenges conceptualising sexual rights activism and its very hopeful glorification of digital spaces as sites for liberatory mobilisation.

The creative navigation of digital spaces by LGBTKHQ activists is not merely some kind of pure transgressive desire that stands in opposition to ideas of digital India, but rather as many of our authors suggest, LGBTKHQ online (as well as offline) activism represents a slow move toward normative *Digital India*. LGBTKHQ online formations are complex contested sites. The figure of Laxmi Naryan Tripathi, founder of the first *Hijra Akhara* (Hijra Hindu collective) next to the iconic *Ganga Arati* ritual at Varanasi on the steps of *Dashashwamedh Ghat* has been circulating throughout diverse digital platforms. In the image, Tripathi stands on the steps of this historic Ghat in Varanasi and announces that if Hijras are given a chance by the Indian government, they would help eliminate Pakistan from the world map. Tripathi's call to removing Pakistan from the map of the world is very similar to that of the soldier we discussed earlier in this introduction. In this sense everyone in (digital) India is engaged in a constant war against Pakistan. In the image Tripathi's location is the iconic Hindu city of Varanasi. Tripathi's facial makeup, golden saree and huge *Sindoor Tilak* (red vermilion marking on the forehead) suggest an excessive desire. The spatiality of her excessive desire for a Hindu nation cannot be contained territorially, but rather takes on a deterritorialised proportion through the viral circulation of her image. Prime Minister Narendra Modi fought the parliamentary elections from Varanasi. Soon after his victory, he launched the *Swaccha Bharat* (#MyCleanIndia) project by cleaning the ghats of Varanasi. The image of Narendra Modi sweeping Jaggannath Gali near Assi Ghat (one of the famous ghats of Varanasi) circulated throughout different digital platforms. The image of Laxmi Narayan Tripathi at the steps of Varanasi comes very close to the desire for a clean and productive India, one that stands in opposition to the nation of Pakistan. These images are exemplary of how some LGBTKHQ bodies are being folded into the new nationalist neoliberal India, whereas certain bodies and certain kinds of sexual behaviours are relegated as dangerous (see also Shah 2014). We map how LGBTKHQ activism for legal recognition hinges around aligning LGBTKHQ formations alongside ideas of a shining, new, clean, Hindu (digital) India. Thus we present queer India as an assemblage of multiple bodies, desires and sensations.

We argue that queering digital India requires disentangling how Hindu nationalism, ideas about economic productivity and visions of a new global India remain entrenched in LGBTKHQ digital activisms (also see Anand 2007, 2011). Anand (2007: 261), writing about Hindutva and sexuality, argues:

> While the patriarchal nature of Hindutva is undeniable, it is not a replica of conventional models of heterosexual masculinity. For Hindutva organizations such as the RSS and VHP, ideal leaders are celibate while the ideal common Hindu men and women are governed by heteronormativity without being too sexual . . . Sexuality is something that is to be controlled and disciplined for the purpose of procreation.

Our intention is to lay out different manoeuvres for the mobilisation of queer desires on digital platforms while also gesturing to the normative possibilities of digital queer spaces. We outline how queer collectivities provisionally assemble on and through digital queer spaces and how they remain entangled with digital nationalisms. In this sense, LGBTKHQ mobilisations remain ambivalently placed on digital spaces. However, as LGBTKHQ activist formations rally for inclusion into the nation-state thereby mapping a queer inclusive digital India, other kinds of bodies are marked as dangerous to the nation state. We present two kinds of bodies and desires as dangerous to a digitally productive India. The first figure of our discussion is the runaway working-class young man who is depicted as the monstrous rapist, one who is improperly gendered and is a threat to the modern Indian productive, rights-bearing (female) subject. The wide media coverage of the spectacular rape case of Jyoti Singh, dubbed 'India's Daughter' and memorialised through a BBC documentary made by filmmaker Leslee Udwin, gestures toward a new gendered crisis in India. The figure of the runaway working-class young man comes to represent a sexual monster who is in need of discipline and regulation. The young men's desire which cannot be contained casts a dangerous spell on the women of the nation. Similarly, the desire for *Azad Kashmir* (free Kashmir) disrupts the map of digital India. The bodies of Kashmiri activists are vilified as terrorists, bodies that need to be subjugated through military occupation. In this way, the desire for *Azad Kashmir* comes to represent a queer desire, one that remains in contradiction to the neat territorial demarcations of *Digital India*. We outline the circulation of digital meme's and chat forums that vilify the bodies of Kashmiri people and young working-class men as aberrations to modern India. In this way we contrast the normative move within the LGBTKQ movements for state recognition with the formation of new sexual monsters in and through digital India.

Theoretical Contours

In conceiving this book, the editors decided to bring three diverse theoretical traditions in conversation with each other, namely: (1) French poststructural thinkers (particularly the *oeuvre* of Michel Foucault, Gilles Deleuze and Félix Guattari, Georges Bataille and the re-articulation of their work in the scholarship of Judith Butler); (2) postcolonial thinkers such as Achile Mbembe and Libby Meintjes, Gayatri Spivak, Sanjay Srivastava (1998 and 2014), Anjali Arondekar and Geeta Patel (2009), Srila Roy, Partha Chaterjee and Nivedita Menon (2010); (3) Queer of Color thinkers such as José Esteban Muñoz (1999 and 2009), Gayatri Gopinath (2005) and Jasbir Puar (2005). These traditions are not distinct from each other, but rather remain in conversation with one another; after all, Spivak's essay 'Can the Subaltern Speak?' emerges from her critique of 'Intellectuals and Power: A Conversation between Michel Foucault and Gilles Deleuze', and Membe extended Foucault's ideas about biopolitics as the governance of life and death through ideas about 'necropolitics', as the works of death in framing the subject (Spivak 1988; Mbembe and Meintjes 2003). Recent scholarship in postcolonial studies emerging from the Indian context has taken up questions of modernity, the emergence of situated cosmopolitanisms and neoliberal social rationalities as they relate to questions of gender and sexuality (Srivastava 1998; Chatterjee and Menon 2010). In their recent introduction to an important collection of articles about area studies and queer studies, Anjali Arondekar and Geeta Patel mention that queer studies notably invoke '. . . queer theory (that) mostly speaks to US mappings of queer, rather than transacting across questions from different sites, colluding and colliding along the way' (Arondekar and Patel 2016: 151). Arondekar and Patel remind us that

> Area studies emerge out of a Cold War era in the US, with a primary focus on areas that were of strategic military interest for the US, an idea that was also propounded by Spivak earlier. Rey Chow contends that area studies in US academia is the peacetime information-retrieval machinery that complements the United States' self-aggrandising foreign policy. (Chow 2006: 14)

Academic scholarship about India has often been housed within Area Studies departments and conferences. Queer Studies has rarely engaged with area studies that has consequences for how 'queer theory' travels transnationally. In this edited volume, we have paid particular attention to the geopolitics of India and Pakistan, particularly the way Kashmir remains precariously situated as a contested territory between India and Pakistan. We take up the question of desire for digitally productive India as a form of nationalistic excess that circulates through digital technologies and frames the ways in which various LGBTHKQ subjects manoeuvre digital spaces. We argue that for queer theory to travel or converse with South Asia studies, postcolonial scholarship and scholarship emerging from India there must be a broader engagement with regional politics and historical contingencies of caste and class in India. Such regional specificities are not merely additives to what queer theory might propose as 'queer', but rather form the basis for rethinking of queer subjectivities and politics.

As mentioned earlier, we were particularly drawn to the 'Queer of Color Critique' as a project that emerges in the US and remains committed to naming the ways sexualisation and racialisation are constitutive of each other. The Queer of Color Critique emerges from Roderick Ferguson's rethinking of Marx's ideas about surplus value (2003). Ferguson argues that queer of colour subjects emerge as racialised remainders within global capitalism (Ferguson 2003). Figures such as African American drag queens and Mexican American female house cleaners are permanent fixtures within commodity capitalism. While Ferguson's work builds upon the analytical tradition in continental philosophy, scholars such as Jasbir Puar (2005), Juanna Maria Rodriguez (2003), José Esteban Muñoz (2009), and C. Riley Snorton (2014) further the hermeneutic tradition through a thorough engagement with the works of Michel Foucault, Gilles Deleuze and Félix Guattari, Judith Butler, Ernst Bloch, Julia Kristeva and Georges Bataille. *Queering Digital India* builds on this extensive body of knowledge by extending the works of many of these critical thinkers within a transnational sexuality studies context. Scholars such as Anjali Arondekar state that 'the lexicon of racial formation is necessarily linked to multiple lexicons of religion, caste, and even literacy, making it a consideration for any geopolitical reality tour of the sexual cultures of India' (Arondekar 2004: 240). In *Queering Digital India* we take up this task of extending ideas about racialisation and sexualisation within an Indian context through a thorough analysis of how caste, class and regional and linguistic politics remain interimbricated within queer (digital) cultures.

Our conception of queerness as an optic through which certain bodies are being folded into the life of the Indian nation-state and certain bodies are being relegated to let die, draws upon Jasbir Puar's notion of *homonationalism* (Puar 2005 and 2013) wherein the folding of certain queer subjects within the folds of normative nationalism is an inevitable aspect of sexual modernity. Puar traces racialisation of the Muslim terroristic figure as excessive to the US nation-state within a post 9/11 national security culture. Puar argues that, as opposed to the Muslim terrorist monster, the rights-bearing homosexual patriotic subject emerges as a normative sexual figure through claims to gay marriage and participation in the US army. In *Queering Digital India*, we build upon Puar's ideas by carefully examining regional, religious, caste, ethnic and linguistic differences that form provisional assemblages on digital spaces. We have argued that Puar's critical intervention arising out of the specificities of post 9/11 USA is useful for the purposes of analysing how sexual modernity is entangled with neoliberal nationalism in India. However, in order for her ideas to travel transnationally, one needs to consider how regional-ethnic, caste, class and linguistic conflicts reshape sexual modernities in India. In understanding how neoliberalism emerges from a specific East Asian and South Asian contexts, the works of Rupal Oza (2006), Srila Roy (Legg and Roy 2013), and Nivedita Menon (2012) provide insights about regional specificities and their entanglements with projects of gender and sexual equality. The authors in this volume bring these conversations to bear upon the nature of digital technologies, Indian nationalisms and queer desires in order to trace an unruly genealogy of how desiring bodies are specifically encoded through regional variations within the present political conjuncture in India.

The Organisation of Chapters

We begin this collection with a roundtable discussion between the editors and four academics as well as practitioners to talk about the intersections between digitality and queer politics within their respective work. In keeping with the unique concept of *adda* (Chakraborty 1999) we gathered together to discuss and critique how we see digital culture and queer politics coming together. *Adda* is literally the practice of friends gathering together on a recurrent basis for extended intellectual informal conversations. All of the contributors to the roundtable come from a unique position of putting their academic work in practical context within community-based research, while coming together provisionally (not always together in one time and space) through digital technologies to 'chat' with each other. Our *adda* is a lyrical fragment of the everyday exchanges that are a part of our digital (tactile) life. The six of us remain tethered with each other and many of the contributing authors through *Facebook messenger*, *Whatsapp*, *Google Chat*, *Facetime* and *Skype*. Our research (media and medium) travels through wires, generating sensations between wires, bodies and now this book. As we move through the chapters, we remain cognisant that many of the authors' 'field research' emerges from the author(s) bodies belonging in digital space that take on the becoming of their (re)search. The next few chapters chart these multiple (digital) becomings and pick up the key themes of queer bodies, spaces and nationalisms.

Gairola's chapter attempts a close reading of two Hindi-language films: Hansal Mehta's *Aligarh* (2016) and Shakun Batra's *Kapoor & Sons* (2016), to show how digital representations of 'outing' members of the LGBTQ community in India consolidate the effects of the Victorian statute of the Indian Penal Code, Section 377. As such, the legal ramifications of this British colonial law police meanings and makings of home in both films. The essay points to the rise of electronic, visual media in recent, queer Hindi cinema to critically engage representations of the digital as indicative of post-millennial masculinities in the two films. Gairola argues that, essential to understanding the politics of queer, contemporary India, are also critical, historical understandings of how and why representations of technology, like their material counterparts, enable imaginings of alternative queer lives in India.

Kareem Khubchandani ends this section with 'Cruising the Ephemeral Archives of Bangalore's Gay Nightlife'. Khubchandani's essay explores the visual and textual promotions of gay parties via digital venues, as well as the interactions, choreographies, soundscapes and organisation of the parties themselves. This essay attends to two understudied and distinctly ephemeral sites of queer Indian cultural production: underground gay men's dance parties and the internet-based communication that promotes them. These parties are designed to elide the production of material evidence of their existence, but as Khubchandani's essay demonstrates, the effects they have on the community, on the psyche and on the bodies of their attendees persist. Given the moral and legal policing of gay men in India, party organisers in Bangalore elide public promotion of their events, opting instead for internet-based advertising. By examining the language and imagery used to promote parties, Khubchadani shows the kinds of pedagogy the parties engage in to curate a 'global gay' aesthetic.

Khubchandani engages with the *ouevre* of José Esteban Muñoz's work, in order to mobilise Muñoz's appeal to the ephemeral archives for reading queer night life. Drawing upon major queer performing artists and Ernest Bloch's ideas about futurity, Muñoz provides us with ways of thinking and 'cruising' through queer archives. Queerness has a vexed relationship with archives, since visibility for queer desires is often connected with policing and legal consequences (as evidenced in the chapter by Singh on the sting operations conducted on PlanetRomeo). Khubchandani employs Muñoz's ideas about cruising on the ephemera of Gay Bangalore nightlife (such as flyers, digital memes, invitation pages, chats on PR and Manhunt) in order to trace how global and local forces shape the nightlife of gay men in Bangalore.

In the second part we turn to digital activisms and advocacy. These chapters trace either mobilisations for and against juridical recognition (Pawan Singh, Ila Nagar), or mobilisations for public health initiatives (Rohit Dasgupta), or modalities of self-representation. These chapters help us in understanding how domination impinges upon certain bodies in order to relegate them for policing and death, how queer bodies assemble against domination, and how multiple kinds of desire are generated in and through diverse digital platforms. Ila Nagar's chapter 'Digitally Untouched: *Janana* (In) Visibility and the Digital Divide' turns the lens away from gay men to trans and *janana* identities. Nagar argues that, while images of queer bodies have penetrated the digital space, especially in the wake of the Section 377 ruling and the subsequent (online) protest and activism, the *janana* is a queer subaltern figure marked through misrecognition or silence or through erasure within middle-class LGBTHKQ activism. Nagar helps us to understand how we can rethink queer subalternity through a keen analysis of linguistic hierarchies that is written into the 'coding' of the digital sphere. Employing ethnography and critical discourse analysis this research uncovers the consequences of illiteracy, class and perverse sexuality on the lives of men with uneven income who have sex with men on the streets of Lucknow. The subjectivity of the *jananas* remain untouched by the debates about juridical equality, since the occasion of their (legal) appearance is marked by violence, while their erasure is performed through the deployment of caste and class hierarchies within queer digital spaces. She argues that queer images in India are circulated through access to technology that the majority of the *jananas* do not have access owing to their irregular income. The images make *jananas* visible and invisible simultaneously. Their experience is effaced by putting them in a media image, where their lack of agency in the production and circulation of images is blatantly visible. This chapter explores the lives, injustices and discourses of people who have not been touched by the digital revolution and who are outside the digital world. The deployment of *koti/janana* images in digital activism is a form of exploitation of the diverse sexual life worlds. Nagar argues that the *janana* body is subjected to domination through religious rhetoric as well as the rhetoric of constitutional equality. For Nagar, the LGBTHKQ juridical activist spaces that have erupted on digital platforms exclude the *janana* subject, by figuratively conjuring the *janana* body as the dancing body, one that performs the visibility of the *janana*, yet relegates their substantive concerns to a liminal space.

This is followed by Rohit K. Dasgupta's chapter on the use of digital and social media for sexual health advocacy in Kolkata, India. This chapter reports on how an HIV capacity-building charity, Solidarity and Action Against the HIV Infection in India (SAATHII), used digital media and the internet to transform HIV prevention across India. The chapter describes the design and launch of the SAATHII website and an online resource centre and illustrates how, through digital media and the internet, SAATHII was able to widen access, advocacy and information dissemination among multiple audiences to complement traditional community mobilisation HIV prevention approaches. To conclude, the chapter reflects on SAATHII's work with digital media and the internet based on the notion of credibility and how credibility is created that allows for mobilisation and advocacy in Kolkata to disrupt dominant approaches to HIV prevention in India so as to better meet the challenges of developing AIDS-resilient communities.

Singh's chapter 'The TV9 Sting Operation on PlanetRomeo: Absent Subjects, Digital Privacy and LGBTQ Activism' ends this section by looking at a television sting operation that took place in February 2011 when TV9, a Hyderabad-based Telugu news channel aired a sting operation conducted by an undercover journalist on the nationally popular online gay dating service PlanetRomeo. The news anchor's sensationalist overtones of moral panic were accompanied by the breach of the service users' privacy whose profile content including pictures was exposed in the story. While such egregious publicity of user information in digital spaces marked a continuity with other local news reporting practices on sex scandals, the incident assumed a particular gravity given that privacy related to same-sex conduct among consenting adults was a legally recognised right under the 2009 Delhi High Court Naz ruling that decriminalised homosexuality. Singh argues that the TV9 sting foregrounds the zonal logic of privacy as more urgent given that the violation occurred in online media spaces that are only ambiguously private. The scandalously public profile users never came forward to claim privacy violation marking a profound absence in an episode in which the same pathologised figure of the online gay man became a signifier of moral corruption and queer empowerment. Drawing upon media studies, critical studies of law, new media studies and the scholarship on the globalisation of sexuality Singh's chapter highlights the stakes in public identification as gay or lesbian in the Indian context within the Naz framework of rights and visibility.

In bringing together a series of chapters about public health campaigns, the policing of gay male chatrooms, young women's self-representation on the internet, and *janana* subjectivity we assemble a range of identificatory regimes that are formed through multiple power-knowledge formations. In this way, our book attempts to map multiple forms of domination and productive mobilisations.

In the third section we move to digital intimacies (also see Dasgupta 2016) and begin with Sneha Krishnan's '"Bitch, don't be a lesbian": Selfies and Same-Sex Desire'. Krishnan examines practices through which young women pose for, take and upload selfies as sites where forms of same-sex play come to materialise. Building on prior research by scholars such as Cohen (1995) and Katyal (2013) who have conceptualised such desires in the idiom of *masti* or play among friends, an idiom that is revealing of the ways in which the notion of the sexual is circulated in this context, Krishnan's chapter seeks to unpack the gendered forms of playfulness through which middle-class women in the city of Chennai in India engage in practices of eroticism with each other. Towards this, it draws on ethnographic research conducted among college-going middle-class students in Chennai. The chapter thus through a study of practices surrounding the selfie unpacks the ways in which digital cultures mediate desire, friendship and subjectivity. Debanuj DasGupta's chapter 'Disciplining the "Delinquent": Situating Virtual Intimacies, Bodies and Pleasures among Friendship Networks of Young Men in Kolkata, India' interrogates the virtual networks of runaway and delinquent young men/boys engaged with a non-governmental organisation (PDS) in Kolkata, India. Dasgupta argues that affective bonds forged between staff, volunteers and the young runaway boys on virtual spaces such as *Facebook* hold the potential to cut through the neoliberal regulation of the runaway boys' bodies. PDS, as DasGupta notes, seeks to reform the lives of the runaway boys through educational, body-hygiene and income-generation projects. However, the volunteers forge intimate bonds with each other on digital platforms such as Facebook, which remain in excess of PDS's territorial dimension.

The screen, body and digital intimacy forged by the young men present a rather queer time and space in contrast to the developmentalist time of PDS, which seeks to facilitate the re-entry of the delinquent boys into mainstream Indian society. DasGupta considers the substance of virtual intimacies forged by the young boys in order to understand the ways their bodies take on a deterritorialiasing and reterritorialising dimension through online and offline spaces. DasGupta engages with the question of the political potential of bodily sensations. The chapter maps how young men are utilising social networking sites such as Facebook to form affective bonds that are in excess of the regulations disciplining the body. DasGupta returns to George's Bataille's ideas about expenditure, and how our bodies always have an excess of energy which cannot be contained.

The final chapter of this section is Inshah Malik's 'Kashmiri Desire and Digital Space: Queering Indian Citizen and National Identity'. In this chapter, Malik argues there has been an 'invisiblising' of Kashmiri desire for 'queer' *Azadi* (Freedom) in response to the Indian postcolonial state's reproduction of a normative 'upper caste', 'Hindu', 'heterosexual' subject and the displacing of the Kashmiri subject. Postcolonial nation-states are patriarchal through the punishing of sexual difference as well as other differences such as ethnic identities, which are considered in contravention to the interests of the nation-state. In this sense, experiences of queerness could be extended to other political identities that do not conform to the 'state-approved' idea of citizenship. Malik begins by mapping out the necropolitics of the Indian state and then problematising the killing of a Kashmiri youth through a conflation of his queer and Kashmiri identity. Examining instances of digital activism and self-assertion on digital spaces, Malik's chapter provides a different way of understanding queerness in India. Malik's mobilisation of Mbembe's 'necropolitics' offers a way of reading how the bodies of Kashmiri men and the desire for *Azad Kashmir* is relegated to (digital/real) death. Malik traces diverse Facebook memes and suggests digital policing and blackouts as necropolitical apparatuses.

Conclusion

Thus this edited volume is an assemblage of a diverse range of theoretical and disciplinary scholarship in order to cross breed between continental philosophy and postcolonial as well as Queer of Color thinking. In doing so, this edited collection presents newer ways of imagining sexual politics and its interimbrication with digital technologies and Hindu nationalism within present-day India. We present a cautionary note toward celebrating the digital sphere as a utopic space of queer freedom, at the same time gesturing to the potentials within intimate formations forged on digital platforms that undercut the neoliberal disciplining of bodies and pleasures. We remain committed to an unruly body of literature that seeks to trace (queer) desires through the ether, and yet remain firmly grounded to question how desiring bodies are arranged along and across the international division of labour.

In assembling this book, our hope has been to suggest ways of disentangling neoliberalism, nationalism, digital technologies and queerness in the Indian context. Our introduction attempts to lay out a theoretical structure that informs the organisation of the book. The following chapters take up questions of how to think about queering digital India and how different queer figurations are assembled through digital formations. We hope to highlight critique that is immanent within diverse queer formations, and thereby offer ways of thinking about productive mobilisation forged within and through digital spaces. We invite our readers to return to this introduction while journeying through the book as a potential road map, or perhaps a flashlight that helps illuminate the haphazard journeying of the desiring subject. Hopefully, our readers will undertake a journey that has neither any beginning nor any ending, but rather multiple becomings. In this sense each chapter might help gather speed toward multiple becomings.

References

Alexander, J. (2002) 'Homo Pages and Queer Sites: Studying the Construction and Representation of Queer Identities on the World Wide Web', *International Journal of Sexuality and Gender Studies*, 7 (2–3): 85–106.

Anand, D. (2007) 'Anxious Sexualities: Masculinity, Nationalism and Violence', *British Journal of Politics and International Relations*, 9: 257–69.

Anand, D. (2011) *Hindu Nationalism in India and the Politics of Fear*. London: Palgrave Macmillan.

Anderson, B. (1991) *Imagined Communities: Reflections on the Origin and Spread of Nationalism*. London: Verso.

Arondekar, A. (2004) 'Geopolitics Alert!', *GLQ: A Journal of Lesbian and Gay Studies*, 10 (2): 236–40.

Arondekar, A. and Patel, G. (2016) Area Impossible: Notes Toward an Introduction', *GLQ: A Journal of Lesbian and Gay Studies*, 22 (2): 151–71.

Banerjea, N. and Dasgupta, D. (2013) 'States of Desire: Niharika Banerjea and Debanuj Dasgupta on homonationalism and LGBT activism in India'. Available at: http://sanhati.com/articles/7185/.

Bataille, G. (1988) *The Accursed Share: An Essay on General Economy*, trans. R. Hurley. New York: Zone Books.

Bloch, E. (2000) *The Spirit of Utopia*. Stanford: Stanford University Press.

Boyce, P. (2007) '(Dis)locating Men Who Have Sex with Men in Calcutta: Subject, Space and Perception', in B. Bose and S. Bhattacharyya (eds), *The Phobic and the Erotic: The Politics of Sexualities in Contemporary India*. Kolkata: Seagull.

Butler, J. (1987) *Subjects of Desire: Hegelian Reflections in 20th Century France*. New York: Columbia University Press.

Campbell, J. E. and Carlson, M. (2002) 'Panopticon.com: Online Surveillance and the Commodification of Privacy', *Journal of Broadcasting and Electronic Media*, 46 (4): 586–606.

Chakraborty, D. (1999) 'Adda, Calcutta: Dwelling in Modernity', *Public Culture*, 11 (1): 109–45.

Chatterjee, P. and Menon, N. (2010) *Empire and Nation: Selected Essays*. New York: Columbia University Press.

Chow, R. (2006) *The Age of the World Target: Self-Referentiality in War, Theory, and Comparative Work*. Durham, NC: Duke University Press.

Cohen, L. (1995) 'Holi in Banaras and the Mahaland of Modernity', *GLQ: A Journal of Lesbian and Gay Studies*, 2 (4): 399–424.

Cooper, M. (2010) 'Lesbians Who Are Married to Men: Identity Collective Stories and the Internet Online Community', in C. Pullen and M. Cooper (eds), *LGBT Identity and Online New Media*. Oxford: Routledge, pp. 75–86.

Cooper, M. and Dzara, K. (2010) 'The Facebook Revolution: LGBT Identity and Activism', in C. Pullen and M. Cooper (eds), *LGBT Identity and Online New Media*. Oxford: Routledge, pp. 100–12.

Dasgupta, R. K. (2015) 'Articulating Dissident Citizenship, Belonging and Queerness on Cyberspace', *South Asian Review*, 35 (3): 203–23.

Dasgupta, R. K. (2016) 'Queering Virtual Intimacies in Contemporary India', in B. Scherer (ed.), *Queering Paradigms VI: Interventions, Ethics and Glocalities*. Oxford: Peter Lang, pp. 197–214.

Dasgupta, R. K. (2017) *Digital Queer Cultures in India: Politics, Intimacies and Belonging*. London: Routledge.

Dasgupta, R. K. and DasGupta, D. (forthcoming) 'Intimate Subjects and Virtual Spaces: Rethinking Sexuality as a Category for Intimate Ethnographies', *Sexualities*, Online First. Available at: https://doi.org/10.1177/1363460716677285.

Dasgupta, R. K. and Dhall, P. (2017) *Social Media, Sexuality, and Sexual Health Advocacy in Kolkata, India*. New Delhi: Bloomsbury.

Deleuze, G. (1988) *Spinoza: Practical Philosophy*. San Francisco: City Light Books.

Deleuze, G. and Guattari, F. (1987) *A Thousand Plateaus*. Minneapolis: University of Minnesota Press.

Drushel, B. (2010) 'Virtually Supportive: Self Disclosure of Minority Sexualities through Online Social Networking Sites', in C. Pullen and

M. Cooper (eds), *LGBT Identity and Online New Media*. Oxford: Routledge, pp. 62–74.

Ferguson, R. (2003) *Aberrations in Black: Towards a Queer of Color Critique*. Minneapolis: University of Minnesota Press.

Foucault, M. (1972) 'Intellectuals and Power: A Conversation Between Michel Foucault and Gilles Deleuze', in D. F. Bouchard (ed.), *Language, Counter-Memory, Practice: Selected Essays and Interviews by Michel Foucault*. New York: Cornell University Press, pp. 205–17.

Foucault, M. (1986) 'Of Other Spaces', *Diacritics*, 16: 22–7.

Foucault, M. (1990) *History of Sexuality: Vol I*. London: Vintage.

Foucault, M. (2003) *Society Must Be Defended: Lectures at the Collège de France, 1975–1976*. New York: Picador Press.

Fraser, N. (2009) *Scales of Justice: Reimagining Political Space in a Globalizing World*. New York: Columbia University Press.

Gajjala, R. and Mitra, R. (2008) 'Queer Blogging in Indian Digital Diasporas: A Dialogic Encounter', *Journal of Communication Inquiry*, 32 (4): 400–23.

Gajjala, R., Rybas, N. and Altman, M. (2008) 'Racing and Queering the Interface: Producing Global/Local Cyberselves', *Qualitative Inquiry*, 14 (7): 1110–33.

Ganguly-Scrase, R. and Scrase, T. J. (2009) *Globalization and the Middle Classes in India: The Social and Cultural Impact of Neoliberal Reforms*. Abingdon: Routledge.

Grewal, I. (2005) *Transnational America: Feminisms, Diasporas, Neoliberalisms*. Durham, NC: Duke University Press

Habermas, J. (1989) *The Structural Transformation of the Public Sphere*. Cambridge, MA: MIT Press.

Hudson, V. and Den Boer, A. (2002) 'A Surplus of Men, A Deficit of Peace: Security and Sex Ratios in Asia's Largest States', *International Security*, 26 (4): 5–39.

Katyal, A. (2013) 'Laundebaazi: Habits and Politics in North India', *Interventions*, 15 (4): 474–93.

Kristeva, J. (1984) *Powers of Horror: An Essay on Abjection*. New York: Columbia University Press.

Kuntsman, A. (2008) 'The Soldier and the Terrorist: Sexy Nationalism, Queer Violence', *Sexualities*, 11 (1–2): 142–70.

Legg, S. and Roy, S. (2013) 'Neoliberalism, Postcolonialism and Hetero-sovereignties: Emergent Sexual Formations in contemporary India', *Interventions: International Journal of Postcolonial Studies*, 15 (4): 461–73.

Leitner, H., Sheppard, E. Sziarto, K. and Maringanti, A. (2007) 'Contesting Urban Futures: Decentering Neoliberalism', in H. Leitner et al. (eds), *Contesting Neoliberalism: Urban Frontiers*. New York: Guilford Press, pp. 1–25.

Liu, P. (2015) *Queer Marxism in Two Chinas*. Durham, NC: Duke University Press.

Mbembe, A. and Meintjes, L. (2003) 'Necropolitics', *Public Culture*, 15 (1): 11–40.

Menon, N. (2012) *Seeing Like a Feminist*. New Delhi: Penguin Books.

Mitra, R. (2010) 'Resisting the Spectacle of Pride: Queer Indian Bloggers as Interpretive Communities', *Journal of Broadcasting and Electronic Media*, 54 (1): 163–78.

Mowlabocus, S. (2010) *Gaydar Culture: Gay Men, Technology and Embodiment in the Digital Age*. Farnham and Burlington, VT: Ashgate.

Muñoz, J. E. (2009) *Cruising Utopia: The Then and There of Queer Futurity*. New York: New York University Press.

Nagar, I. and Dasgupta, D. (2015) 'Public Koti and Private Love: Section 377, Religion, Perversity and Lived Desire', *Contemporary South Asia*, 23 (4): 1–16.

Ninan Thomas, P. (2012) *Digital India: Understanding Information. Communication and Social Change*. New Delhi: Sage.

Oza, R. (2006) *The Making of Neoliberal India: Nationalism, Gender and Paradoxes of Globalisation*. Abingdon: Routledge.

Povinelli, E. (2011) *Economies of Abandonment: Social Belonging and Endurance in Late Liberalism*. Durham, NC: Duke University Press.

Puar, J. (2005) 'Queer Times, Queer Assemblage: What's Queer About Queer Studies Now?', *Social Text*, 84/85 (3–4): 21–139.

Puar, J. (2013) 'Rethinking Homonationalism', *International Journal of Middle East Studies*, 45 (2): 335–9.

Pullen, C. (2010) 'Introduction', in C. Pullen and M. Cooper (eds), *LGBT Identity and Online New Media*. London: Routledge, pp. 1–13.

Rheingold, H. (1993) *The Virtual Community: Homesteading on the Electronic Frontier*. Cambridge, MA: MIT Press.

Rodriguez, J. M. (2003) *Queer Latinidad: Identity Practices, Discursive Spaces*. New York: New York University Press.

Roy, S. (2003) 'From Khush List to Gay Bombay: Virtual Webs of Real People', in C. Berry, F. Martin and A. Yue (eds), *Mobile Cultures: New Media in Queer Asia*. Durham, NC: Duke University Press, pp. 180–200.

Shah, S. (2014) *Street Corner Secrets: Sex Work and Migration in the City of Mumbai*. Durham, NC: Duke University Press.

Shahani, P. (2008) *GayBombay: Globalisation, Love and Belonging in Contemporary India*. New Delhi: Sage.

Snorton, C. R. (2014) *Nobody Is Supposed to Know: Black Sexuality on the Down Low*. Minneapolis: University of Minnesota Press.

Spivak, Gayatri Chakravorty (1988) 'Can the Subaltern Speak?', *Marxism and the Interpretation of Culture*, ed. L. Grossberg. Urbana: University of Illinois Press: pp. 271–313.

Srivastava, S. (1998) *Constructing Post-colonial India: National Character and the Doon School*. London: Routledge.

Sunder Rajan, K. (2006) *Biocapital: The Constitution of Postgenomic Life*. Durham, NC: Duke University Press.

Swiss, T. and Hermann, A. (2000) 'The World Wide Web as Magic, Metaphor and Power', in T. Swiss and A. Hermann (eds), *The World Wide Web and Contemporary Cultural Theory*. London: Routledge, pp. 1–4.

Woodland, R. (2000) 'Queer Spaces, Modem Boys and Pagan Statues: Gay/Lesbian Identity and the Construction of Cyberspace', in D. Bell and B. Kennedy (eds), *The Cybercultures Reader*. London: Routledge, pp. 417–31.

1 Digital Performance and Politics

Chapter 2

Queering Digital Cultures: A Roundtable Conversation

Niharika Banerjea, Debanuj DasGupta, Rohit K. Dasgupta,
Aniruddha Dutta, Radhika Gajjala, Amit S. Rai and Jack
Harrison-Quintana

Rohit and Debanuj: In this roundtable we discuss the role of digital cultures and 'queering' them in contemporary India within the backdrop of Section 377 (see Introduction), which frames the dominant legal discourse on sexual rights in India. This roundtable brings together academics and activists: Dr Niharika Banerjea whose research and teaching interests are in the areas of queer activisms, transnational feminisms and collaborative ethnographies. She is a member of Sappho for Equality, one of the organisations working with Lesbian, Bisexual women, and Trans men in Eastern India. Dr Aniruddha Dutta who works on non-metropolitan working-class networks of Kothi, Hijra and transgender communities; Dr Amit S. Rai who is both a media philosopher as well as an organiser and founder of the autonomous Tech fetish Group in East London, Jack Harrison Quintana, who is currently working with Grindr for Equality, the human rights wing of the popular gay dating app Grindr, and Professor Radhika Gajjala, a feminist researcher of digital media spaces working on issues related to women and globalisation at the intersection of NGO-isation and IT-isation since the 1990s. Thank you all for agreeing to take part in this roundtable. At the outset we must say that we have purposefully not defined terms such as digital cultures, queer and queering for all of you. Instead, we are allowing your responses to uphold the diverse ways academics and activists conceive of digital technologies, digital spaces, queer as a marker for non-normative identity, and queering as different modes of doing gender and sexuality politics.

I guess we would like to start off this discussion with thinking about digital culture in our own lives and especially thinking about

29

what has been the role of digital culture and digital technologies in the last few years in the various groups that we currently work with.

Niharika: Let me first answer this question by thinking through the terms 'digital culture' and 'digital technologies'. I do not have any scholarly expertise on these concepts, but am wondering if digital culture indicates that the use of certain technologies over time becomes part of a habitus, and/or cultural habit. And what are these technologies? Are they only limited to groups on the internet or can I include messaging services such as Whatsapp and email?

Allow me to elaborate with the example from Sappho for Equality (SFE), an activist forum in eastern India for the rights of lesbians, bisexual women and transmen. I am closely associated with this collective as a member, an academic-activist and as a queer kin. SFE's digital habitus has emerged over time to include varying practices of documentation, archiving and activist exchanges about events, histories, publications and posts through its website, Facebook page, archive and Whatsapp group. While the first three are more public and part of a wider network of persons, the Whatsapp group is a more intimate space to carry on the face-to-face interactions of its weekly meetings. I became a member of SFE in 2009, during this time I was located in the United States and developed my personal as well as work bonds through online modalities such as Skype and emails; today I continue to do so through my location in Delhi. It would have been impossible for me to be a part of this collective, without the digital modalities.

The communication of organisational goals, events, visions, and missions, sharing publications and photographs, discussing a current event (not always LGBTQ related), developing a layered digital archive (the first of its kind in eastern India), and a rich array of documentary and feature films and media documentation of events – all of these practices and modalities are crucial to SFE's advocacy and awareness goals. Such sites are rich tapestries of identity formation, narration of selves, dialogues across differences that allows activism to continue as an ongoing practice beyond face-to-face interactions. Activism, after all, is not a finished product that begins and ends with a face-to-face meeting, but continues online, which often provides a space to rest, recover and renew.

Jack: What I see among activists is a lot of ambivalence about the digital. On the one hand, the digital is increasingly imbedded (embedded?) in our cultures, our workplaces and our everyday lives. On the other, social media has allowed us to connect, build relationships and share information in a way that literally wasn't available to prior generations. We have borne witness to the role Twitter has played in uprisings in Iran and the movements of the Arab Spring. We've even seen brand new organisations come together on Facebook and other platforms that have more mass support and engagement than many of the traditionally constituted NGOs that have been around for years. But on the other hand, many of the most effective and powerful advocates who I see in the field today have an extremely limited relationship with these spaces. In a way that makes sense because most of us have never pursued formal study of technology. If we had, our lives might have gone in very different directions. And, of course, we haven't left behind the questions of the digital divide and who has financial access to hardware. Even as cell phones have become the world's primary computing device, a true digital grassroots movement of economically abused peoples remains elusive in many countries.

Rohit and Debanuj: Thanks for that response, Niharika and Jack. We think the point you make about digital technologies as modalities for space building is a vital theme for this book. However, as mentioned by Jack, the digital divide is a very important one especially in the context of India where digital literacy and especially media affordance plays such a huge role about who can have access or not which in turn creates different forms of gated communities within queer, transgender/Hijra/Kothi and MSM groups.

Aniruddha: My research project studies how contemporary communities and political identities of gender-variant and/or same-sex desiring persons have emerged in eastern India, and what this process tells us about broader phenomena such as transnational capitalism, globalisation and development. In particular, I am interested in how urban LGBT activism and the transnational development industry interface with non-metropolitan and working class/Dalit community networks of *kothis*, *dhuranis*, *metis* and *hijras* – terms connoting a trans feminine spectrum including trans women, feminine-identified same-sex desiring males and persons who identify as a separate gender.

Digital culture and digital technologies have had important roles to play across the aforementioned urban–rural and class–caste divides, but these roles vary in relation to the class–caste position and geographic location of users. Digital media, particularly social media sites such as Facebook and cruising websites and apps such as PlanetRomeo and Grindr, have played a major role in both urban LGBT community formation and in LGBT organising and activism, and this is where most of the current research on queering digital media is focused. However, there is much less research on digital media usage in semi-urban and rural areas, and even among urban working class/Dalit sections. While digital media has had a historically less important role in *kothi-hijra* community formation, there is increasing evidence of such usage in these community networks over the last decade or so. In particular, the burgeoning availability of cheaper smartphones and phone-based data connections has facilitated the use of phone-based apps such as WhatsApp and the mobile version of Facebook among working class/Dalit and rural users. In my fieldwork, I've also come across much evidence of inter-class and urban–rural contact enabled through these applications and websites, as manifested in the usage of *kothi-hijra* idioms among urban gay networks and the adaptation of anglophone LGBT terminology in *kothi-hijra* networks. Future research has much to explore in terms of studying such intermingling, and how they challenge and/or sustain class-caste and locational hierarchies.

Rohit and Debanuj: We think Aniruddha's point is spot on about there being very little work done on non-metropolitan communities especially in the rural and suburban. While there has been some work done (Dasgupta, 2014; DasGupta and Banerjea, 2013) and attempts made to rectify some of this it is still quite urban centric. Amit comes from a slightly different background and might have an interesting take on this question.

Amit: I organise out of a queer feminist anti-racist Marxist social centre in Bethnal Green, the Common House (http://www.commonhouse.org.uk/). I, along with ten other researchers, digital activists, journalists, designers, artists and radical educators, founded Autonomous Tech Fetish (ATF) in East London (http://www.commonhouse.org.uk/whos-involved/autonomous-tech-fetish/). ATF is an open space for gathering, sharing and making. We explore how digital technology is fetishised and how we can respond – to defetishise it and repurpose technology in emergent collective forms, where the magic of the fetish is activated both in the reality of the embodied processes of digital experimentation and invention, and in activist social reproduction within and against neoliberal accumulation and global oligopolies. ATF seeks new configurations, assemblages and collective expressions of desiring machines of silicon- and carbon-based life that better serve our needs and solidarities. In this way, can we question why technology has been made a certain way? Who has it been made for, and who has been excluded or captured? How does or can it restructure our bodies, minds, desires, perceptions, habits, time-spaces and movement?

As part of the Common House, ATF is looking to work with different groups to affirm the technological autonomy of political activism, helping it overcome surveillance and control. Beyond this, we are committed to co-education, creating spaces where pitfalls and hidden potentials of technologies can be explored without assumptions, to play with the innards of the physical and abstract machines that surround us. Autonomous Tech Fetish has also set up a number of PCs in the Common House for the use of all. They have internet and are set up with Linux Mint and a range of free and open source software. Many have celebrated the supposedly flat hierarchy organisational structures and management cultures in the digital industries (Florida 2012; Pratt 2013; Hesmondalgh and Baker 2010). Play in and through the digital is an ascendant entrepreneurial value of neoliberal accumulation: the value realised in the circulation of licensed intellectual property through monopoly rents in digital logistics, for instance, is itself part of the accumulation strategies developed in the major global oligopolies (which have become increasingly concentrated since the 1970s – see Nolan and Zhang 2010). In what way would a queer activist engagement with these logistics ontologically reshape the dominant experience and material organisation of the digital?

Through such questions, ATF has developed a specific practice of solidarity through hacking, or commoning digital and analogue resources for a post-capitalist, and anti-imperialist and post-heterosexist future. For me, and here I speak for myself as a member of the group, what ATF has developed is solidarity through re-contextualising political struggles in relation to data-bodies, bio-surveillance, cyber security and techno-perceptual assemblages, and so to develop in collaboration with others specific solutions that work around and resist, sabotage or refuse forms of normalising control that characterise more aspects of more societies globally. What does the exchange of value in the digital have to do with the transvaluation of all values? ATF is very conscious of the monopoly rents at the heart of contemporary intellectual property rights-imprisoned discourses and practice of the creative industries, the app economy and futurist-gurus. ATF heralds with others the advent of a new economy: the economy of money as a commons (see Sachy 2016). But then what specific values are generated and circulate through its practice? These values would be the values of solidarity through the co-creation of work-arounds or new practices of commoning techno-perceptual resources. Another value, therefore, would be experimentation itself. How does the value of experimentation circulate through ATF practice? This is something that affects each member differently but affects ATF as a whole continually. So in that sense there is 'exchange' of value, there is the irreversible, and non-linear circulation of values such as commoning, experimentation, tinkering, speculating, that, with specific force and sense, affect our sociality, bodies, perception, capacities, durations and becomings.

Thus, if central to contemporary forms of neoliberalism is the extraction of rents through monopoly licensing of intellectual property, ATF affirms open-source computing and its cultures; some have argued that this is simply another form of neoliberalism (see Chiapello and Botanski and others) and there are dangers that the cry of open source can become a neoliberal mantra just as easily as disruption has become. So radical politics is like brushing your teeth, as Gayatri Spivak once said, you have to get up every day and do it again. In that sense, the practice of commoning has to be examined carefully and ecologically and in terms of its different domains, value forms, processes and parameters of change only then will a politics of commoning have remained lively to another future, unpredictable but intuited emergent properties, in the post-capitalist present.

More generally, I teach courses in the Creative Industries in a left-leaning business school in London, with all the contradictions that formation entails. In these courses, and in the field of business and management itself, digital technologies have both transformed educational practice and the curriculum under discussion. Of course, I have benefitted from conversations with colleagues associated in various ways with autonomous Marxism and postcolonial queer studies such as Matteo Mandarini, Arianna Bove, Erik Empson, Stevphen Shakaitus, Denise Ferrera Da Silva, Manuela Zeuchner, Bue Hansen, Camille Barbagallo, Matteo Pasquinelli, Sadhvi Dar and Stefano Harney who have shaped the political culture where I teach. These colleagues have pushed me to consider digital technologies as one domain of what Marx called the general intellect, and its the political ecology of that domain that develops questions of global supply chains for creative products and design, the context of cognitive labour (and work more generally), the realisation/accumulation of capital through the circulation of digital commodities and their monopoly rents, and the value form in the digital. These questions help to diagram the tendencies, forces, senses and values that any radical queer politics in the digital in India and elsewhere must assemble in the affirmation of minor becoming minor compositions of the queer in subaltern India.

Rohit and Debanuj: That is a great response, Amit. The point you make about 'commoning' is indeed important and something that would actually push us to think about different kinds and possibilities and digital futurities.

Radhika: I am currently engaged in looking at how domestic space and digital publics reveal nuances of 'ghar' and 'bahir' and of the shaping of economic and consumer subjectivities in neoliberal market logics. I do this through an examination of various gendered spaces including online microfinance as well as ethnographic research on craft communities and on care-givers both in domestic settings and institutional settings. I see the intersecting forces of NGOisation and ITisation as playing a crucial role in all these contexts. Gender, Queer, Class, Race, Caste, Geography – these are identity terms that I work with, among others, in my exploration of what I broadly (for lack of a clearer term) refer to as 'digital subalternity'. My concern with digital queer therefore arises out of my exploration of the interwebs as spaces of 'outsideness' – and what these spaces of outsideness come to mean – to activate, to release or to control – at different temporal and socio-political moments. Where, when and how do the interwebs rupture to provide escape routes? Who escapes and into what? It is in such a framework that I encounter and engage the digital queer. In further discussion with you in this roundtable I hope to unpack more around these issues.

Rohit and Debanuj: To move on a little bit, what does 'queering' mean for each of you. How does it have an impact on your work. Would you say similarly there are different ways to think about the 'digital'?

Aniruddha: In relation to its history of usage as a term for articulating a critique of normativity in various forms, 'queer' has largely become a politically vacuous term as deployed currently, particularly within metropolitan LGBT communities and activism both in India and transnationally. Often, as in websites like Queerty (with its tagline 'free of an agenda, except that gay one'), it merely becomes a synonym for cisgender – indeed, gender-normative – versions of gay and lesbian identity. In other instances, like the annual Delhi Queer Pride Parade, 'queer' serves more as an umbrella term subsuming the large variety of terms used in India, though its representative capacity as an anglophone usage largely unknown outside of metropolitan activist communities is debatable. Thus using 'queering' as a scholarly and activist term for articulating forms of non-normativity is fraught with the danger of reinforcing cis LGB and elite metropolitan hegemonies. However, it is also a handy usage with a rich history in scholarly and activist archives, including ones that seek to disrupt the aforementioned hierarchies.

If its non-normative potential is to be retained in the South Asian context, 'queer' and 'queering' need to be thought of not just in terms of gender and sexuality, but must factor in class–caste and linguistic divides as well. As Narrain and Bhan (2005) remind us in the pioneering LGBT anthology *Because I Have a Voice* (2005), in the Indian context, many heterosexual relationships – particularly cross-caste and cross-class ones – also disrupt heteropatriarchy and may be thought of as 'queer'. In the ensuing decade since the anthology, it has become increasingly clear that many ostensibly 'queer' relationships and forms of community formation, on the other hand, may reinforce class-caste and gendered hierarchies. Thus, 'queering' in the digital context has to mean not just the articulation of LGBT identities in digital media; one would need to simultaneously question whether and how such articulations disrupt or reinforce class-caste and locational hierarchies.

Amit: The modern global Queer movement began with the refusal of normative identity imposed on violently pathologised populations cutting across (but also thereby affected by and in ecology with) race, gender, class and ability-based forms of power, production, value and exploitation. Its history of a novel intersectional politics is rooted in the liberation of the oppressed that in critical projects of solidarity connect queer movement to decolonisation, feminism and the civil rights and Black Power, Asian American and American Indian movements. Its moment is thus marked by this struggle for recognition in civil societies in the global North. (Of course same-sex, non-heterosexual, non-unitary trans-desire and practices are a global and ancient phenomenon, with regional, linguistic and cultural expressions that cannot be universalised under the recent political moniker queer.) A certain *ressentiment* marks, if not dominates, all identity politics, social constructivist-based activism, and left social formations, even the intersectional queer formation, throughout the world for the past fifty years: we should remember and affirm that the term 'political correctness' was used first in the radical left as a self-critique. We should understand the processes beneath this product of *ressentiment*: a bourgeois struggle for recognition. For most of its history in the capitalist West, the minority has struggled for recognition, i.e. struggled for (historically objective) justice rooted in (partial and exclusionary) ressentiment, rooted in the negations, for instance, in being 'anti-heteronormative'. In India's Queer movement, because of its historically specific and socially complex formations of sexual and desiring individuation, these processes immediately took the form of developing sympathies and solidarities between hijiras, Westernised queers, feminists, secularists, NGOs, liberals and leftists more generally. In the West it has been the work of Foucault, Fanon, Butler, Grosz, Puar, Clough, Muñoz, Lorde, Burroughs, Massumi, Manning and others to show the genealogy of a becoming minor of the queer, a becoming with other emergent properties, affordances, capacities, senses and so other solidarities. In India, it has been the feminist and women's movement that for the past thirty years have engaged most intensely with queer formations in the West, and the histories of subaltern desire. Critics and activist such as Nivedita Menon, Ruth Vanita, Gayatri Spivak, Ann Stoler, Dipesh Chakravarty, Vandana Shiva, Svati Shah, Shilpa Phadke, Madhu Kishwar and many others have drawn attention to the historically specific emergence of the norm in eighteenth-century Western Europe, focusing thought and action on the dominant schema of desire tied to the social reproduction of value and order in patriarchal and heterosexual matrices in South Asia. These are only some of the dynamics that have shaped contemporary practices of queering.

Today, the key question is: In this postcolonial genealogy what is the becoming minor of queer identity? What is its diagram and practice of that becoming minor of the queer? That becoming is affect itself. Queer identity as a line of flight, a multiplicious becoming expressed in desiring practices, subaltern culture, strategic and essentialist politics, material ontologies, mutating perceptions and co-evolving technologies. These expressions have pushed the limits of the body beyond humanism, into the techno-perceptual assemblages through which silicon- and carbon-based life have creatively evolved together. The recent work in queer ecologies is an important intervention in several of these methodological and political debates.

Jack: To me, queering is about the centring of diversely sexed and gendered bodies whose differences create crises and opportunities. And, for a long time, the digital felt like it was about disembodying. I wasn't entirely sure how to think these two things together because of this distinction about the flesh itself. But, at the same time, I always knew in my bones and in my flesh that for me as a mixed race, bisexual-gay-queer man, the digital has never felt like a place of disembodiment. These days, rather than thinking about disembodiment, I find myself thinking more about projection – that we project our bodies across space and time in a novel way through the digital. And that, in and of it, is neither revolutionary nor retrogressive. It simply changes the terrain over which the crises and opportunities of queerness can take place.

Niharika: Queering for me, briefly, is the dislocation and interruption of a dominant (or to-be dominant) narrative and/or a way of work and/or life. It may or may not be tied to LGBTQ activisms. It is an orientation that is deeply unsettling but rife with possibilities, all of which may not be rewarding. To be oriented as a queer subject in my work (beyond the sexuality question), has meant a few things:

1. being an academic-activist, and thereby engaging myself in activisms on the ground that may not always emerge in academic publications;
2. leaving a privileged tenured position in the US to locate myself in activist circles and with colleagues and friends with whom I dialogue and work;
3. keeping myself engaged with friends and colleagues outside of my immediate national boundary in continuing to do collaborative work.

These engagements I think have been queering, because I have and am straying from a well-recognised path. Perhaps in a small way, such straying will interrupt dominant institutional narratives.

Digital for me is a space that, while disembodied in one sense, is also an embodiment of voices, often faceless, at other times with faces of objects and others. In this sense, the potential of the digital is immense. If I am able to converse, dialogue and connect with objects and others that may or may not have a face, the political as practice will have a much more expansive scope across given boundaries.

Radhika: I agree with Aniruddha that the term 'Queer' has lost its political valence in contemporary times. How might we trouble it? Anyway let me answer your question directly.

My scholarly/academic interest in the internet of the early 1990s began to take form around the same time as I began producing scholarship about the digital, the postcolonial nation and gender after I started my doctoral work a couple of years later. Heteronormative gender clashes online were the most visible to me in those days. Issues of subalternity and the nation were repeatedly engaged in classroom settings and I began to see how the diasporic populations were reconnecting and shaping home-nation politics through discourse and capital flows. Queer South Asian spaces began to surface as early as the late 1980s. As Shahani (2008) has noted Trikone began in 1986 and in the early 1990s when I was working with listproc founding and moderation through the spoon collective (see http://www.driftline. org/spoon_collective.html) and through SAWnet (http://www.sawnet. org), Trikone and the Khush list were very much in my field of digital vision and intellectual conversation space. Thus not very surprisingly, my entry into the digital was also my entry into the investigation of gender beyond just heteronormative, liberal equal access concerns that come from and were most vocally expressed in the 1970s middle- and upper-class educated spaces in India. Heternormative liberal feminist discourse became easily co-opted into right-wing national politics and into neoliberal individualisation where some women's privilege – coming from heteronormative caste/class space – went uninterrogated. The queer spaces of the internet, however, were engaged in far more complex struggles and brought out further nuances and struggles around gender, nation and subalternity. Yet in the 1990s, published academic scholarship about the South Asian and Indian digital was still mostly about 'the Anglophone world'.

Not only was published work about the South Asian and Indian digital diasporas mostly in English, cyberqueer formations mostly relied on and globalised Western queer formations, resulting in the emergence of LGBTQ cyber-subject position possibilities that bypassed global South based non-heteronormative identities. Coming out via the internet resulted in entering the global North oriented subject positions. The political Internet was – then – as is the marketised internet even now – situated in a neocolonial hierarchy where the 'developed' countries had access first and set the standards and protocols for not only the technical infrastructure, but the sociality within internet-mediated spaces. Access from various other locations continues to negotiate these neocolonial technical, socio-political and economic infrastructures.

Oddly enough, the example that Ruth Vanita starts her introduction to the collection on *Queering India* (2002) – taken from film – works to describe the dilemma of cyberqueer origins in relation to global South locations such as India. Vanita notes the moment in Deepa Mehta's film *Fire* when one of the two women comments on the lack of a word in 'our language' to describe their feelings for each other. 'To which language does she refer,' asks Ruth Vanita:

> Punjabi, some variant of Hindi, Urdu, or more likely some combination of all three? We do not know because on screen the characters speak English. In this metanymic moment two things happen. English is disowned as 'our language' (even though Indians have been speaking English for two hundred years) and 'our language' is framed as a catch-all unnamed Indian language that lacks any word for same-sex identities or relationships. (Vanita 2002: 1)

Rohit and Debanuj: Thanks for that response, Radhika. The point you make about language and the ways in which it articulates but also obfuscates certain identities is especially important for us to think about in the digital realm. Amit can we press you to tell us a bit more about the 'digital' especially as this is your field of research and creative projects . . .

Amit: The digital is an object-oriented ontological construction of human beings that divides living movement into binary pairs. The digital expresses what Bergson would call an intellectual understanding of the world.

Thus when looking at the movement of an arm, intelligence, in the form of analytical science, breaks it down into a series of discrete points which can be mapped in space. However, no matter how sophisticated the measurement and how close together the points, this can never capture the movement itself. For this reason, argues Bergson (1960 [1911]: 174), 'The intellect is characterized by a natural inability to comprehend life' (in Mutch 2016: 3).

Thus the digital, in its ontology as binary code – in a way, like human perception itself – is the subtraction necessary for durational movement to become measureable, mapable, fungible and probable. The durations that constitute the time of living labour and that flow in and through this capture of movement by capitalist measure are, as Negri once said, immense and immeasurable but susceptible to control. This is why the term digital should be given back its own technology, which is *practice*. Digital practices are constituted in embodied durations of habituation, communication, expression, work and play. These practices are folded into our sensory motor circuits by and large for the oligopolistically controlled valorisation of capitalist commodities through prosumer-oriented circulation, and increasingly through the ontopowers of neurology. The digital is a global tech fetish, the processes of which are queering all the time. The work of the Why Loiter movement which was begun by feminists like Sameera Khan and Shilpa Phadke comes to mind. Shilpa claims that public space for women has spread to many other formations throughout South Asia, some queer, some mixed-generation and all self-organised. Social network organising has been central to this feminist, queer project of commoning. Queering and commoning must invent new solidarities (especially today in India across caste, class, ability and religion) and compose with emergent properties (in habits and perception).

Rohit and Debanuj: We think what is clear from all your responses is there is a general consensus on what queering could mean as a way of creating new forms of solidarities but also forging new possibilities across the intersectional spectrum of identities in a place like India. Niharika and Debanuj mention this in their recent article about homonationalism and LGBT activism in an Indian context (Banerjea and DasGupta 2013). Both of them argue that 'queering' is a kind of doing, a state of flux and constant becoming. Queering as an affinity politics is an entanglement between unlikely communities

such as Lesbian, Gay, Bisexual, Koti and Queer (LGBTKQ) friendship formations, and precarious urban workers who live in same gender communities within settlement units. Both of them point out that
the present LGBTKQ movement is moving toward a certain kind
of gendered normativity by wanting to fold within the citizenship
rights framework. Citizenship (rights) in the Indian context is built
through the violent exclusion of Kashmiri and many North-Eastern
communities. Do you feel there is any relationship between nationalism, regionalism and queer politics in India?

Amit: I think this question needs to be posed from the politics of
the digitalisation of politics in India. What does this digital politics
look like? It is regional, deeply linguistic, ethnically, gender, class
and caste stratified in terms of access, globalisation, representation,
energy, mobility, resources, property and spectacle. The political
economy of digital capitalist processes, the cognitive labour central
to its emergence, and its forms of value have not broken, in fact,
from the value form of the monopolistic commodity. At this level of
subjectivation-in-habituation digitalisation are having effects of disruption and ramification for all forms of politics in India, from queer
to Dalit to Hindutva. The new Brahminism that has slowly come to
ascendancy since the first storming of the Babri Masjid in 1990 has
shaped the politics of recognition that marks the dominant forms of
queer politics in India today.

And yet it is undeniable that a new perceptual dominance has come
into being in India in the past twenty years or so. What indications
do we have of that new dominant perceptual matrix? Certainly the
jugaad (workaround, life hacking, wit) cultures thriving in the millions
of pirate kingdoms proliferating in India today pre-dated the advent
of neoliberal restructuring. Consider the case of Salman Khan. Being
reviled for his violent and elitist masculinity is central to his brand;
like brand Bachchan before him, Khan has repeatedly rebranded his
meme, down and out romantic, avenging lover, humanist simpleton,
steroid-driven bodybuilder, etc. Gay icon and masculinist fetish are
unified through his rebrandings. A radical queer politics would disrupt
not only this representational regime, but experiment in and beyond
its ecologies of sensation and attention. It is this 'neuro-communism'
that queers the sensory motor diagram of capitalist habituation to
develop capacities that are untimely, that is in sympathy and solidarity
with a time to come.

Rohit and Debanuj: Thank you bringing up upper class, upper-caste
masculinity and its rebranding within Indian neoliberalism. Niharika,
you had some thoughts about masculinity and regional politics. Will

you please elaborate on the relationships between upper-caste masculinity, demand for state recognition, and regionalism and queer politics in India?

Niharika: I am not sure if there can be a queer politics without a conversation with the nationalist and regional question, either explicitly
or implicitly in any part of the world! I would refrain from using
'ism' here, as I think it is more useful to think how different versions
of queer politics and LGBTQ activisms in India are situated in complex and deep ways with both nationalist and regional concerns. The
production of Hindu, *savarna* masculinities – integral to a certain
version of nationalism – is not outside of some versions of queer
activism in India. Involvement with the Indian state has always been
a conundrum with most social movements. The question I would like
to ask is – what is our role as queer academics and activists? I am not
proposing an exit from engaging with the state for our rights but asking for a more hard-hitting engagement where our demand for rights
is also tied to our demand for a more accountable state.

As far as the regional question is concerned, I think that our realities, while inflected with global forces, are also very regional, more
specifically local. Given the diverse experiences around class, language, caste, gender, religion, the question of the local is part of our
political practices. I do not see how such differences can be addressed
by subsuming queer activisms around a 'national' agenda. Having
said that, I also feel that regional and local voices have to be in dialogue with each other, not to put forward a 'national agenda', but to
keep violent and even benevolent nationalisms accountable.

Radhika: The queering of the internet precedes the racing of the
internet. Digital divides of the 1990s were clearly socio-economic,
and access for raced bodies was clearly based in a global political
economy of histories of access to capital and dominant forms of
accepted literacy and practice.

In the early 1990s, my interest was both in finding immigrant
South Asian women and also in searching for new writing spaces/out-
lets where my creative work could be shared, where my intellectual
abilities could be freely expressed. As it turned out it several familiar
and unfamiliar issues of gender, nation, culture and class emerged in
South Asian usenet spaces – and several South Asian women formed
their own list spaces (such as SAWnet - http://www.sawnet.org/list/)
while queer oriented women and men formed their own (such as
the Khush list – http://www.sawnet.org/khush/). We were all aware
that all this was possible through the privilege of internet access and

the ability to enter/create textual English typing spaces online. These were not spaces that were comfortable to all who entered, however. But the communities were forming. And the ability to think of them as our own safe spaces. Until the question of who belonged erupted every now and then (see Gajjala 2002).

Virtual communities are formed as much out of assumptions of belonging and not belonging – inside/outside – as are communities formed in physical place. In fact as Benedict Anderson's work on imagined communities reveals, even national, religious and other communities formations are 'imagined' in a way that makes them as virtual and real as the internet mediated communities we used to label as 'virtual communities'. The early years of my research looking into what I termed 'cyborg-diaspora: the virtual imagined community' of South Asians, I began with the hope noted by scholars 37

This is highly ironic considering that in subsequent years – and something I discovered even through my cyberethnographic research in mid-1990s – the internet-mediated communities in fact further extended the possibilities for fetishising Indianness in a particular form that intensified discourses and brought about renewed and implicit allegiances to conservative readings and practices of what it means to be Indian (i.e. a Hindu Indian). Amit Rai (1995) wrote about the proliferation of Hindutva discourse through the production of India online, and in more recent times, Hindutva nationalist political discourse in online media continues as organised social media responses by non-experts from Hindu nationalist political party workers harass feminist activists online through what Udupa (2015) refers to as 'Gaali cultures' as they appropriate social media's 'subversive' techniques to talk back to and build archives towards a revisionist Indian history. Thus for instance, when, in the face of the Indian Apex court's decision to continue with the criminalisation of homosexuality, there was twitter protest against this by prominent people:

> An alert online group of right-wing Hindu nationalists . . . launch[ed] an offensive . . . Working briskly to substantiate this as a case of contempt of court, the online workers for Hindu nationalism assembled legal precedents, case studies, and Court pronouncements, and posted its 'findings' on 'Indiafacts.com,' a website with an avowed mission to 'act as a watchdog by closely monitoring anti-India and anti-Hindu propaganda, distortion and slander. (Udupa 2016: 212)

Aniruddha: Let me pick up from Radhika. Yes, nationalism and regionalism do modulate 'queer' or LGBTKHIQ . . . politics in India, but we may first need to interrogate the construction and (in)stability of the very categories of 'nation' and 'region'. My field-work and collaborative activism with both metropolitan and rural/semi-urban communities has made it increasingly clear to me how hegemonic forms of LGBT politics, like the broader phenomena of transnational capitalism and national developmental agendas within which they are embedded, construct and reinforce hierar-chies of scale where certain discourses and categories emerge as 'transnational' or 'national' while others – such as *kothi-hijra* terminology and idioms – are positioned as 'regional', 'local' or 'vernacular', even though they might be part of alternative translo-cal, transregional and even transnational scales (stretching across Bangladesh, Nepal and Pakistan) which are not reducible to the aforementioned scalar hierarchies. In my work, I term this pro-cess as 'vernacularisation', to understand the processes through which categories like 'vernacular' and 'local' get produced and how particular sites (both spatial and discursive) are positioned within such scales.

Queer politics in India is a site where hegemonic scales of the nation and transnationalism may be both reinforced and disrupted. While participants of 'regional' linguistic spheres such as Tamil have publicly resisted the imposition of Hindi as the 'national language', the resistance to the hegemonic imposition of a trans/national LGBT lingua franca has been subtler and less visibly articulated in terms of public politics, and yet evident in the discursive practices of non-elite and non-metropolitan communities. Teasing out and bolstering these resistant practices remains a major challenge as well as oppor-tunity for a critical queer politics that is attuned to linguistic and class-caste hierarchies in South Asia.

Rohit and Debanuj: What about you Jack? You have worked in many different countries as an activist.

Jack: I have witnessed a strong relationship between nationalism, cul-ture and the digital in every country where I've worked. This imme-diately brings to mind Pornhub Insights's analytics on pornographic search terms by country. Almost everywhere in the world outside of the United States, the number one searched word is the demonym for that country. So for India, the most searched term is 'Indian' (http://www.pornhub.com/insights/pornhub-india). In Colombia, the top three are Colombia, Colombian and Colombiana (http://www.pornhub.com/insights/pornhub-colombia). And in Uganda, black is first, African is third and Uganda is sixth (http://www.pornhub.com/insights/pornhub-rwanda). Sub-nationally within India, the most searched term for Kolkata is Bengali and for Chennai it's Tamil (http://www.pornhub.com/insights/indian-cities). To me, this underscores my point above that the digital is not as much about disembodiment as we once believed.

In terms of a relationship between the national, regional and queer politics, it's clear to me that where we are matters, that histories of colonialism, enslavement and migration have created wells of power that must be militated against by queers and communites who are continuously being othered.

Rohit and Debanuj: We do not want to aggrandise the utopic possibilities of the internet (Dasgupta 2014; Dasgupta 2015) but in relation to the ongoing movement for decriminalisation and related movement for greater trans visibility do you think digital media plays an important role or would you say it debilitates the movement by showcasing some voices over others.

Amit: It debilitates by showcasing some voices, definitely, almost always. Visibility is a trap (Foucault, Rai). It is never the answer – it's a field of struggle for recognition within with which the social democratic requirement for citizenship to be extended is negotiated. Visibility is also, however, a potentiality, as it emerges within definite systems of force, sense and value. If we think of transvisibility not as the entrance of a subalternised identity onto the world stage of universal politics, but rather as one (sometimes not decisive, nor strategic) emergent property of a political, biological and social assemblage of transdesire within definite systems of force, sense and value, i.e. the internet's political ontology, then other questions become urgent: what politics can turn and transform this force, make monstrous its normative sense, and transvalue the bourgeois value of heterosexual privilege? This is why visibility in a radical politics should be a practice of networked solidarity, bringing to bear the full force of commoning and workaround digital strategies beyond copyright and the security weaponised internet, turning visibility into a moment of collective study (Harney and Moten 2012), a call to solidarity across oppressions, and one moment in an ongoing ontological experiment.

Jack: I think the digital can cut both ways so easily. I'm less concerned about the amplification of certain voices over others, although that is without a doubt true, and more concerned with how the digital is used by those who already hold power to further consolidate that power over us. I think about the tightening of control over foreign funding for LGBT organisations coming into India from donors in other countries and how much less that was possible prior to the total digitalisation of all world banking, for example. But I also see organisations that have sprung up to create communities of resistance through the digital. For instance, I work with a digital formation from India that helps LGBT people in major Indian metropolitan locations to find other potential flat mates with whom they can create queer households rather than being stuck with their straight cousins or friends of the family when and if they are able to convince their parents to let them move out of the family home.

Aniruddha: In the context of queer-trans politics in South Asia, digital media seems to have both democratising and hierarchising tendencies, depending on the users and context of usage. For example, with reference to the aforementioned politics of scale, digital media may be deployed in ways that construct and reinforce linguistic and scalar hierarchies. Social media spaces such as Facebook LGBT groups often mandate English as a common trans/national language rather than fostering equal multilingual translation and exchange, thus resulting in the disenfranchisement and silencing of working-class, Dalit and rural voices with less access to an anglophone education. However, the last five years or so have also seen an exponential increase in South Asian language-based content in social media and blogging websites, and language-specific forums and online collectives have also emerged that to an extent challenge the aforementioned modes of silencing, though class-caste hierarchies are certainly operative within South Asian languages as well, and middle-class users who deploy relatively sanitised, Sanskritised registers of these languages may end up dominating non-anglophone online spaces.

Even so, the expansion of linguistic possibilities in social and communicative media such as Facebook and WhatsApp harbours strong democratising potentials, as it enables greater access across class–caste and urban–rural divides and non-metropolitan communities can use such media in ways that disrupt linguistic and scalar hegemonies, whether of English or of the Sanskritised versions of South Asian languages. *Kothi-hijra* subcultural languages such as Ulti (eastern India) and Farsi (north India, Pakistan) may appear on Facebook threads, and disrupt or modify institutionally recognised cartographies of LGBT identification. However, there are hierarchised layers of archival permanency and institutional support within the digital sphere; much of the non-metropolitan and/or working class-Dalit usages take place in formats that are more ephemeral and harder to preserve (such as WhatsApp groups, public or private Facebook comment threads, etc.), whereas more stable and retrievable content such as blog posts and online articles are in English or more standard, Sanskritised versions of South Asian languages. Thus the democratising potentials are structurally constrained by the inequalities between the various layers and formats of digital media and the unequal levels of access to more stable forms of digital publishing.

Niharika: Digital media indeed is playing a crucial role in bringing together voices for decriminalisation. For instance, Voices Against 377 is a group where matters other than decriminalisation is discussed to share, connect and strategise issues related to LGBTQ discriminations and violence. Having said that, it is also a reality that such discussions are carried on in English because of which many voices are unable to participate, leaving alone the fact that not all have easy access to the internet. I think digital media has to engage itself with the role of language and translation in more proactive ways. While it is true that we have keyboards that are available in regional languages, yet how comfortable is one in writing in a language other than English and expect to be understood? How much are digital platforms ready for that?

Rohit and Debanuj: Thanks for those responses. We agree that digital media can be Janus faced – on one hand it does amplify some voices as Jack mentioned but within the caste/class hierarchy of India, especially within the digital divides that exist, it also leads to the silencing of others who do not have access to these spaces. To conclude this conversation I would like all of you to focus a bit on the academic side of it and how might we be able to bridge this gap (if there is a gap that is) between the digital and the queer. We believe digital studies in India need to focus on 'queer' and queer studies need to focus on the 'digital'. Do you necessarily see these as boundaries? How has your own work contributed to the scholarship and practice in this area?

Jack: My response to this will be quite short. As mentioned in question one, it feels like those working in all areas of inquiry are increasingly compelled to integrate the digital as it becomes further imbedded in our cultures, nations and everyday lives.

Amit: I don't respect the boundaries between the two, although the two have very different morphogenesis, unless you limit yourself to academic boundaries – which historically neither queer studies nor digital studies have done. My aim today is to develop collective experiments in dehabituation and commoning in and beyond the digital. This involves experimenting with capacities more than identities, ontologies more than epistemologies, diagrams more than representations. It is to bring queer digital politics into strategic convergence with different kinds of Marxisms and postcolonial problematics; in what way would a queering of digital logistics overturn the value form, that is in and through what politics, alliances, compositions, becomings?

Aniruddha: I agree somewhat with Jack and it is certainly true that there needs to be more cross-fertilisation and overlap between digital and queer studies in India. However, in my view, just greater interchange across whatever boundaries may exist between these fields is not enough, rather the question is also about the kinds of sites that are taken up by digital queer studies and how far these sites are overdetermined and constrained by systems and relations of power. For example, far too often, studies of urban queer politics (whether online or offline) in a few metropolitan cities stand in for Indian queer politics as a whole, and there is far less attention and resources expended on suburban, semi-urban or rural sites and on marginalised regions such as the north east. Further, sometimes the 'digital' (however understood) also stands in for the 'new' and the 'emerging' in queer-trans politics, thus obscuring other sites and spaces (such as offline cruising spaces and networks) that may persist and be recreated anew, but get consigned to the 'old' or the 'disappearing'. Thus the formation of a more integrated field of digital queer studies would also need to interrogate its own investments and interests and how far they reinforce or resist relations of power and inequalities across fields and archives. In my own work, I try to do this by remaining attentive to offline non-metropolitan spaces, and how such spaces intersect (or not) with digital media. In doing so, I hope to arrive at a more non-linear, non-teleological understanding of the 'digital' wherein the 'digital' does not merely stand in for elite-dominated and metropolis-based forms of queer modernity, but is also studied as a site of potential rupture and resistance to hegemonic narratives of queer politics.

Niharika: While I am aware of some existing scholarship on the subject that is trying to question this boundary, yet I am not sure it's interconnected to an extent where both digital and queer studies automatically incorporate each other.

In my own work, in a collaborative project, called 'Making Liveable Lives: Rethinking Social Exclusion' with Sappho for Equality and the University of Brighton, we have tried to engage the digital by creating a website that includes surveys, discussion boards and news events, the purpose of which is to connect activists and academics and LGBTQ persons across India and the UK, in an effort to understand the modalities and forms of liveabilities. Yet, while doing this we have seen that the response has been more from persons based in the UK than in India, and we are yet to draw a final conclusion about that. Nevertheless, I would say that this has been a significant 'experiment' in trying to create a dialogue across 'first' and 'third' world hierarchies about places and lives beyond questions of judicial gains and losses.

The digital then is an orientation toward both self and other, and could be an important mobilisation of the same for advocacy and awareness. However, we also need to question as we mobilise ourselves, narrate ourselves through digital modalities, if we are reproducing hierarchies that normalise us in certain ways, or are we deeply engaging ourselves enough to interrupt such hierarchies?

Radhika: As Niharika does, I question this idea of the digital being a rupture. It may have had that potential at one time – however, as I recently noted on my twitter feed: When social media itself is part of the configuration of control it is no longer an escape route. We must look elsewhere for the ruptures. Yet – can I say that as an absolute? Ruptures and escape routes have always existed in the in between. Perhaps we have to examine our methodologies for understanding these phenomena. As academics are we complicit in the capture and contain process that misses shifts perhaps? The bodies evade our classification when in motion. Some of this motion is what the term queer may have attempted to capture – in all its contradictions. Yet motion is neither escape, freedom or liberty in and of itself.

Between the now of social/mobile media, app-based digitality and the then of the listproc and USEnet days 'the web' exposed us all to the world. Early World Wide Web days allowed even amateurs to code. Hypertext markup language (invisible and inaccessible from the back end of the Java and various GUI software interfaces we engage in as we 'build' our web presences in the present day) was comparatively accessible – at least to English-educated global middle classes worldwide. What changed? Typing and coding ourselves into existence became a bit more separated than before. Even though complex backend coding had been invisible to the average user during the days when html was visible and accessible to amateur coders, the typing of the self into existence relied on some forms of coding. Typing the self in existence meant simultaneously learning a minimal amount of coding and – even if briefly – glimpsing some code pass by and be cognisant of being coded into existence. Present-day minimal computing movements (http://www.globaloutlookdh.org/minimal-computing/kickstart-workshop/) try to take us back to the political economy of those days and make us aware of the inequalities made invisible in today's political economy of digitality.

Jenny Sunden (2003) writes of the typing into existence that is a requirement for any sustained online identity. However, while the action of *producing one's self* in such an environment is enacted through typing, the particular participant's *subject position* is produced both through the act of typing combined with pre-existing code. The political economy of presence and absence in this production of online selves is investigated by Linda Leung in her work where she goes beyond looking at what she refers to as the Asian 'Techno-Elites' (Leung 2008). A key question she asks is: 'What happens when information and communication technologies (ICTs) are provided to those who would otherwise not have access to them?' Leung focuses on unpacking a case study of two south Asian women in the UK and she reconceptualises the notion of digital divide by noting the contradictions that emerge through this 'unlikely couple of novice computer users' and their participation in virtual communities.

> While there is potential to participate in Asian virtual communities, to feel close to and part of something familiar, there is also the capacity for claustrophobia and discomfort. In the relationship between technology and ethnicity, gender and class interrupt the smooth transition between the online and offline. Being women in a socioeconomically deprived region of London exacerbated Rosie and Noori's minority status, not only within the South Asian digital diaspora but in the wider cyberspace. (Leung 2008: 23)

Yet, these sorts of contradictions in present social media times are glossed over in a renewed sense of celebration of social justice movements through Twitter and Facebook and the so-called possibilities for subaltern access through smart phones. Thus as the web shifted to becoming algorithm driven and began providing us apparently seamless user/consumer interfaces, the texting, typing, imaging, recording, selfie-ing into being began to be separated from the cognition involved in semi-coding selves into being. The embodied actions and literacies required shifted to different combinations of pre-existing offline/online sociality, requiring socio-cultural and technical literacies based in various other external gadgets and hardware in addition to the visible circuitry associated with a computer of the 1990s. Further layered political economies and contradictions of access and digital divides surfaced. Tetteh, Birzescu and I have written about some of this in the context of the marketing of M-pesa (Gajjala et al. 2015) while my several collaborators and I have also examined these contradictions and neocolonial underpinnings in relation to microfinance onlined in the book *Cyberculture and the Subaltern* (Gajjala 2012).

Rohit and Debanuj: Thank you friends for coming together for this roundtable. It was indeed a thought-provoking conversation about some of the issues that we are trying to grapple with in this volume. As our introduction will highlight, many of these themes raised by all of you have been elaborated by our authors. Issues about regionalism, digital hierarchies, creative manoeuvring of digital space by multiple communities, as well as the policing of digital spaces are addressed in this anthology. We are opening this book with the roundtable in order to honour the 'adda' sociality (Chakrabarty 2007) of Kolkata intellectuals. As elaborated by Chakrabarty, *adda* is an exchange of ideas, dialogue and debate between friends within household and public spaces. *Adda* is a form of sociality, a form of postcolonial political culture, one that queers public and private division of political space. We hope this 'adda' will lyrically resonate through print and digital spaces creating multiple meanings of queering digital India.

References

Banerjea, N. and Dasgupta, D. (2013) 'States of Desire: Niharika Banerjea & Debanuj Dasgupta on Homonationalism and LGBT Activism in India'. Available at: http://sanhati.com/articles/7185/.

Bergson, H. (1960 [1911]) *Creative Evolution*. London: Macmillan.

Bergson, H. (2007 [1912]) *Matter and Memory*. New York: Cosimo.

Butler, J. (1997) *The Psychic Life of Power: Theories in Subjection*. Stanford: Stanford University Press.

Butler, J. (2004) *Precarious Life: The Powers of Mourning and Violence*. London and New York: Verso.

Castells, M. (2012) *Networks of Outrage and Hope: Social Movements in the Internet Age*. Cambridge: Polity Press.

Chakrabarty, D. (2007) *Provincializing Europe: Post Colonial Thought and Historical Difference*. Princeton: Princeton University Press.

Chiapello, E. and Boltanski, L. (2007) *The New Spirit of Capitalism*. New York: Verso.

Dasgupta, R. K. (2014) 'Parties, Advocacy and Activism: Interrogating Community and Class in Digital Queer India, in C. Pullen (ed.), *Queer Youth and Media Cultures*. Basingstoke: Palgrave Macmillan, pp. 265–77.

Dasgupta, R. K. (2015) 'Articulating Dissident Citizenship, Belonging and Queerness on Cyberspace', *South Asian Review*, 35 (3): 203–23.

Deleuze, G. (1988) *Spinoza: Practical Philosophy*. San Francisco: City Light Books.

Deleuze, G. and Guattari, F. (1987) *A Thousand Plateaus*. Minneapolis: University of Minnesota Press.

Fanon, F. (2001) *The Wretched of the Earth*. New York: Penguin.

Florida, R. (2012) *The Rise of the Creative Class Revisited*. New York: Basic Books.

Foucault, M. (1976) *Discipline and Punish*. New York: Vintage.

Gajjala, R. (2002) 'An Interrupted Postcolonial/Feminist Cyberethnography: Complicity and Resistance in the "Field"', *Feminist Media Studies*, 2 (2): 177–93.

Gajjala, R. (2004) *Cyber Selves: Feminist Ethnographies of South Asian Women*. AltaMira Press, Kindle Edition.

Gajjala, R. (2012) *Cyberculture and the Subaltern: Weavings of the Virtual and Real*. Lanham, MD: Lexington Press.

Gajjala, R., Tetteh, D. and Birzescu, A. (2015) 'Staging the Subaltern Self and the Subaltern Other: Digital Labor and Digital Leisure in ICT4D for Producing Theory in a Digital World', in R. Lind (ed.), *The Intersection of Audiences and Production in Contemporary Theory*. New York: Peter Lang.

Grosz, E. (2005) *Time Travels: Feminism, Nature, Power*. Durham, NC: Duke University Press.

Hardt, A. and Negri, A. (2000) *Empire*. Cambridge, MA: Harvard University Press.

Harney, S. and Moten, F. (2012) *The Undercommons*. Wivenhoe: Autonome.

Hesmondhalgh, D. and Baker, S. (2008) Creative Work and Emotional Labour in the Television Industry', *Theory, Culture and Society*, 25 (7–8): 97–118.

Hesmondhalgh, D. and Baker, S. (2010) '"A Very Complicated Version of Freedom": Conditions and Experiences of Creative Labour in Three Cultural Industries', *Poetics*, 38 (1): 4–20.

Karamcheti, I. (1992) 'The Shrinking Himalayas', *Diaspora*, 2 (2): 268–9.

Khan, S., Phadke, S. and Ranade, S. (2007) *Why Loiter?* London: Penguin Books.

Lazzarato, M. (2009) 'Neoliberalism in Action: Inequality, Insecurity and the Reconstitution of the Social', *Theory, Culture and Society*, 26 (6): 109–33.

Lazzarato, M. (2012) *The Making of the Indebted Man: An Essay on the Neoliberal Condition*. Los Angeles: Semiotext(e).

Leung, L. T. (2008) 'From "Victims of the Digital Divide" to "Techno-Elites": Gender, Class, and Contested "Asianness" in Online and Offline Geographies', in R. Gajjala and V. Gajjala (eds), *South Asian Technospaces*. New York: Peter Lang, pp. 7–25.

Malabou, C. (2008) *What Should We Do with Our Brain?* New York: Fordham University Press.

Manning, E. (2014) *Thought in the Act: Passages in the Ecology of Experience*. Durham, NC: Duke University Press.

Massumi, B. (2002) *Parables for the Virtual*. Durham, NC: Duke University Press.

Mehta, D. (1996) *Fire*. Bobby Bedi and Deepa Mehta Productions.

Menon, N. (2011) *Seeing Like a Feminist*. London: Penguin.

Mutch, A. (2016) The Limits of Process: On (Re)reading Henri Bergson', *Organisation*, January, pp. 1–15.

Narrain, A. and Bhan, G. (2005) *Because I Have a Voice*. New Delhi: Yoda Press.

Negri, A. (1999) 'Value and affect', *Boundary 2*, 26: 77–88.

Nietzsche, F. (2003) *Beyond Good and Evil*. New York: Penguin Classics.

Nolan, P. and Zhang, J. (2010) 'Global Competition after the Financial Crisis', *New Left Review*, 64: 97–108.

Nolan, P., Zhang, J. and Chunhang, L. (2007) *The Global Business Revolution and the Cascade Effect: Systems Integration in the Aerospace, Beverages and Retail Industries*. Basingstoke: Palgrave.

Pratt, A. C. (2006) 'Advertising and Creativity, a Governance Approach: A Case Study of Creative Agencies in London', *Environment and Planning A*, 38 (10): 1883–99.

Pratt, A. C. (2013) 'Space and Place in the Digital Creative Economy', in R. Towse and C. Handke (eds), *Handbook of the Digital Creative Economy*. Northampton: Edward Elgar, pp. 37–44.

Puar, J. (2009) *Terrorist Assemblages*. Durham, NC: Duke University Press.

Rai, A. (1995) 'India On-Line: Electronic Bulletin Boards and the Construction of a Diasporic Hindu Identity', *Diaspora*, 4 (1): 31–57.

Sachy, M. (2016) *Money as a Commons*. PhD Dissertation, University of Leicester, University of Leicester Press.

Shahani, P. (2008) *Gay Bombay*. New Delhi: Sage.

Sunden, J. (2003) *Material Virtualities: Approaching Online Textual Embodiment*. Oxford: Peter Lang.

Udupa, S. (2015) 'Abusive Exchange on Social Media: The Politics of Online Gaali Cultures in India. EASA e-seminar draft. Available at http://www.mediaanthropology.net/file/udupa_abusive_exchange_final2.pdf.

Udupa, S. (2016) 'Archiving as History-Making: Religious Politics of Social Media in India', *Communication, Culture and Critique*, 9 (2): 212–30.

Vanita, R. (2002) *Queering India: Same-Sex Love and Eroticism in Indian Culture and Society*. New York: Routledge.

Chapter 3

Digital Closets: Post-millennial Representations of Queerness in *Kapoor & Sons* and *Aligarh*

Rahul K. Gairola

Introduction: (G)hosts of the Past

The past two decades have been particularly significant for representations of non-heteronormative subjects in Hindi cinema despite the persistence of Section 377 of the Indian Penal Code, an 1860 law that criminalises sex 'against the order of nature' (Kalra and Barupal 2013: 318). Despite the anti-queer law whose history traces back to the heyday of the erstwhile British Empire in India, contemporary images of erotically intimate wives, queer children, incestuous relatives, brutal rapes and hushed sexual liaisons between men have proliferated in Hindi cinema as the more popular, global Bollywood brand continues to produce more films than other film industry in the world (Desai 2004: 373). However, Deepa Mehta's critically-acclaimed film *Fire* (1998) and Kaizad Gustad's *Bombay Boys* (1998), both released in the late 1990s, faced sharp criticism for portrayals of Hindu lesbians caught in unfulfilling marriages in joint families and effeminate, gay partygoers in Mumbai. In Mehta's *Fire*, Hindu matrimony is a patriarchal pivot that compels lesbian desire between protagonists Radha and Sita, while sexually confused Xerxes (Alexander Gifford) of *Bombay Boys* and his ultra-campy landlord Pesi (Roshan Seth) are 'classically gay' characters (often cast for slapstick humour like Sean Hayes' character Jack in the popular American sitcom *Will & Grace*) who conform to, rather than challenge, the most mundane stereotypes of emasculated men (Gairola 2001).

Virulent protests over *Fire* resulted in torched cinema halls in Delhi and Mumbai upon release of the film in 1998, but the Censor Board re-released the film in 1999. This historical contradiction today signals to the ongoing tension created by a colonial-era law in a country that promises to have the world's highest population by 2025. India's booming youth population growth, on the one hand, and techno-logical innovations in the rapid dissemination of global media on the other seem to have empowered the production of filmic narratives that challenge cultural conventions of heteronormativity. These Hindi films include Mira Nair's *Kama Sutra: A Tale of Love* (1996), Sridhar Rangayan's *The Pink Mirror* (2003), Vinod Pande's *Sins* (2005), Quashiq Mukherjee's *Gandu* (2010), Saad Khan's *Hide and Seek* (2013), Raj Amit Kumar's *Unfreedom* (2014), Shonali Bose's *Margarita With a Straw* (2014) and Pan Nalin's *Angry Goddesses* (2015). While these films offered filmic agency of queer in India during the tumultuous run-up to global debates on gay civil unions and marriage, they also came to define popular stereotypes of homosexuality in contemporary India – being used as comic asides such as Tarun Mansukhani's queer Bollywood extravaganza, *Dostana* (2008). As usual in Hindi cinema, the intertwined issue of colourism and casteism is clearly visible -- for example, Gustad's Bombay boys' 'fair' complexions and toned physiques that undergird hegemonic stereotypes of gay men.

And this is perhaps one of the biggest problems of films like *Fire* and *Bombay Boys*. While the former gives South Asian lesbians filmic agency (Gairola 2002: 322) and the latter does the same for diasporic South Asians returning to the homeland, both films heavily depend on clichés influenced by colonial and Hollywood norms. In particular, in both films, the rehearsed notion of 'following one's heart to discover one's true desires' stretches thin to justify queer love that, ironically, sounds familiar in many brands of orientalist desire. While this critique is indeed important, it is not one on which I extensively linger upon here though it is the object that is indeed transmitted by my subject. Rather, I would like to begin by observing that both *Bombay Boys* and *Fire* share a common visual-ideological feature: both films' plots also feature forms of visual technology including cameras, film recorders and VCR which release suppressed identities mired in transgressive sexual desires. That is to say, within the very medium of independent Hindi cinema, the gradual turn to digital media as the arbiters of queer sexual relations is depicted on the big screen as it impacts us in real life. From photographs in *Bombay Boys* to pornographic VHS tapes in *Fire*, these technological mediums are the precursors to digital media that viscerally shape sexuality and identity on the big screen in, literally, larger than life ways.

This essay points to the rise of electronic, visual media in recent, queer Hindi cinema to critically engage representations of the digital as indicative of post-millennial masculinities in two recent, Hindi-language films: Hansal Mehta's *Aligarh* (2016) and Shakun Batra's *Kapoor & Sons* (2016). In what follows, I shall argue that essential to understanding the politics of queer, contemporary India are also critical, historical understandings of how and why representations of technology, like their material counterparts, enable imaginings of alternative queer lives in the world's largest democracy. Indeed, this essay shows that representations of technology are inextricable from representations of queer India at a time when the Victorian, punitive mandates of Section 377 continue to police the erotic lives of young Indians. In conceptualising what I call 'the digital closet' as an electronic structure of both opening and concealing contemporary, queer identities in India, I conclude that representations of technology in such films suggest to how best mobilise technology with identity politics in the interest of compelling social justice movements around gender and sexuality in post-millennial India. In the conclusion, I return to the nascent studies of digital humanities in South Asia to chart an activist path forward.

Digital Technologies and Queer Hindi Cinema

A brief literature review offers many helpful methodological and theoretical paradigms that inform the concerns of this essay and my opening reading of technological representations in Hindi language films. For example, Parmesh Shahani's *Gay Bombay: Globalization, Love, and (Be)longing* (2008) offers an ethnographic tour de force of urban sexualities both off and online, and their interface in material worlds. Another ethnographic study that tracks male queerness is Shaka McGlotten's *Virtual Intimacies: Media, Affect, and Queer Sociality* (2013), in which the author explores how sexual intimacy is forged online in arguments that explore 'the Janus-like effects of networks on intimate encounters' (6). The effect of simultaneously looking ahead while gazing into the past as suggested by the Roman god Janus is, for twenty-first-century Hindi cinema, a formidable crucible within which technology births new gender and sexual possibilities which are impossible to ignore. Such ethnographic work mediates against the sometimes homogenising effect that visual representations and theory can have in the rights of their own abstractions. Indeed, Pradip Ninan Thomas writes in *Digital India: Understanding Information, Communication and Social Change* that 'the digital is making itself present and felt in intended and unintended ways as innovation and creativity are unleashed in both formal and informal environments' (2012: 3).

Thomas's observation aptly describes what we see in *Fire* and *Bombay Boys* as it cites the pervasive agency that digital media and products have in many social articulations of representation, from digital advertising to product placement in music videos. Queer desire is facilitated and released in both films by what we now consider relics of technology – for Radha's (Shabana Azmi) servant, Mundu, it entails masturbating to VHS tapes of American pornography when his lesbian mistresses are away, while for Xerxes (Alexander Gifford) it means capturing a part of India on film so that he can figure out if he is gay or bisexual. These technologies of the self reflect back to characters, as they do for us, in the words of Gilles Deleuze and Félix Guattari, a libidinal

> infinity of different and even contrary flows. Everything depends on the way in which these flows – whatever their object, source, and aim – are coded and broken according to uniform figures, or on the contrary taken up in chains of decoding that resect them according to mobile and nonfigurative points (the flows-schizzes). (Deleuze and Guattari 2004: 385)

Deleuze and Guattari's 'infinity of different and even contrary flows' permeates not only the ways in which technologies of the self release, mediate and disavow erotic desires, but more and more how we reveal, hide and experience sexuality through digital mediums in the twenty-first century.

These queer digitalities surface in unexpected and contradictory ways within other digital forms, creating mirrored vectors of online subjectivity that must be maintained, controlled, even hidden. These are also in some ways today dependent on 'the flows-schizzes' of electricity, and where and when it and an internet network are available. Indeed, these queer digitalities seem strange bedfellows with the 'cyberqueer space' that Nina Wakeford describes as a liberatory domain with activities and research emanating from the United States (2000: 413). Representation, as with revolution, has always been a site of contestation and resistance. From the mobilisation of cultural studies in Black Britain to the rise of subaltern studies in postmodern India, digital and social media have compelled us to intercept and interpret images and sounds at a faster rate than ever before. The works of many others including Chandan Reddy (1998), Jigna Desai (2004), Gayatri Gopinath (2005), Jasbir Puar (2007), Amit Rai (2009), Rajinder Dudrah (2012) and Rohit K. Dasgupta (2015) have contributed to a formidable and urgent archive of queer diasporic film readings by South Asians that explore the complexities of cinematic agency. In bridging these earlier texts to the pervasiveness of digital forms of queerness, Radhika Gajjala and Rahul Mitra argue that the LGBTQ South Asian community is a 'situated [original emphasis] practice – at radically varying contextual disjunctural and conjunctural online-offline intersections' (Gajjala and Mitra 2008: 402).

In other words, queer blogging in South Asia facilitates a number of electronically mediated interactions with the possibility of even more when the posting author is offline. Such is the discourse of queer digitality in post-millennial India with a population of 1.3 billion which substantially consists of people below the age of thirty. Nascent, critical dialogues on establishing a field of postcolonial Digital Humanities (#DHpoco), as well as a field geographically rooted in South Asia (#SADH) are taking shape as global struggles for social justice are met with hailstorms of bullets. In arguing to expand scholarship from *traditional* postcolonial archives to postcolonial *digital* archives, Roopika Risam writes, 'To define the imperial archive simply by its textuality is to miss the inextricable relationship between preservation, knowledge production and the colonial apparatus. To understand such links – or, indeed, to undo them – we must understand the colonial archive as a dynamic force in the production, distribution and construction of history' (2015: 36). Like LGBTQ blogging for South Asians, Risam's insistence on forging a digital archive of postcolonial resources that can be accessed through hashtags that collate and unify content across communications platforms. Moreover, like queer South Asian blogging, postcolonial Digital Humanities and its production of counter-archives in the digital milieu indeed constitute what Gajjala calls a 'situated practice' with the potential of casting global developments of how we recast the Global South.

Digital Closets in *Aligarh* and *Kapoor & Sons*

Such developments of how we recast the Global South, I would argue, not only compel us to think critically about the modes of production of digital identities at home and beyond South Asia, but also the colonial histories that have shaped them with respect to race. Sexuality in this case is viewed as constitutive of rather than additive to such identities. Queer representation in post-millennial Hindi cinema, I would argue, is most profoundly shaped by the convergence of the fast-paced and forward looking trajectory of technological innovation, on the one hand, and the backwards-looking persistence of the British Raj's 1860 statute on queer sexuality today. In the historical context of lively debates in India concerning the role of technology in contemporary society, as well as the Supreme Court's legal recognition of 'third sex' people in April 2014 and ongoing efforts to strike down the colonialist Section 377, the digital milieu has become the primary battleground for social activism and representation of alternative genders and sexualities in post-millennial India. Hansal Mehta's *Aligarh* (2016) and Shakun Batra's *Kapoor & Sons (since 1921)* (2016) offer compelling portraits in which digital technology is narratively entwined in and constituent of the ways in which queer sexuality is masked, manipulated, marshalled and materialised publicly by well-off, Hindu subjects.

Indeed, both films arguably construct digital closets around Professor Shrinivas Ramchandra Siras and Rahul Kapoor, the two queer protagonists, which are breached by coming-out confessionals. In offering the term 'digital closets', I would argue that these are in-between spaces that interface with material spaces which are shaped and informed by Section 377's colonial afterlife. Digital closets are the pivot points upon which hinge public disclosure of one's queer lifestyle practices, and the protective shadows of life online that obscure gender and sexuality identities. Such closets, which are distinct from and deeply complicate those described by Eve Kosofsky Sedgwick in her pioneering study the *Epistemology of the Closet* (1990), allow a new way for queer identities to slip and slide around technological interfaces wherein the evidence of transgressive sexuality only exists in cyberspace when it is targeted for postcolonial policing. Against a backdrop of queer identities masked or revealed by digital closets, *Aligarh* and *Mr. Kapoor & Sons* offer poignant portrayals that potentially reify the marginalisation of queer narratives in Hindi cinema. Ashley Tellis writes that 'both films only reaffirm the fact that homosexuality has to be airbrushed into heteronormativity for it to be acceptable or tolerable at all. Homosexuality has to be made as heterosexual as possible and framed by the logics of heterosexual representation for it to merit screen time at all' (2016).

While I would agree with Tellis's critique that these films certainly sanitise the most socially contentious aspects of their protagonists' social transgressions of heteronormativity to render the subject matter palatable to a wide swath of Hindi movie-goers in India, such readings are far more complex when we take into account the ways in which digital closets and their openings render queer sexuality to the public gaze. These experiences with digital closets and electronically facilitated revelations of these characters' 'real' sexual identity compels viewers to reconsider how and under what conditions others dwell in erotic anonymity or publicly stake a claim to erotic autonomy (Alexander 2005: 22–3). Mehta's *Aligarh* certainly

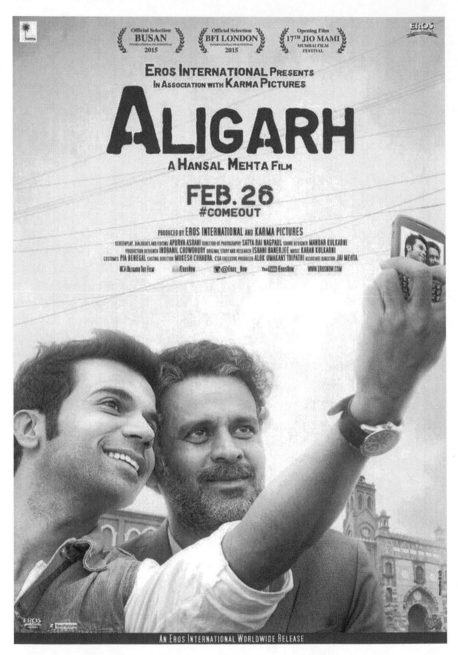

Figure 3.1 Poster from *Aligarh* (author's collection)

strives to render a compassionate and lyrical portrayal of Professor Siras, who was suspended from his professorship and deprived of his accommodation at Aligarh Muslim University, one of India's most prestigious colonial-era institutions of higher education, when his colleagues happened upon him undressed in his bedroom with a rickshaw cycler. As might be expected in this film and although it is not the main thrust of this study, Mehta's film frames situated protests against the professor that seem to implicate Mehta's film in a sort of pink washing against the backdrop of India's most prestigious Muslim university.

While the film problematically justifies Siras's illicit sexual tryst with his rickshaw-cycle lover by showing the metrosexual journalist Deepu Sebastian (Rajkummar Rao) hooking up with his lovely supervising editor ('all love is equal'), perhaps what is even more alienating are the ways that the camera, cell phone and laptop produce queerness in contemporary India. For example, Mehta is very conscious of ensuring that viewers see the trauma and strife of public shame through the mechanical eye of the digital camera. It seems, in fact, that the only way viewers can intercept Professor Siras's transgressive sexuality is through its digital reproduction although his poetic, 'more human' side is observed by the cinematic eye unmediated by other digital media. For example, there is a palpable tension that viewers feel when the audience's point of view is mediated by the digital camera, whose omniscient gaze punctuates the filmic narrative with exposure and revelation of punitive queerness. Yet while the digital camera's eye is sharp and instantaneous, it is not foolproof. At the same moment that technological capture confirms to viewers the intimacy between Siras and his male lover, the camera is also the source of their most extreme terror of being outed as it also captures for viewers the tenderness of queer sex.

The threshold of the closet pivots on the digital apparatus. Early in the film, the chirpy Deepu and his photographer from the *Indian Post* seek out the professor, who Deepu finds haggard and in poor health. Upon helping the man up to his apartment, Deepu refrains from revealing his identity as a journalist or his intention of soliciting an interview from the professor about the campus gay sex scandal. The digital camera and its possibilities of public exposure make clear Deepu's intentions when his *Indian Post* colleague begins snapping pictures outside, looking through the drawing room's windows. When he confesses to Siras that he is a reporter hot on the trail of his story, the professor drives him out of his house with a menacing umbrella. While back downstairs Deepu scolds his friend for deploying the digital camera to break the air of amicability that he is trying to establish with Siras before convincing him to consent to an interview, digital closets and their public openings seem to haunt Mehta's tragic protagonist and film. The fear of being recorded as a sexual transgressive echoes in Siras's aversion to saying the word 'gay' or even talking about MSM (men who have sex with men); the closest he comes to doing so is by alluding to homosexual erotics as intimate poetry. The potential of digital closets to privately record and publicly display the truth of queer sex in post-millennial India seems to haunt Siras throughout the film while they lay open for exposure by Deepu.

This overarching, romantic and even homonormative rendition tends to subvert the socio-political message that gay people are humans, too, who have sexual impulses and desires. While Mehta ostensibly punctuates most dialogue in the script with this rehearsed thematic undercurrent, the 'different and even contradictory flows' described by Deleuze and Guattari are apparent in Siras's sexual subjectivity the digital closet. The same camera from which he angrily flees when he ousts Deepu from his flat is the one that he shyly smiles for when Deepu later insists that they take a selfie together, thus indulging his own straight narcissism. The digital camera thus seems to have a life of its own as it becomes the omniscient hermeneutic through whose eye we see and do not see. From inducing anger, anxiety, duty, pleasure and even sheer terror, the camera threatens the digital closet with a loud and public outing – and one for which Mehta suggests in a number of ways that Siras is not ready. In one scene, while he is the subject of a televised talk show during which callers vociferously attack indict his 'immorality', a visibly petrified Siras is only able to speak about how he feels – an abstraction that allows him to cling to the digital closet while he is live on air, even while skirting the socio-political differences that shape the parameters of sexual encounters.

Gajjala et al. collectively write:

> Race, gender, sexuality, and other indicators of difference are made up of ongoing processes of meaning-making, performance, and enactment. For instance, racialization in a technologically mediated global context is nuanced by how class, gender, geography, caste, colonization, and globalization intersect. Raced subjectivities thus get produced against the specific contextual backgrounds incorporating local and global economic and social processes. (Gajjala 2008: 1111)

The presence of both digital closets and digital cameras in *Aligarh*, I would argue, produce a viewing experience which relies on the implied omniscience of the digital eye to render tangible the professor's sexual transgressivity in addition to class, caste and other vectors of identity. In fact, both Deepu and Siras's class, caste and sexuality are enabled and emphasised by digital apparatuses that suggest transcendence of identitarian difference even as they serve as electronic renditions of the truth of one's identity. Nowhere in the film is this juxtaposition of affect more striking than Mehta's shift in the reaction of Siras to the goons who break into his home and film him and the rickshaw-cycler embracing in the bedroom.

This tightly framed sequence feels like a collision between the presence of the digital eye and homophobia on the professor's expendable, queer life. While Mehta's film is problematic in the sense that its empathy at times touches on what could be argued as latent Islamaphobia and/ or cinematic pink-washing in the script, the terror on Siras and his partner's face as captured by the video camera registers the horror of being outed from the digital closet which also provided comfort, support and amiable silence. We must recognise that in the film, as it was in real life for Siras, the digital archive of sexual transgression is a script of electronic testament that results in personal and professional destruction. Indeed, this reconfiguration of queer subjectivity – how gay identity is both masked and revealed by the digital apparatus – compels us to seriously consider how queer subjectivities shape and are shaped by so-called 'Digital India'.

The ripple effect of the reconciliatory technology wielded by the boyish Deepu in the form of a digital voice recorder and mobile camera are juxtaposed against the more 'official' digital eyes of exploitative media (held by Deepu's photographer colleague) and the electronic gaze of the disciplinary state that is symbolised by the two men who film Siras and his sex partner in utter, naked humiliation and terror. The trauma and tears here seem to turn the digital closet inside out, emptying it of all secrets and tacitly promising utter ruination of both men, which is exactly how the poignant story, based on a the life of a professor of Marathi at Aligarh Muslim University, ends with the exiled, absent rickshaw-cycler and the ostensible suicide of Shrinivas Ramchandra Siras. While Mehta's film strives to humanise the embattled professor and lionise the charismatic, young journalist, the star at the centre stage of *Aligarh* seems to be the digital closet upon whose threshold the very life of Professor Siras pivots, spins and crumples into death. That is to say, the digital eye here is constituent of 'contemporary forms of subjugation of life to the power of death (necropolitics) profoundly reconfigure[ing] the relations . . . [between] resistance, sacrifice, and terror' (Mbembe 2003: 39).

The notion of a necropolitics, in Achille Mbembe's above formulation, as being mediated by digital apparatuses that calibrate surreptitious, queer subjectivity in South Asia surfaces in Shakun Batra's *Kapoor & Sons (since 1921)*, and also features a character who experiences extreme emotional vicissitudes through digital apparatuses. Electronic and digital media mediate same-sex sexuality in deeply traumatic ways in both films: in *Aligarh*, as I have above outlined, the camera and video camera provide the digital evidence of the professor's sexual deviance while the computer and mobile phone facilitate the outing of Rahul in the film *Kapoor & Sons*. In contrast to Mehta's empathetic yet sanitised biopic of the months leading up to Siras's death, Batra's composedly deceptive Rahul (portrayed by Fawad Afzal Khan) not only manages to hide his partner and sexual orientation from his family, but likewise uses digital apparatuses to veil his partner from becoming too familiar – dare we say intimate? – with his doting parents and envious brother Arjun (portrayed by Sidharth Malhotra). The ruse of straightness is facilitated by a digital closet that Rahul carefully constructs with the help of technological apparatuses and the timing that it affords us.

In fact, Rahul's homonormative sexuality seems to be a function of both technological connection to veiled gayness in India juxtaposed by his bourgeois lifestyle as a 'hot', metrosexual fiction writer living in London with his partner. Rahul's sanitised desires and sexuality are not a threat to the economic order that allows him to profit from stealing his brother's story ideas, engaging in a homonormative lifestyle that perpetuates stereotypes of gay men, and have at his fingertips the flashy gadgets that allow a deceitful flexibility to one's sexual identity. While I do not intend here to reduce the impact of this character in Batra's film on wider questions of representation of South Asian diasporas in Hindi cinema, we should note, as Gajjala et al. have above, that the technological apparatus does not simply render queer agency possible but rather also enfolds questions of race, gender and class into the fold of representations in the film. Indeed, Batra's film makes clear that all of the characters' lives are mediated by digital closets of sorts that collide with the image of the happy, Westernised family in contemporary, upper-class India. While Batra's film seems to borrow many of its themes and even the birthday party sequence from Mira Nair's 2001 family drama *Monsoon Wedding*, the technological interface also mediates queer sexuality.

The life and death of the digital closet centres around the family home of Arjun and Rahul, both aspiring fiction writers though the latter has experienced commercial success. In a sense, the countryside bungalow operates as a handsome maze of deceptions in which the brothers' father is hiding an affair with Anju, a family friend and former colleague, while their mother conceals a terrible secret about the success of one over the other son. As such, there are many closets in the film that revolve around heteronormative kinship and its cracks and fissures for this family in Coonoor, Tamil Nadu. Even the brothers' elderly grandfather, Amarjeet Dadu (Rishi Kapoor), delights in the clips of Mandakini clad in a wet, white sari on the tablet computer that the brothers introduce to him. Yet ultimately it is Rahul's deception that is revealed by his own laptop and cell phone when his mother is trying to check email on it and is instant messaged by her son's partner in London. In other words, in Batra's film, the queer transgression of Hindu heteronormativity, even for the diasporic hipness of Rahul and his chic, second life in London, becomes the primary betrayal of family that is unresolved, and perhaps ultimately unforgiveable, as it is revealed and then silently retracts back into the digital closet. His sexual transgressions are not portrayed as mortal sins, but are indeed the least speakable as they constitute a dual assault on heteropatriarchal masculinity and reproductive kinship.

A close and critical analysis of *Kapoor & Sons* demonstrates that Rahul's hidden sexuality is completely mediated by his smart phone, on which he is constantly chatting with his invisible partner 'Nikki' (a name that escapes gender specification). Here, there is indeed a kind of speaking of the 'sexual subaltern', in legal scholar Ratna Kapoor's words, despite the subject's ability to speak freely beyond the safe channels of his international, digital phone; here, as in colonial days, difference is threatened by laws that promise 'strict discipline and punishment' (2013: 23). Indeed, Batra vastly contrasts the glitzy liberalness of London against the putative prohibitions of queer sexuality in contemporary, rural India. The mobile phone as the point source of a digital closet that Rahul has constructed likewise serves as a conduit for his affection and yearning to share his ancestral homeland with his British partner Nick. This diasporic desire, which many scholars of postcolonial, diaspora and transnational studies have explored at different lengths, produces tension with the digital closet it because it enables leaks and cracks in the composure of the protective discourse. For Batra's Rahul, who is closeted within the heteronormative kinship networks at home in India, his mobile phone is the transnational lifeline that literally and figuratively connects him to his partner across the globe.

Rahul's mobile phone is, moreover, a time portal that mediates contradictory identities in the palm of his hand compelling us to reconsider not just the way in which we think about closets in the twenty-first century, but also how digitality reshapes their components and functions. For Rahul, the closet door seems to open both ways, and perhaps more accurately is a revolving door that enables him to have varying social articulations of what he wishes to present to his brother, family and friends while he is at his parents' homestead. His cell not only allows him to speak with Nick in private conversations, but also allows him to show in real time the writer's retreat he is considering buying – even when briefly introducing him to lovely local Tia Malik who seems to be dev eloping a crush on the dapper metrosexual from London. The digital interface in his hands thus in some ways allows for sexual play and the illusion that the special person in his life is a white, British lady rather than a good, 'Hindustani girl who can give his mother grandchildren. It strategically perpetuates, that is, the hegemonic straight myth for which Tellis (2016) critiques both films while also allowing release from it. As such, representations of upstanding, gay men in society who are respected for their knowledge, wealth or both, is an affront to the entire kinship system of the Coonoor community in contrast to the unbridled flows of desires in cyberspace.

The mobile phone, however, is not the digital point of contact wherein Rahul's mother Sunita discovers her son's sexual aberrations. She casually opens his MacBook Air laptop to view some receipts in her email account, wherein she stumbles upon his open Google chat windows with his partner Nick. In response to seeing that Rahul is online, his partner Nick sends him romantic, holiday pictures of the couple with notes describing how much he misses him to boot with blowing-kisses emojis. While this doesn't put the nail in the coffin of Rahul's family life as the 'perfect child', it is his cell phone that ultimately betrays him: a concerned Nick calls Rahul back after sensing that something is awry with the discrepancy between the chat bubbles marked as 'Read' and Rahul not even being in possession of his laptop. As would be good family drama, Sunita picks up the phone as she demands he tell her who the person in the 'disgusting' photographs is. The same mobile phone that links Rahul to his partner while he navigates his homestead is the very mechanism that verifies, for his mother, that her perfect son was never – and can never be – perfect in her and greater society's eyes. Batra's likeable character suddenly becomes the focus of the ire of his family members with his unforgiving mother and standoffish brother when he proclaims his sexual identity.

The functioning of the mobile phone in its facilitation of digital closets and the multiple ways in which their portals open reflects Nishant Shah's intentions to separate sexuality from queerness 'to characterize the mobile as a queer technology as it transcends, transgresses, and renders different bodies and events queer' (Hjorth and Khoo 2015: 10). The image of Nick's face illuminated on Rahul's smart phone reveals the depth of deception, even with this breakdown of the digital closet and overdetermined exposure, for Sunita. Yet while she leaves her son to pick up the pieces of mid-life rejection by one's own mother, a different tragedy unfolds soon after when she decides to call Harsh on his mobile after a terrible fight. His vehicle is demolished head on by a truck as he is answering her call. Here, Mbembe's 'subjugation of life to the power of death' is totally orchestrated around the digital closets – whether straight or gay – that mobile phone cultures make possible in contemporary India. Rahul is lucky at the end of Batra's film to reconnect with his Coonoor family, presumably through the good graces of benevolent heteronormativity and upper-class civility, although his father's life is permanently erased from the material world on account of his ill-fated actions with mechanisms of the digital world. Both father and son, however, pay through life and death scenarios for their transgressions of hegemonic heteronormativity as mediated by digital closets made possible by data-revealing mobile phones, tablets and laptops.

Conclusion: Pink Screens in Digital India

Digital closets structure queer subjectivity in Mehta's *Aligarh* and Batra's *Kapoor & Sons*, although with different affect. While the representations of Professor Siras and Rahul Kapoor are emotionally fraught and somewhat stereotypical, there can be no denying that the real star of these films is the digital closet. As it engages Indian viewers' voyeuristic tendencies in the wake of Section 377's most taboo topic, the digital closet also reigns throughout *Aligarh* and *Kapoor & Sons* as the dominant fulcrum for queer trauma and agency. It shows, in other words, a side of Digital India that is both unexpected and innovative for Hindi cinema – that sexuality is technologically mediated despite how organically rooted we are to our organs, that in these two films queer sexuality in India is coextensive with technological apparatus like mobile phones, laptops, video recorders, and digital cameras. While there can be no doubt that these films ideologically upset the dominant stereotypes of gays in India at a crucial, historical juncture in the post-colony's afterlife from the British Empire, they also do so by making clear that queer subjectivity in post-millennial India depends on technology in complicated and deeply nuanced ways. It remains to be seen in which ways the viewing public of both films will be swayed by the painfully empathetic portrayals of their gay protagonists. While the bourgeois and male-centric queer narratives seem to justify approaching the topic through patriarchal and bourgeois privilege (i.e. queerness is OK for men and the upper-middle class), the digital closet anchors us back down to the console and the ways in which it shapes libidinal desire.

The other great impact, indeed queer activism, of *Aligarh*, *Kapoor & Sons* and other queer, Hindi films ranges beyond the representations of technology in the films themselves and involves the potential for social change in the lives that the films have online following theatrical release. For example, availability on YouTube, Netflix and a universe of third-party live streaming websites will revolutionise the accessibility and viewership of these films and the audiences to whom they might forge the most identifications with. Digital media is perhaps the most effective medium in how and why viewers around the globe encounter representations of itself, and in what ways it can enable us to hide and reveal different aspects of our identities. As Roopika Risam and Adeleine Koh have outlined in their Mission Statement for Postcolonial Digital Humanities:

> The mid-2000s transmedia shift began changing digital practices by eliding boundaries between media producers and consumers. Such shifts have raised questions of possible epistemological differences in the articulation of identities in digital spaces . . . Taking these assessments of digital space as its basis, postcolonial digital humanities brings critiques of colonialism, imperialism, and globalization and their relationship to race, class, gender, sexuality and disability to bear on the digital humanities. (2013)

As we continue to survey the shifts in media and how they reshape sexual identities in post-millennial India, we will be better able to survey also the shifting terrains of digital closets that expose and conceal illicit sexual trysts. I have elsewhere argued that the Cold War period of queer representation in the US was arguably characterised by 'the white closet . . . [which] consolidates white skin's privilege as an epidermal marker of manifest male homosexuality by emanating its own cultural capital as the point of origin for what is sexually desirable' (Gairola 2012: 2). In contrast to those earlier forms of exclusion based on race and nation, contemporary Hindi cinema ostensibly links digital technology with queer identity formations as both a nexus of great terror and pleasure as we see with Siras and Rahul. My hope and intention here is that the focus of these cinematic trends in India will shift from permitting queer sexuality's public lives as an affect of failed digital closets to recalibrations of flesh and metal in the era of pervasive technoculture. Perhaps then we may evolve from dwelling on the limitations of the material life of digital closets to possibilities they can catalyse in data networks and online communities.

References

Alexander, M. Jacqui (2005) *Pedagogies of Crossing: Meditations on Feminism, Sexual Politics, Memory, and the Sacred*. Durham, NC: Duke University Press.

Batra, Shakun (2016) *Kapoor & Sons (since 1921)*. Karan Johar Productions

Campbell, John Edward (2004) *Getting It Online: Cyberspace, Gay Male Sexuality, and Embodied Identity*. London: Routledge.

Dasgupta, Rohit K. (2012) 'Queering the Cyberspace: Towards a Space/Identity Discussion', *Bhatter College Journal of Multidisciplinary Studies*, 2. Available online at http://bcjms.bhattercollege.ac.in/queering-the-cyberspace-towards-a-spaceidentity-discussion/ (accessed 21 March 2016).

Dasgupta, Rohit K. (2015) 'The Visual Representation of Queer Bollywood: Mistaken Identities and Misreadings in Dostana', *Journals of Arts Writing*, 1 (1): 91–101.

Deleuze, Gilles and Guattari, Félix (2004) *A Thousand Plateaus*. London: A & C Black.

Desai, Jigna (2004) *Beyond Bollywood: The Cultural Politics of South Asian Diasporic Film*. New York: Routledge.

Dudrah, Rajinder (2012) *Bollywood Travels: Culture, Diaspora and Border Crossings in Popular Hindi Cinema*. London: Routledge.

Ferguson, Roderick (2003) *Aberrations in Black: Towards a Queer of Color Critique*. Minneapolis: University of Minnesota Press.

Gairola, Rahul K. (2001) 'Watching with Ambivalence', *Popmatters. com*. Available at http://www.popmatters.com/review/will-and-grace/ (accessed 27 June 2016).

Gairola, Rahul K. (2002) 'Burning With Shame: Desire and South Asian Patriarchy, from Gayatri Spivak's "Can the Subaltern Speak?" to Deepa Mehta's *Fire*', *Comparative Literature*, 54 (4): 307–24.

Gairola, Rahul K. (2012) 'White Skin, Red Masks: Playing "Indian" in Queer Images from *Physique Pictorial*, 1957–67', *Liminalities: A Journal of Performance Studies*, 8 (4): 1–17.

Gairola, Rahul K. (2016) 'Migrations in Absentia: Multinational Digital Advertising and Manipulation of Partition Trauma', *Revisiting India's Partition: New Essays on Memory, Culture, and Politics*. New York: Lexington Books, pp. 53–70.

Gajjala, Radhika (2008) 'Racing and Queering the Interface: Producing Local/Global Cyberselves', *Qualitative Inquiry*, 14 (7): 1110–33.

Gajjala, Radhika (2013) *Cyberculture and the Subaltern: Weavings of the Virtual and Real*. New York: Lexington Books.

Gajjala, Radhika and Mitra, Rahul (2008) 'Queer Blogging in Indian Digital Diasporas: A Dialogic Encounter', *Journal of Communication Inquiry*, 32 (4): 400–23.

Gajjala, R., Rybas, N. and Altman, M. (2008) 'Racing and Queering the Interface: Producing Global/Local Cyberselves', *Feminist Media Studies*, 14 (7): 111033.

Gopinath, Gayatri (2005) *Impossible Desires: Queer Diasporas and South Asian Public Cultures*. London: Duke University Press.

Gustad, Kaizad (1998) *Bombay Boys*. Kaizad Gustad Films.

Hjorth, Larissa and Khoo, Olivia (2015) 'Intimate Entanglements: New Media in Asia', *Routledge Handbook of New Media in Asia*. London: Routledge.

Kalra, Kush and Barupal, Priyanka (2013) *Law, Sex and Crime*. New Delhi: Vij Books.

Kapur, Ratna (2013) *Erotic Justice: Law and the New Politics of Postcolonialism*. London: Routledge.

Khan, Saad (2013) *Hide and Seek*. Saad Khan.

Landzelius, Kyra (2004) *Native on the Net: Indigenous and Diasporic Peoples in the Virtual Age*. New York: Routledge.

McGlotten, Shaka (2013) *Virtual Intimacies: Media, Affect, and Queer Sociality*. Albany: SUNY Press.

Manovich, Lev (1999) 'What Is Digital Cinema?', *Digital Dialectic: New Essays on New Media*, ed. Peter Lunenfeld. Cambridge, MA: MIT Press, pp. 172–96.

Mansukhani, Tarun (2008) *Dostana*. Karan Johar Films.

Mbembe, Achille (2003) 'Necropolitics', *Public Culture*, 15 (1): 11–40.

Mehta, Deepa (1996) *Fire*. Zeitgeist Films, India/ Canada.

Mehta, Hansal (2016) *Aligarh*. Hansal Mehta Films.

Mowlabocus, Sharif (2010) *Gaydar Culture: Gay Men, Technology, and Embodiment in the Digital Age*. London: Routledge.

Nair, Mira (2001) *Monsoon Wedding*. Mirabai Films.

Nakamura, Lisa and Chow-White, Peter A. (2012) 'Introduction – Race and Digital Technology: Code, the Color Line, and the Information Society', *Race After the Internet*, ed. Lisa Nakamura and Peter A. Chow-White. London: Routledge, pp. 1–18.

O'Riordan, Kate (2007) 'Queer Theories and Cybersubjects', *Queer Online: Media, Technology and Sexuality*. Bern: Peter Lang, pp. 13–30.

Puar, Jasbir (2007) *Terrorist Assemblages: Homonationalism in Queer Times*. London: Duke University Press.

Rai, Amit (2009) *Untimely Bollywood: Globalization and India's New Media Assemblage*. Durham, NC: Duke University Press.

Reddy, Chandan (1998) 'Paris Is Burning', *Burning Down the House: Domesticity and Postcoloniality*, ed. Rosemary Marangoly George. Boulder: Westview Press, pp. 359–79.

Risam, Roopika (2015) 'Revising History and Re-authoring the Left in the Postcolonial Digital Archive', *Left History*, 18 (2): 35–46.

Risam, Roopika and Koh, Adeleine (2013) 'Postcolonial Digital Humanities: Mission Statement'. Available online at http://dhpoco.org/mission-statement-postcolonial-digital-humanities/ (accessed 14 July 2016).

Sedgwick, Eve Kosofsky (1990) *The Epistemology of the Closet*. Berkeley: University of California Press.

Shah, Nishant (2015) 'Queer Mobiles and Mobile Queers: Intersections, Vectors, and Movements in India', *Routledge Handbook of New*

Media in Asia, ed. Larissa Hjorth and Olivia Khoo. New York: Routledge, pp. 275–84.

Shahani, Parmesh (2008) *Gay Bombay: Globalization, Love, and (Be)longing in Contemporary India*. New Delhi: Sage.

Spivak, Gayatri Chakravorty (1988) 'Can the Subaltern Speak?', *Marxism and the Interpretation of Culture*, ed. Lawrence Grossberg. Urbana: University of Illinois Press, pp. 271–313.

Tellis, Ashley (2016) 'How *Aligarh* and *Kapoor & Sons* Reaffirm that Homosexuality Is Acceptable Only When Made as Heterosexual as Possible'. Available online at http://www.gaylaxymag.com/blogs/aligarh-kapporand-sons-reaffirm-gomosexuality-has-to-be-heteronormative/#gs.yGb8=sw (accessed 22 June 2016).

Thomas, Pradeep Ninan (2012) *Digital India: Understanding Information, Communication, and Social Change*. New Delhi: Sage.

Wakeford, Nina (2000) 'Cyberqueer', *The Cybercltures Reader*, ed. David Bell and Barbara M. Kennedy. London: Routledge, pp. 403–13.

Chapter 4

Cruising the Ephemeral Archives of Bangalore's Gay Nightlife

Kareem Khubchandani

Cruzin D FMrl Rkivez of Blr's G Nitelife

On 31 December 2012, two gay party groups, Heatwave and Pink Nation, collaborated to host simultaneous gay parties in Goa and Bangalore. Pink Nation's founder hosted the Goa party, which was a bust because the owners changed the name of the bar without informing anyone and attendees could not find the place. The party in Bangalore was held at Seven Hotel, in Marathahalli on the outskirts of the city. Seven, a boutique hotel owned by a white French gay male couple, was always amenable to parties, and usually hosted them at its rooftop Pink Sky Bar. When the French couple sold Seven to an Indian family business, Heatwave could no longer host parties there. This New Years Eve, the gay party was relegated to the basement bar, The Box, as a straight DJ had booked the regular space for a higher price.[1] Mihir's ad for the Bangalore Heatwave party read as follows:

> N.U.D.E. 2012: N-ew year's eve U-nderground D-ance E-xtravaganza | Our party's called NUDE but v wont b rude if u dress in nothin. HAHA! | But wen v call it a NUDE party, do v really take u fr granted? | Here v r stripping it down 2 bare essentials u must hv fr the party mood. | 1) MEN'S LINGERIE SHOW: Hunky models in International brand lingerie! | 2) DARK HOUR frm 11PM til stroke of midnight. | [. . .] | Cum the way u were born – not NUDE but UNINHIBITED!

Gay party invitations, and not just NYE events, are often encumbered with detailed explanations of what to expect and what attendees will 'avail'. 'Hunky models', 'International brand lingerie' and 'the way you were born' signal the preference for masculinity, foreign

72

products and Western pop culture – the last line recalls Lady Gaga's essentialist gay anthem, 'Born This Way'. The overtly explanatory nature of this advertisement – clarifying that 'nude' does not necessarily mean naked – speaks to the intentionality of the organiser to fashion a particularly sexy affect. His text is littered with internet and text-message style abbreviations, writing 'we' as 'v' to mimic an Indianised pronunciation of the English word, and 'come' as 'cum' to evoke ejaculate. This invitation is at once hypersexual and modest, international and local, elaborate and flippant. It generates extensive expectations for what to expect at the party, while still leaving a patron unsure of what interpretation of 'nude' to arrive with.

The promise of the 'men's lingerie show' has the sweaty crowd of dancers excited, and there is an eager buzz when the ugly fluorescent lights turn on. Mihir escorts two straight male models to the stage, draped in full length, white, terrycloth robes. Neither cracks a smile. One pulls at his belt, and his robe opens up to reveal a smooth muscular, fair-skinned body and cheetah-print underwear. Gaining confidence from the audience response, the other removes his robe completely and smiles. More screams and cheers. In less than sixty seconds, robes are back on and the models are gone. The crowd groans in disappointment; was that all? Suddenly cheers erupt for Subodh, skinny and dark skinned, scampering from the bathroom to the stage. He mischievously runs on stage in a woman's red bathing suit, wiggling his exposed ass; his cock is dangerously close to falling out. Subodh is escorted off the stage by Mihir, who brings back the models; they have new underwear to show off beneath their robes. Again, they stiffly exhibit their bodies for a minute and disappear. Their departure is quickly followed by several men packing the small stage to dance, removing and unbuttoning their shirts to show off their muscles, tattoos, hairy chests and jiggling bellies while fluorescent lights are still on them. The room darkens and the party continues.

When I asked Mihir why the underwear show was so short, he said that the models were afraid the audience would snatch their underwear off. He signals the models' unspoken homophobia, as well as the absence of rules in interacting with go-go boys in Indian bar spaces. In lieu of the disappointing show, partygoers, prompted by the recently released item song 'Chikni Chameli,' claimed the stage and became their own go-go boys and strippers. Subodh and the 'Chikni Chameli' dancers seized the stage, riffing on the party's invitation to be 'nude,' while also refusing the propriety generally expected of partygoers. Their skinny, fat, hairy, feminine and dark bodies contrasted with the fair-skinned, masculine, muscular, hairless models, as well as the white muscle clones on the party invitation.

This essay explores the visual and textual promotion of gay parties via digital venues, as well as the interactions, choreographies, soundscapes and organisation of the parties themselves. My descriptions of the N.U.D.E. party gesture to the subject (nightlife ephemera), method (ethnography and interview) and analytic focus (interruptions, linguistic games, cancellations, punctuations, repetitions) I employ. I position digital promotion and party happenings as ephemeral archives, venues without long-lasting material evidence of their presence. These cultural spheres resist meticulous documentation and comprehensive studies, so I attend to smaller moments of communication. While a distinctly cosmopolitan ethos is curated for partygoers via digital communication, attendees themselves negotiate pleasures of language, choreography, music and intimacy that potentially refuse the heavy pedagogy of the party. I suggest that it is in these aesthetic and material breaks – interruptions, stumbles, skips, blackouts – that we see the negotiation of local and global gay sensibilities, what Eng-Beng Lim (2005) refers to as 'glocalqueering' and Alyson Campbell and Stephen Farrier (2016) describe as 'translocal'. Like Bobby Benedicto's (2014) beautiful ethnography of gay Manila, this essay is concerned with the ways that postcolonial queers aspire toward western, white and upper-class performances of global gayness. But where Benedicto is consistently critical of his interlocutors' aspirational tendencies, I look for those breaks and failures in deftly performing global gayness. Whether intentional or unintentional refusals, they have performative consequence that allow for alternative habitations of queer space.

Gay nightlife in Bangalore is difficult to institutionalise because of the stigmas attached to gay identities and communities that keep these parties underground, as well as the conservative entities – police, bureaucrats, politicians – that keep a tight leash on the nightlife entrepreneurs. Bangalore is a quickly globalising city known for its information technology industries and overseas business processing services that arrived prior to economic liberalisation but have boomed since (Heitzman 2004; Nair 2005). Rapid economic, commercial, demographic and infrastructural changes have resulted in backlashes against nightlife and other seemingly western importations that supposedly corrupt traditional sensibilities and ways of life (see, for example, Bhaskaran (2004) on the Miss World pageant in Bangalore). There is no bar or club that caters primarily to a gay clientele; however, a handful of event organisers host parties on Saturday nights at various bars across the city. They promote parties exclusively to gay men via various digital platforms: phone-based apps, personals websites and SMS lists.

I use the term 'gay' with caution. The parties draw on globally hegemonic gay styles, while also eliding the word 'gay'; instead, they speak of 'G-parties' and advertise 'hundreds of guys'. Further, a subsection of men at these parties are married to women and do not identify as gay, although they enjoy the sexual, social, emotional and romantic company of other men. I choose not to use MSM (men who have sex with men) as these parties eschew the aesthetic and political rhetorics of the non-profit industrial complex from which 'MSM' emerges (Dutta 2012: 118; Khan 2014: 177). My use of 'gay' signals the privileging of desire between male and masculine persons in these party spaces, as well as the citation of recognisable white, Western gay subcultures. By no means am I suggesting that gay is incompatible with localised formations of sexual subjecthood; rather this essay follows queer media studies scholar Christopher Pullen's call to chart how non-Western queer folk ground gay subcultural practices in aesthetics and sensibilities that are not incompatible with local sexual and moral economies (see also Reddy 2005 and Boellstorff 2005 among many others).

Discretionary acts and ephemeral archives

PlanetRomeo.com, colloquially referred to by my interlocutors as 'PR', is a primary online platform in Bangalore, and across India, for men interested in making romantic and sexual connections with other men. Party organisers create 'Clubs' within PR's interface to send invitations to people interested in their events. On 10 December 2015 I received an email from the PR's adminstrators:

> you were a member of the PINK_NATION Club.
>   The Club Admin didn't log in since 06.09.2015. [. . .] So today we're writing to let you know that unfortunately the Club has been automatically deleted.

This deletion of a club within PlanetRomeo is a reminder that the internet is far from an ideal archive. Without the foresight to screenshot, copy and paste, and print out pages, we completely lose content that accumulated in the Pink Nation Club. Moreover, PR's merging with the Guys4Men.com – a significant resource to gay Indian publics – in 2009 signals the loss of a whole online archive, with a very different user interface from PR. Party groups such as Heatwave have been reported as offensive to Facebook; though organisers have rebuilt or renamed their pages, earlier content has been lost to public access. As Brian Herrera poignantly points out, queer sites on the internet such as Rentboy and BillyWorld are more likely to disappear without trace and documentation: 'contrary to popular cliché, the internet is *not* forever' (Herrera 2016: 48).

In discussing gay party promotion as ephemeral, I am signalling not only the uncertain longevity of internet-based content, but also its immaterial quality that limits access and circulation. For a variety of reasons, party organisers use digital platforms to advertise their events: access can be controlled through private groups so that homophobic strangers do not stumble on event information; event locations are often not secured until a day or two before the party; digital gay resources (PR, Grindr, Scruff) can target and attract new audiences; organisers may need to reach their audience on short notice to cancel a party due to a police raid, political emergencies or loss of venue. Where Pride month celebrations and NGO outreach efforts deliberately use posters, fliers and public listings to access a wide audience, gay parties are almost never promoted in print. Utilising online, login-based venues does not provide complete privacy from public scrutiny as the TV9 debacle indicates (see Singh, this volume). But party organisers labour to provide some sense of discretion by respecting pseudonyms, limiting publicity and avoiding the use of terms such as 'gay' and 'queer' (Mowlabocus 2008: 426).

It strikes me that the TV9 footage of Hyderabad's gay club night is some of the only footage of gay Indian parties I've seen in circulation. Where drag queens and club kids have been the muses of artists and filmmakers in East Asia, the Americas and Europe, there exists a very limited (tele)visual archive of gay Indian nightlife. Indian pride marches are featured in (inter)national and regional news coverage and NGOs take meticulous minutes of their meetings but there is little documentation of what happens at parties. Though not advertised on promotional material, filming and photography are generally disallowed at gay parties; organisers will request DJs to announce, 'No photography please!' if they see anyone taking non-personal pictures.

Rohit K. Dasgupta (2014) shows, in the case of India, that an ethnography of nightlife must consider both online discourses and embodied interactions in order to perform critical social analysis of party spaces. If we rely on the heavily detailed promotional materials – already an ephemeral digital collection – to provide an idea of what parties are like, researchers might be misled in imagining the quality of the party itself. José Esteban Muñoz, a pioneer of contemporary queer nightlife studies, reminds us that research on queer life and politics must remember the trouble of the archive itself: 'Queerness has an especially vexed relationship to evidence. Historically, evidence of queerness has been used to penalize and discipline queer desires, connections, and acts' (2001: 423; see also Muñoz 1996; Marshall et al. 2015). He moves us to think about ephemera – those immaterial moments and inconsequential objects that are too incriminating to circulate or archive – as vital pieces of queer subculture that have long-lasting effects. It is with this imperative that I assemble my strange collection of Bangalore's queer nightlife, pursuing an intricate and aesthetically oriented online/offline ethnography modelled by Parmesh Shahani in his study of gay Indian community spaces.

Cruising in the Breaks: On Method and Analysis

Muñoz's *oeuvre* also offers us a method of 'cruising' with which to accrue and analyse an ephemeral archive by trusting small moments, scenes and objects. For queer people, the labour of cruising – congealing most poignantly in the backward glance – involves the search for pleasure, intimacy, recognition and mutual desire in plain sight of an unknowing or even phobic public. Some moments of recognition are made strange by the fact that they are in Bangalore when I recognise them from my American life. Others are strange because they hail me as a queer subject, even when I am unfamiliar with the cultural context. Particularly relevant to the scope of this book, Maya Ganesh and Sharif Mowlabocus both argue that the move toward technology in facilitating sexual and romantic meetings has not eliminated cruising as a social and public practice, but has been adapted to facilitate public intimacies and erotic recognitions.

Cruising, as a method, taught me to collect data in both intentional and opportunistic ways: relying on anecdotes, isolated incidents, small objects, little gestures and offhand remarks, alongside regular attendance at parties over two years with consistent ethnographic transcription of choreography, conversations and music paired with formal interviews. By registering those points of frictive recognition, I ask why they arrest me, stop me in my tracks and make me look back, break my familiar, learned and rehearsed rhythms of queer nightlife. These breaks include grammatical misfires and typos in party descriptions, interruptive announcements by DJs during music sets, unexpected choreographies on the dance floor and back-pedalling and stutters in ethnographic interviews.

This analytic mode is not to police the subjects of my fieldsites for how they get nightlife 'wrong' – this would be tantamount to suggesting that gay Indian nightlife is merely flawed mimicry or a 'delayed modernity'. Nor am I making fun of linguistic or choreographic flubs.

Jillana Enteen argues in her study of Thai women using online community spaces that though an English language medium signals class privilege and mobility, the presence of spelling and grammatical mistakes does not necessarily indicate 'errors' (2005: 436). Rather they can be read as articulations of locality or resistance. Moreover, Roy Pérez's (2012) meditation on the online-based art and writing of trans cultural worker Mark Aguhar argues that seemingly flippant abbreviations by queer and trans people in internet language in fact work to undermine the authority of colonial and patriarchal pedagogies. Following such approaches, my analysis is premised on the ways that postcolonial subjects take 'license to play with form and refigure function according to the exigencies of the situation' (Gaonkar 2001: 23).

I am interested in the performative qualities of moments in which Western referents run up against local practices; they are productive frictions. Various performance scholars imagine the performative and philosophical possibilities of such punctuations, understanding them as sites of self-making, when subjectivity is sutured with, through and against social scripts (Smith 2000: 36; Hewitt 2005: 95; Moten 2003). I rely on these breaks to evidence the productive possibilities that emerge from such 'frictive encounters' (Rivera-Servera 2012 195) between archive and repertoire, global and local, regional and national, digital and embodied. In these halting moments of online and party cruising, often missed and easily dismissed, we might find more textured theorising about the nature of gay identity, desire and becoming in India.

Pedagogies of Global Style

The graphic flier (see Figure 4.1), sent to members of Heatwave's PR Club, is accompanied by the following text:

> 'NOCHE CALIENTE, FIESTA LOCA' @ SEVEN HOTEL on November 19th, Saturday from 8PM – 1:15AM hosted by HEATWAVE & PINK NATION
> A Pride Fund Raiser Party!
>
> ==
>
> Noche | Caliente | Fiesta | Loca
>
> These are the words which can be associated with any rocking party. But what are they? Don't say they sound Greek to you! They are certainly not Greek but Spanish!
>
> Spanish is a sexy and romantic language! And so are Latino men. Spanish music is equally sensual.

Figure 4.1 Graphic flier sent by Heatwave

Well 'Noche Caliente, Fiesta Loca' means 'Hot Night, Crazy Party'! So now you know what we are talkin' bout.

Get ready to gyrate on the erotic Spanish tunes and other club numbers this Saturday as The Dirty Trio spin their best tracks.

Bring out the Spanish in you by dressing up as a matador or a bull!:-)

Or just dress up in a cool outfit and party like the Spanish for they sure know how to party big!

The best outfit would win a cool prize.

Enjoy the night and get tipsy with Mojitos, Margaritas and Sangrias.

Also, feel good coz this party is for a cause. A portion of the entry amount would be donated towards this year's Bangalore Pride Funds. So make sure you bring all your friends along and party in style and contribute to the cause and say 'Hola'!

We also have a special discount for students if they bring their IDs.

Hasta pronto amigos!

DATE: November 19th 2011 Saturday

TIME: 8PM – 1:15AM

VENUE:
Pink Sky Bar, Seven Hotel, 4th Floor
Beside new total shopping mall, Outer Ring Road, Between Marathahalli & KR Puram Bridges, Doddanekundi, Bangalore

ENTRY: 299/-

DEAL:
1) 250+ crowd 2) Great ambience 3) 2 party groups together 4) Great crowd 5) Gay-friendly venue 6) Cool Spanish theme 7) Prize for best costume

Like most party invitations, that for Noche Caliente offers both a heavy dose of pedagogy about how to be a cosmopolitan subject alongside reassurance that paying the entry fee will guarantee a good time. The promoters capitalise on the 'economies of passion' associated with Latin America and Spain (Savigliano 1995), while also missing important differentiations between American Latino ethnicity and Spanish nationality. Noche Caliente rides on the coat-tails of the Hindi film *Zindagi Na Milegi Dobara*, released earlier in 2011, exposing Indian publics to Spanish spectacles such as the Running of the Bulls and the Tomatina festival. The message promises drinks that are unavailable at the bar and music that is 'erotic' and 'sensual' but generally unfamiliar to its audience. The flier itself features an image – one quickly found with a Google Image search of 'gay matador' – of white muscular men placed against an abstract, sparkling background. With the rarest exception, every model featured on gay party fliers, like the matadors and bull in this one, is white-passing, muscular and avowedly masculine; even the 'Pink Diwali' and 'Desi Glamour Nyt' party fliers feature white men. Encouraging patrons to dress as a 'matador or bull' organisers buy into clichéd notions of

Spanish culture while also inviting some possibly strange and exciting sartorial styles.

Meredith McGuire (2011), studying India's new middle classes, argues that the performance of class status is not only an unconscious rehearsal through consumption practices in new commercial spaces such as malls, coffeeshops and pubs. Call centres and IT firms actively instruct and cultivate bodily disposition through trainings called 'Personal Development and Enhancement modules'. Like PDE modules, party invitations in Bangalore offer sartorial and performance scripts that engender and regulate class performance. The regularity of party themes structured around style – 'The Hipster Ball', 'Umbrella Party', 'Black Tie Edition', 'Ripped Jeans Party', 'Raincoat Party', 'T-Shirt Party', 'Waistcoat Party', 'Lockets and Jackets', 'Dudes in Boots', 'Uniform Party' – invites patrons into shared global fashion sensibilities through lengthy descriptions about the appeal of these garments and styles. Fashion statements are not only cultural capital at these parties, there is material incentive to participate in these visual economies as they might get you a discount at the door.

A flier for The Hipster Ball in 2011 offers a long explanation about hipsters, including rather obscure information such as: 'they can be found in the Williamsburg, Wicker Park, and Mission neighborhoods'. On the one hand this presumes a well-travelled patron, and on the other it creates aspirational desires to visit these specific US neighbourhoods. The 2015 Hipsteria Party contradictorily notes, 'Today's hipsters are more individualistic and nonconformist than ever. Mass market style and manufactured trendiness just won't do for them,' while also dictating how to achieve such individualism through conformist practices, 'flaunt your suspenders, bow ties, cool facial hair and quirky styles'. At the Fashionista party, a cash prize was given to the best dressed (as chosen by the organisers), a man repeatedly announced as 'Rohit from London' – foreign fashion is always deemed better.

It became clear as I regularly attended parties that despite the rigorous style instructions, most attendees flouted the invitation's recommendations and wore what they felt like. Now, Heatwave's elaborate dress codes conclude with '. . . or just dress hot!', succumbing to the refusals and laziness of patrons. At an Indian themed night, the only man who dressed up in a dhoti and embroidered vest was utterly embarrassed to be overdressed. At a Persian Night, five different men (myself included) wore drop-crotch black pants – a staple in any hip desi's closet – this was the most attendees I've seen heed the theme. Even when partygoers conform to the high-end aesthetics that organisers try to cultivate, they may not be to the liking of other patrons. As one PlanetRomeo user writes:

> Most of them were Hi5 [hi-fi, an Indianism meaning upscale] people from rich families. [. . .] Most of them looked like Models!! Slim body, White skin, Black Dress (Black dress was the dress code), very height [tall] and they had every qualities to be a models in Fashion TV. There were also muscled men, but I did not like their faces [. . .] I don't like such people . . ;) I like Mass! [variously meaning popular, local, regional] [. . .] There was a guy standing next to me who was sexy too. Oh he was too 'south-Indian-ish' which I love.

This user's post on the Heatwave Club's message board suggests that while the upscale crowd conformed to both upper-class North Indian standards of beauty, he was more interested in South Indian men with a local flair.

Cosmopolitan Travels, Bangalorean Locales

Abhishek's desire to start Pink Nation came from both his admiration of Bangalore's thriving nightlife in the early 2000s that earned it the moniker 'pub city', as well as his disdain for gay farmhouse parties that took place at private residences, far from the city's centre. 'Why these parties have to be done in secluded places? Why can't they be done in mainstream venues?' His vision for the parties was particularly cosmopolitan and respectable, and he conceived of a gimmick to create this ethos:

> I came up with the concept of a pink passport. It had exactly the same number of pages in an actual passport, but the size was of credit card size so that people could put it in the wallet. Everyone had to fill in whatever, put their photograph in that, and they had to bring that along to the party. Only if you bring the pink passport you get a free entry.

During my fieldwork, Pink Passports were no longer in operation, although Heatwave recently instituted membership cards due to security breaches at parties. However, several of my interviewees fondly recollect having Pink Passports and the discount they provided. Around 2009, Abhishek chatted with Kartik on PlanetRomeo, telling him about his parties; Kartik reminisces, 'I wanted that Pink Passport, but I didn't want to give out my name or number.' The name of the party, and the fake passport, suggest the possibility of escape from the mundanity of India, or at least Indian work life. However, during my interview with Kartik, he expressed concerns about documentation even while desiring inclusion in this 'Pink Nation'. Kartik also describes the exigent materialities of arriving at his first party: the bouncers kept asking who he knew at the party and he only had Abhishek's online pseudonym to go by; there was a Bachata dance lesson going on when he arrived so he wasn't sure he was in the right place; the presence of women made him unsure of whether this was a gay party; and he was relying on buses to commute so he couldn't stay for more than an hour.

Despite the resourceful planning on the part of party organisers, the experience of these parties is mediated by a variety of material conditions: what patrons can afford; getting to or from remote party locations, especially given opportunistic auto drivers and irregular buses; police regulations, etc. This premise – that the promise of escape from realms of heteronormativity and respectability that the club affords is always tempered by material contexts – has been at the core of much scholarship on queer nightlife (Rivera-Servera 2012; Vogel 2009; Buckland 2002; Han 2015; Bollen 2001). Bangalore's geography, infrastructure and politics shape the night. Sometimes patrons arrive at a shuttered door because the bar fears a police raid; liquor service has to stop early because of citywide religious observances; a power outage ends the party early; or the music and lights must pause for ten minutes because police have arrived to take a bribe.

These material limitations are most apparent in the location of a party. It is clear to partygoers that events happen primarily at the city's peripheries: Marathahalli, Domlur and Bellandur. While bars in these areas, in proximity to multinational business campuses, might be convenient to some gay men who live close to work, they do not offer the trendy atmosphere of central Bangalore, nor the upscale ethos of the Indiranagar neighbourhood. One PR user adds on his profile that he can host sex partners at his home very close to Shah, a lesbian-owned restaurant in the suburbs where parties were held for a while. In the absence of gaybourhoods, party locations, however ephemeral, become useful markers for a gay geography.

Organisers acknowledge the appeal of central locations, for when they do manage to secure a club in Indiranagar or Brigade Road, they actively advertise: 'Party in city central for all our guys ☺.' Often, these parties share space with straight clientele and bouncers are present to direct traffic to one room or another. Sometimes organisers are not invited back to first-time locations when bar owners realise that there was a gay party on their premises. The limited spaces available to party organisers has often meant renting out hotel party rooms for events. The indecorous make-do location, with white fabric-covered chairs along the walls, peanut snacks on side tables and a makeshift bar and DJ station led Piyush to comment, 'Are we at a fucking wedding?' and later and more incredulously, 'What is this? A Texas high school party? I came out for real urban life, not for a night in Phoenix.' Similarly, Amar comments at the same party, 'This is like being in Iowa!' Comparing this party to the US Midwest, South and Southwest, as well as the pageantry of a wedding, Amar and Piyush evaluate the party's success through a model that ascribes proper gay modernity to coastal and urban America (for critiques of such 'metronoramative' tendencies, see Gray 2009; Herring 2012; Halberstam 2005; Tongson 2011). For patrons who arrive with cosmopolitan sensibilities, or general snobbery, the organisers' failure to provide the trendy ethos so thoroughly developed in their promotional materials becomes doubly disappointing.

Stuttering Soundscapes

I asked Mihir how he arranges his DJs:

> 'Through contacts. Just friends. I change a lot of DJs'
>   'Do they care about the gay crowd?'
>   'They care. They like [doing this], as far as they get money they don't [care about] anything. If you don't say anything, they play 'straight' party music. Not 'our' party music. Our people like more commercial. [It's a] devas [divas] music crowd: like Lady Gaga, Shakira, Jenny [Jennifer Lopez]. This kind of music our people like, like Pitbull, Akon. Straight party is only House music type. That music I'm sure our people don't like. People keep coming out [of the party to the lobby], 'Mihir change the music.'
>   'What about Bollywood?'
>   'Fifty-fifty. If in case DJ is playing his own music [electronica/techno], I tell him directly people don't like it and immediately they change it. You remember sometimes [you have seen me] come inside and talk to the DJ.'

Music at gay parties is contested and negotiated, between the organisers, straight DJs and gay partygoers. The frequency with which gay parties rotate DJs means that a new queer subcultural sound, produced in conversation with regular attendees, does not develop at these parties.

Though Mihir talks about '*our* party music' as 'commercial' and 'diva' music, he in fact privileges electronica as more tasteful club music; during our interview he revealed that he is learning to be a techno DJ himself. The classification of electronic dance music as

classier music than Bollywood is evident in mainstream DJs' preference for these forms. When they do play nostalgic Hindi music, it is
heavily remixed; a 'Choli Ke Peeche' remix only sampled the chorus
and never built up into the verses of the song, leaving dancers eager to
queen out disappointed. Attempts to vary the music, such as spinning
Spanish tracks at Noche Caliente, quickly clear the dancefloor. At the
Retro Metro Party, the DJ played contemporary commercial music
for most of the time. Only following a white American's request did
the DJ announce over the PA system 'We're switching to Retro,' and
played Boney M, ABBA and Haddaway before switching to Hindi
music. At a party that invites patrons to 'Dust off your bell bot-
toms [. . .] Wear your disco threads,' the songs that filled the dance
floor and elicited the most excitement over the night were 'Bachna
Ae Haseeno', 'Waka Waka' and the Dropkick Murphy's 'Shipping to
Boston' that corralled dancers into small circles, holding hands, and
doing an Irish jig. Such uncanny moments of collectivity refuse the
nostalgic pleasure that the party invitation attempts to dictate.

DJ Grim's announcement 'We're switching to Retro,' was not
unfamiliar. At most parties, DJs actively use the microphone: 'OK
guys, we're switching to Bollywood now,' 'We're going back to
commercial!' 'Come on you guys, make some noise!' and even
'Have a good night! Practice safe sex!' Like the party invitations,
these frequent announcements perform a didactic pedagogy that
attempts to shape the party experience. These announcements
often feel like deliberate exertions by the DJ to produce a relationship with a gay audience that he is unable to fully woo with his
music. At one party the DJ shouted into the mike, 'Do you want
Commercial and Bollywood, or do you want Dubstep?' Dubstep,
techno, electronica have gained popularity via the Goa EDM scene
and have become a dominant sound in most Bangalore nightclubs
(on the dominance and contestation of whiteness in the Goa EDM
scene see Prasad 2012; Saldanha 2007). 'Commercial' music is
seen as a concession to these genres, Hindi music is low on the
list and South Indian film music is a virtual no-no. To the chagrin
of the gay men in the space, the DJ's entourage of straight friends
loudly chanted 'Dubstep! Dubstep! Dubstep!' while jumping in a
circle. DJs open up a dialogue through their (over)use of the mike,
but their inability to read a gay crowd's pleasure and response
leads to moments such as this, where their straight friends become
more legible than queer dancers. His transition to dubstep led a
flock of gay men to leave the bar space and hang out on the patio.

The makeshift arrangement of gay party spaces allows for a proximity and dialogue between DJ and audience. Often, DJs are stationed
at tables set up on the party dancefloor instead of in nicely protected

booths. This allows dancers to pester DJs with their requests, which they do with abandon. Whether or not DJs succumb and play Bollywood or *koothu*, by harassing the DJ with requests, patrons take advantage of the makeshift club arrangement to feel some ownership of the space.

Feminine Fissures

Because Hindi music is not the dominant sound in the space, short bursts of it tend to be capitalised on. Shubha Mudgal's 'Dholna' unexpectedly came on after a mostly electronic set and Mayuk's friend whines, 'Indian steps *karo na yaar!*' ['Come on and do Indian steps!']. Mayuk switches to a simple and common step: right hand repetitively extends across chest to meet extended left hand, and then back behind shoulder. His friends join in to make a circle of hands blossoming in and out while right feet softly tapped back and forth to keep the rhythm. The circle that formed draws Mayuk to the centre; he wants to queen out but is worried about frightening away the tall, muscular straight boy he brought along as his date. After peering around, however, he mouths, 'Fuck it,' and pulls the bottom of his t-shirt through its collar creating a bra/*choli*. He launches into quick turns, his graceful hands stretching above his head as his wrists turn against each other, much to the pleasure of the rest of the circle.

While such feminine performances are praised, they are not the norm in such a masculinist space. Party descriptions and the imagery that accompany them rarely represent or extol femininity. Organisers tell me that they only disallow cross-dressing – clearly noted on the online invitations – when it is the club's policy (see Gupta 2005: 135; Shahani 2008: 85 for critiques of this phenomenon in Mumbai). However, their preference is for the most appealing club space, not the one that is most inclusive, i.e. they will choose a club with a great ambience and location over one that permits cross-dressing. These under-defined cross-dressing policies also work to police class at these parties; a hipster with nail polish and heavy jewelry will still be let in, but a *hijra* or *kothi* in a sari will not be welcome.

For the westernised gay party, drag acts are seen as 'down market' (Shahani 2008: 25). Only once did I see a drag performance – albeit an impromptu one at the end of the night to 'Chikni Chameli' by a cross-dresser who removed her sari to reveal a bejewelled bikini. The faggotry and femininity danced by Mayuk above, or Pravin as he stripper-sidles down a pillar à la Tyra Banks, or Alex as he *jhatka*s [hip thrusts] to 'Munni Badnaam' are not the kinds of performances that the party anticipates in theme, promotion or description.

Dancing in feminine ways and capitalising on small bursts of *desi* divahood are small protests against the masculine and Western hegemony of gay parties.

Virtually Partying

Party organisers have been innovative in combining technology and parties: 'Grindr Party', 'Facebook Summer Party', 'Selfie Party' and 'Bluetooth party'. The information for the Grindr Party includes:

> As all knows, GrindR is an mobile application where you can find your Mate & Date by using this unique GPS application which is specially designed for gay crowd. [. . .] If you are shy to talk to the

Figure 4.2 Grindr party poster

person you like, Install GrindR application in your mobile and create your profile with your details and picture, then you will see all guys who are near to you in some feet away those are having the GrindR profile . . . Its awesome na ;p | then let's chat, share and get the dream guy you required. After that you know what to do man NOTTEE! [naughty]

Not only this, Show your GrindR profile after you entered to the party and get 100Rs discount in the entry fee.

This message is written with Indianisms, typos, emojis and homonyms that hail Indian users of Grindr and Whatsapp (another phone app named on the flier). At the same time, asking patrons to interact via phone applications works to regulate class at the party, suggesting that one must have a smart phone to acquire citizenship in the space. As Maya Ganesh argues in her study of *kothi* uses of mobile technologies, the cell phone functions as both a symbolic marker of class as well as a tool with which to participate in queer Indian community spaces (2010: 23). The Selfie Party encourages patrons to send in photographs via Whatsapp so that they can be projected at the party, whereas the Facebook Party asks users to post pictures to the Facebook page and images with the most likes will win a cash prize.

These integrations of the virtual into the party space are not perfectly seamless however. While Bluetooth and app-based connections might allow for new forms of mingling at the party, they may not actually result in the hook-ups that the party invitations encourage. On gay websites and apps, it is typical for a person looking for a sex date to say whether they 'have place' or not, i.e. if they live alone, have a place to themselves for some period of time, or live with roommates that are amenable to hook-ups coming over. The living constraints placed on single men – hostels do not allow visitors; apartment buildings don't like to rent to 'bachelors'; single incomes in a booming city require living with roommates – place limits on 'having place'.

One party attendee wrote in a post on the Heatwave PR Club page after he tried to flirt with someone who already had a date, 'he said that he came with his partner and said that it would be bad if he leaves his partner alone. I understood . . . :(I learnt a lesson. I now know that I shouldn't go alone!!' I too learned this lesson during fieldwork – many partygoers pre-arrange their dates, ensuring that one of the couple has place. While I exchanged numbers with many cute men at the parties, they never led to an immediate hook-up because neither of us 'had place'. The one time I left the party with someone and we made out in his car, police rapped on the foggy windows and sent me home alone in an autorickshaw. Many patrons simply come to dance, drink and socialise, knowing that a hook-up isn't foreseeable without further negotiations about place – their time at the party is better spent gossiping and dancing. As Shaka McGlotten writes about Grindr, hooking up is not necessarily the primary use to which the app is put (2013: 135). Similarly, the many parties that are advertised to facilitate dates and hook-ups are used for different kinds of pleasure.

In 2012, Manhunt.net started sponsoring Pink Nation's parties, sending a large banner and a cardboard cutout of a muscular white man to place outside the party entrance. Abhishek's events advertised free Manhunt giveaways; the Manhunt lipbalm I procured was a local brand with a printed MH sticker wrapped around the tube. Similarly, when the gay networking site sponsored a hunky Indian model in an MH tank to strut around the party, he disaffectedly handed out MH beer mugs, which were in fact locally purchased glass pint mugs with a tiny paper sticker awkwardly placed on the glass. At the end of the night, the prized Manhunt mugs advertised in the party invitation were left scattered around the bar. Like the unsold afro wigs after the Retro Party, or the abandoned yellow roses at the Friendship Day party, the discarded Manhunt mugs were a testament from patrons that they were not interested in cheap gimmicks.

Manhunt's attempt to sponsor parties in India with cheap gifts and thus to drive traffic to its website reflects the paternalism that other gay websites espouse. PlanetRomeo sent me a message when it detected my India-based IP address, explaining that my membership would be free because this Netherlands-based company was committed to 'furthering the cause of gay rights' globally (Johri 2013). Similarly, the Scruff app notified me to be careful because of India's criminal codes. These apps thus enforce hierarchies that render western countries (the US in particular) exceptional in their acceptance of LGBTQ people (Puar 2007).

A moment of unruly silence

In the wake of the 2016 mass shooting at a gay club's Latinx night in Orlando, there followed an outpouring of grief from people whose queer lives felt even more precarious than they already were. I landed in Bangalore the week of the Orlando attack, and attended a Heatwave party at Chili's (an American chain restaurant) in Indiranagar (a trendy upscale neighbourhood). Things had changed; no longer were we relegated to the city outskirts of Marathahalli and Bellandur, or the no-name bars that needed business, even gay business. But the oddities of Bangalore gay nightlife persisted. A makeshift banner of red fabric protected the virtuous families dining upstairs from looking down at the gay debauchery below them. However, aunties descending the staircase in saris to exit still had to listen to Demi Lovato and watch boys with too much product in their hair locking lips.

The party theme, 'Love is Love: Stop Hatred, Spread Love', advertised solidarity with the victims of the Orlando shooting and mentioned that there will be a moment of silence in their memory. A man on Grindr I talked to earlier that day appeared apprehensive about going to the party 'after Orlando and all'. The moment of silence was indecorous. The person trying to get everyone's attention to observe the moment of silence shouted throatily into the mic, 'Orlando! We are with you! We remember! Ok now let's see if we can be quiet!!!' This moment of ritual had not been carefully thought out, and the buzz of the still-open restaurant and the close-by street made silence unachievable. Moreover, the chatter in the party crowd never stopped. A British Indian visitor standing next to me fussed, 'People here just don't know how to listen.' He became further annoyed when the himbo next to him trying very hard to flirt asked him cluelessly, 'This is for what? That Orlando thing?'

To me, the lack of silence did not indicate disrespect. Partygoers ignored announcements over the crappy sound system as they always do. The turning off of the music was par for the course at a party. The makeshift emcee didn't have the control of the mike to woo the audience. This unruly moment reminded me that these Saturday night parties in Bangalore engender a habitus different from many global party circuits.

The following week the party theme was 'International Love', where Indian men who brought an 'international date' could get free entry – another reward for cosmopolitan desire and performance. I just couldn't bring myself to go.

Note

1. The names of some interlocutors, parties and party locations have been changed in this essay. I have retained to names of defunct locations and organisations in order to offer readers familiar with the city and scene a sense of geography and intimacy.

References

Benedicto, Bobby (2014) *Under Bright Lights: Gay Manila and the Global Scene*. Minneapolis: University of Minnesota Press.

Bhaskaran, Suparna (2004) *Made in India: Decolonizations, Queer Sexualities, Trans/National Projects*. New York: Palgrave Macmillan.

Boellstorff, Tom (2005) *The Gay Archipelago: Sexuality and Nation in Indonesia*. Princeton: Princeton University Press.

Bollen, Jonathan (2001) 'Queer Kinesthesia: Performativity on the Dance Floor', *Dancing Desires: Choreographing Sexualities On and Off the Stage*, ed. Jane Desmond. Madison: University of Wisconsin Press, pp. 285–314.

Buckland, Fiona (2002) *Impossible Dance: Club Culture and Queer World-Making*. Middletown, CT: Wesleyan University Press.

Campbell, A. and Farrier, S. (2016) *Queer Dramaturgies: International Perspectives on Where Performance Leads Queer*. London: Palgrave Macmillan.

Dasgupta, Rohit (2014) 'Parties, Advocacy, and Activism: Interrogating Community and Class in Digital Queer India', *Queer Youth and Media Cultures*, ed. Christopher Pullen. New York: Palgrave Macmillan, pp. 265–77.

Dutta, Aniruddha (2012) 'Claiming Citizenship, Contesting Civility: The Institutional Lgbt Movement and the Regulation of Gender/Sexual Dissidence in West Bengal, India', *Jindal Global Law Review*, 4 (1): 110–41.

Enteen, Jillana B. (2005) 'Siam Remapped: Cyber-interventions by Thai Women', *New Media and Society*, 7 (4): 457–82.

Ganesh, Maya Indira (2010) *'Mobile Love Videos Make Me Feel Healthy': Rethinking ICTs in Development*, IDS Working Paper 352. Brighton: Institute for Development Studies, pp. 1–43.

Gaonkar, Dilip Parameshwar (2001) *Alternative Modernities*. Durham, NC: Duke University Press.

Gray, Mary L. (2009) *Out in the Country: Youth, Media, and Queer Visibility in Rural America*. New York: New York University Press.

Gupta, Alok (2005) *'Englishpur Ki* Kothi.' *Because I Have a Voice: Queer Politics in India*, ed. Gautam Bhan and Arvind Narrain. New Delhi: Yoda Press, pp. 123–42.

Halberstam, Judith (2005) *In a Queer Time and Place: Transgender Bodies, Subcultural Lives*. New York: New York University Press.

Han, C. Winter (2015) *Geisha of a Different Kind: Race and Sexuality in Gaysian America*. New York: New York University Press.

Heitzman, James (2004) *Network City: Planning the Information Society in Bangalore*. New York: Oxford University Press.

Herrera, Brian Eugenio (2016) 'Evanescence: Three Tales of the Recent Queer Theatrical Past', *Theatre Topics*, 26 (1): 47–51.

Herring, Scott (2010) *Another Country: Queer Anti-Urbanism*. New York: New York University Press.

Hewitt, Andrew (2005) *Social Choreography: Ideology as Performance in Dance and Everyday Movement*. Durham, NC: Duke University Press.

Johri, Vikram (2013) 'From Earth to Planet Romeo', *Business Standard*, 1 January. Available online at http://www.business-standard.com/article/opinion/vikram-johri-from-earth-to-planet-romeo-113011200014_1.html (last accessed 10 April 2014).

Khan, Faris (2014) 'Transgender Activism and Transnationality in Pakistan', *South Asia in the World: An Introduction*, ed. Susan Snow Wadley. New York: Routledge, pp. 170–84.

Lim, Eng-Beng (2005) 'Glocalqueering in New Asia: The Politics of Performing Gay in Singapore', *Theatre Journal*, 57: 383–405.

McGlotten, Shaka (2013)*Virtual Intimacies: Media, Affect, and Queer Sociality*. Albany: State University of New York Press.

McGuire, Meredith (2011) '"How to Sit, How to Stand": Bodily Practice and the New Urban Middle Class', *A Companion to the Anthropology of India*, ed. Isabelle Clark-Deces. Oxford: Wiley-Blackwell,.

Marshall, Daniel, Murphy, Kevin P. and Tortorici, Zeb (2105) 'Queering Archives: Intimate Tracings', *Radical History Review*, 122: 1–10.

Moten, F. (2003) *In the Break: The Aesthetics of the Black Radical Tradition*. Minneapolis: University of Minnesota Press.

Mowlabocus, Sharif (2008) 'Revisiting Old Haunts Through New Technologies: Public (Homo)sexual Cultures in Cyberspace', *International Journal of Cultural Studies*, 11 (4): 419–39.

Muñoz, José Esteban (1996) 'Ephemera as Evidence: Introductory Notes to Queer Acts', *Women and Performance*, 8 (2): 5–16.

Muñoz, José Esteban (2001) 'Gesture, Ephemera, and Queer Feeling: Approaching Kevin Aviance', *Dancing Desires: Choreographing Sexualities On and Off the Stage*, ed. Jane Desmond. Madison: University of Wisconsin Press, pp. 423–44.

Muñoz, José Esteban (2009) *Cruising Utopia: The Then and There of Queer Futurity*. New York: New York University Press.

Nair, Janaki (2005) *The Promise of the Metropolis: Bangalore's Twentieth Century*. New Delhi: Oxford University Press.

Pérez, Roy (2012) 'Mark Aguhar's Critical Flippancy', *Bully Bloggers*, 4 August. Available online at https://bullybloggers.wordpress.com/2012/08/04/mark-aguhars-critical-flippancy/ (last accessed 31 July 2016).

Prasad, Pavithra (2012)'The Baba and the Patrao: Negotiating Localness in the Tourist Village', *Critical Arts*, 26 (3): 353–74.

Puar, Jasbir K. (2007) *Terrorist Assemblages: Homonationalism in Queer Times*. Durham, NC: Duke University Press.

Pullen, Christopher (2012) *LGBT Transnational Identity and the Media*. New York: Palgrave Macmillan.

Reddy, Gayatri (2005) *With Respect to Sex: Negotiating Hijra Identity in South India*. Chicago: University of Chicago Press.

Rivera-Servera, Ramón H. (2012) *Performing Queer Latinidad: Dance, Sexuality, Politics*. Ann Arbor: University of Michigan Press.

Saldanha, A. (2007) *Psychedelic White: Goa Trance and the Viscosity of Race*. Minneapolis: University of Minnesota Press.

Savigliano, Marta (1995) *Tango and the Political Economy of Passion*. Boulder: Westview Press.

Smith, Anna Deavere (2000) *Talk to Me: Listening between the Lines*. New York: Random House.

Shahani, Parmesh (2008) *Gay Bombay: Globalization, Love and (Be)Longing in Contemporary India*. Thousand Oaks, CA: Sage.

Tongson, Karen (2011) *Relocations: Queer Suburban Imaginaries*. New York: New York University Press.

Vogel, Shane (2009) *The Scene of Harlem Cabaret: Race, Sexuality, Performance*. Chicago: University of Chicago Press.

II Digital Activism(s) and Advocacy

Chapter 5

Digitally Untouched: Janana (In) Visibility and the Digital Divide

Ila Nagar

Introduction

On 11 March 2016 Shashi Tharoor, a Member of Parliament from
the Indian National Congress, introduced a bill[1] in the parliament
that would decriminalise homosexuality. This was Tharoor's second attempt at trying to have this bill passed. The bill was defeated
again on 11 March to Tharoor's and many other people's frustration. On 20 March 2016, Aatish Taseer wrote an op-ed for the *New
York Times*[2] in which he described the frustration of a gay lawyer
with Section 377, authoritarian government and the idea of a rright
to love' which could be the loophole when the Supreme Court of
India decides on Section 377 again. Since December 2013 when the
Supreme Court of India upheld Section 377, the 1860 colonial law
that criminalises homosexual activity came to the forefront of international media attention. There has been much interest in the role
of social media and media in general in moving the LGBTQ rights
movement in India forward. Social media became the site for protest and also the study of protests. Growth of social media sites like
Facebook, WhatsApp, etc. is celebrated for fostering the formation
of popular queer publics. The passage of legal verdicts related to the
anti-sodomy provisions (specifically Section 377) and transgender
identity in India has garnered much transnational internet activism
in the form of blogs, Facebook posts and the viral circulation of
images from protest rallies. Images of queer bodies are circulating
in the digital space. Yet, janana as a queer body is missing from this
space. I argue that while the digital is freely accessible and visibil-
ises queer bodies in India, and it should be celebrated as a space for
activism and protest, it is not the utopian space that it is framed as.

The digital space leaves behind bodies, jananas specifically, that do not have access to this space, that do not know the perils of being in the digital space and that do not have the language to communicate in or about the digital space. Images of desiring or longing bodies are circulated through access to technology that jananas do not have. The images make jananas visible and invisible simultaneously – their experience is effaced by putting them in a media image, their lack of agency in the production and circulation of images being blatantly visible. The circulation of ideas, protests, voices and images on social media leaves behind jananas. The idea of protesting for a right to love or any legal rights to have sex with men are foreign to some jananas who find fighting for rights outside the scope of their lives. In this chapter I discuss jananas in the media, the role of Facebook and PlanetRomeo in making jananas visible without giving them agency of their visibility, and how affected jananas are by technology. I argue that while social media and the increasing availability of social media have fostered discussions of rights within and outside of the LGBTQ movements in India, it has also made communities like jananas more invisible in their marginalisation because janana identity is subsumed under larger pressures exerted by neoliberal cultures and ideas.

Jananas, also called kothis (Hall 2005; Cohen 1995, 2005), are men who have sex with men, some take or give money in exchange for sex and most maintain a heterosexual status for the sake of family or honour or both. Jananas, then, lead a double life in which their identities as heterosexual males are not necessarily compromised because of their desire to be janana/Janani.[3] Navigating the distinction between being a heterosexual family-oriented man and a man who engages in sexual relations with other men, sometimes even for money, results in a constant process of self-definition and re-definition. Most jananas I met in Lucknow where I did fieldwork were in poverty with little education or means. Some jananas associate themselves with hijra households. Hijras (Hall 1995a, 1995b; Reddy 2005) are visible and recognised, and are sometimes referred to as a third gender category in South Asia. Hijras have a ritualistic presence where they bless newborns and newlyweds with their presence in exchange for money. Since jananas are often in need of money and uncomfortable with their desires, hijras become a haven of non-judgement for the marginalised jananas. Many jananas frequent hijra households but say that there is no honour, or izzat, in being a hijra or even being seen with one. Jananas are not part of urban gay identities, they are not part of hijras and janana association with hijras highlights the invisibility of jananas because jananas can be subsumed in the hijra category and left out of the urban gay categories. The visual and historical appeal of hijras continues in the neoliberal times as the debate about sexuality moves towards rights, personhood and the right to love.

I present research based on ethnography in Lucknow, India during 2014. The research started with questions about the impact of Section 377 on the lived experiences of jananas. I interviewed ten jananas for this study which is part of a larger study that spanned over thirteen years and started in 2003. Ethnographic research with janana communities reveals a disjuncture between the juridical sphere and digital activism conducted by the gay and lesbian movement which is exemplary of the neoliberal rights-bearing citizens (Nagar and DasGupta 2016) on behalf of the janana communities. None of the informants of this study held knowledge of the substantive contents related to anti-sodomy and the transgender decision, neither do they identify as transgender. The janana lives that I discuss have not been touched by the digital revolution and live outside the digital world. Ethnography and critical discourse analysis uncovers the consequences of illiteracy, class and non-metropole locations on the lives of these men. Jananas come to represent a kind of subaltern figure whose subject formation is untouched by sexual modernities (hailed through juridical and digital activism). Rather, the formation of janana subjectivities gesture to a complex interplay between nationalisms and articulation of desire through linguistic horizons which do not find semiotic coding on digital spheres such as Facebook, PlanetRomeo and WhatsApp. The deployment of janana images in digital activism is an attempt to accommodate the subaltern as a popular figure.

I now turn to the interaction that India has had with technology in the last decade. Cell phone use and affordability has been a story in and of itself. A Forbes report[4] from 2014 suggests that there are about 243million cell phone users in India, of which 220 million are smart phone users. With 243 million cell phone users and 220 million smart phone users,[5] India is the largest market for cell phones and smart phones – 243 million is about a quarter of the population. Cell phones are very affordable and if used only for purposes of calling people, adult literacy (at about 70 per cent now) is not a big issue. Using smart phones and social media on the phone or on a computer does require literacy, and some literacy in English. The figures presented here indicate definite progress in the reach of technology and media. What we must consider is using a phone to make a phone call requires skills that are markedly different from using a phone for activism. Activism requires a smart phone if not a computer, the ability to formulate and access ideas, a belief in the validity and strength of these ideas, and a willingness to share ideas. Activism and activism on social media also requires putting oneself out there – for everyone to access. The number of people with ability to access social media has revolutionised ways of being heard and ways to connect with information. Yet, many people are not part of this revolution. They are left behind due to reasons of poverty, illiteracy and perhaps lack of interest in the specific types of rights that activism generally propagates. It is these parts of the population that I speak about in this chapter.

Ethnographic setting

I started working with jananas in 2003 at which time I was a graduate student. I spent summer semesters in India from 2003 to 2007 with substantial time in Lucknow. After 2007, I did not carry out any fieldwork for a few years, though I still visited Lucknow and met jananas with whom I had established relationships. I started fieldwork again in 2013 and my last fieldwork trip to Lucknow was in 2015. My relationships with a number of jananas in Lucknow has lasted more than a decade at this point. The data in this paper is from ethnographic interviews conducted in 2014. The informants for this study were all part of my longitudinal project.

In 2014 when I left to carry out fieldwork, I imagined learning a lot from jananas who I had known for more than a decade about the impact of Section 377 and the media coverage of that section from jananas. My trip to Lucknow was in July 2013, a few months before the Supreme Court of India up held Section 377 and the world looked at this regressive decision. This event was covered widely in national and international media. My own Facebook newsfeed frequently showed memes, articles, news about rallies and protests, the coming together of activists from around India, and the outrage this issue had garnered. I wondered where my janana informants fitted into this revolution. How did they feel about their rights being crushed and their practices being questioned? I was aware that many of the jananas that I knew in Lucknow did not have regular phone connections. Many of them had a simple, affordable phone but they did not often recharge in. Many phone plans in India are pre-paid and some charge for incoming and outgoing calls. Many jananas and people with limited resources paid for minutes only when they had extra money. The cell phone revolution in India is only about ten to fifteen years old and jananas fall into the demographic where many of them have cell phones but their access is still limited as a result of income which is uneven at best. Smart phones are an entirely different issue for jananas. While some jananas who do not know how to read or write have memorised important patterns in order to use numbers to dial on simple phones, smart phones are out of their reach for reasons of literacy or lack thereof, and more importantly of affordability.

My association with jananas was through a non-profit orgaisation in Lucknow. Over the years the non-profit changed names and the management changed but the jananas associated with it stayed the same. In the course of my fieldwork, I met jananas who had no association with the non-profit. Janana interactions with the non-profit also decided whether they knew or had opinions about Section 377. My argument that jananas are rendered invisible in the movement for rights for the LGBTQ communities in India holds true even for jananas that knew about Section 377. In the case of jananas who knew about Section 377, knowledge of the law or the Supreme Court of India upholding the law did not mean any material changes in lived experiences – in interactions with male partners, with the police or with friends and family. They had information about Section 377 which had come down from the non-profit but there were no consequences to knowing or not knowing about section 377. In the next section I will present some conversation with jananas about Section 377.

Janana stories about Section 377

When I started talking to jananas in Lucknow, I did not expect to find what I did. I had expected sea changes in the way jananas perceived their rights, the responsibility of the government towards citizens, the law and the lived implications of the law. Instead, I found that an overwhelming number of jananas did not know what Section 377 was. A lot of them had heard something about 377 but did not have a specific opinion on the impact or the existence of such a law in India. The example below is from a conversation between Namrita,[6] a janana who I had met through other jananas a few years back, and me. Namrita and I did not know each other too well but we had met before. I had interviewed her a while ago and she remembered my visits to Lucknow over the years. Namrita was associated with the non-profit that I worked with.

1. Ila: Aap 377 ke baare me jante hain?	Ila: do you know about 377
2. Namrita: haan ma'am jaante hain.	Namrita: yes ma'am I know
3. Yehin humne thoda bahut padha hai	here I have read a little bit
4. Ila: Yehan se?	Ila: from here?
5. Namrita: Yehin se padha hai. Yehin.	Namrita: I have read from here. Here
6. Is se pehle nahi jaante the.	I did not know before here
7. Yehin pe hume malum hua	I came to know here
8. Ila: Jaise log aur ye apne	like people, like our people
9. baba aur maulavi,	*babas* and *maulvis*
10. is type ke log jaise kehte hain ki ye	people like that when they say
11. homesexual sex jo hai wo galat hai.	homosexual sex is wrong
12. Unnatural hai. Uske baare	it is unnatural. About that
13. kaisa lagta hai ye sab sun ke?	how do you feel when you hear that
14. Namrita: ma'am, agar wo kehte hain	ma'am if they say that
15. unnatural hai to hum log fir	if it is unnatural then we
16. bana ke bheja hai bhagwan ne hume.	God has sent us here
17. Humari feeling hai jajba	we have feelings, emotions
18. To wo kya hai fir?	What is that then?
19. Hum log ko ye hai ki	we have this that
20. hum natural hain.	we are natural.
21. Sab agar wo galat kaam hai to	If that is wrong then
22. wo hum log ko to	people like us
23. paide nahi hona chahiye.	should not be born.
24. Dekhiye bhagwan ki marji hai.	This is *bhagwan's* will
25. Is me Allah ki marji hai.	It is Allah's will
26. Agar wo humko bana ke bhejta hai	if [God] sends us here
27. to uski kudrat ko	then his will
28. koi nahi samajh paya hai.	no one is able to understand

Namrita says that she heard about 377 from the non-profit. When I pressed more about the details of Section 377 and Namrita's feelings about those details, Namrita said 'if' people talk about such things as the illegality of homosexual sex, they are not right. Namrita did not confirm that she had heard of such things were said and such arguments made, they were baseless. Namrita also talked about the right to be janana but her theory about this right was based on her mere presence and on the presence of her desires as we see in lines 14–20. Section 377 did not come into our conversation after this brief showing and Namrita's response.

Imrana and Anuradha were both jananas I had known for more than a decade. In 2014, I was meeting them after a gap of four years. We almost started where we had left and discussed major life changes that had happened in the last four years. Anuradha was living in the park, Imrana was living with family and was usually on the verge of poverty but had a roof over her head. The conversation about Section 377 did not go far with them. I asked if they had heard about the section. Imrana said:

Koi dhara hai suni   it is a section/law, I have heard

Anuradha agreed. I explained Section 377 to them. They nodded and I drew the implication that further discussion about the impact of something that Imrana and Anuradha barely knew about was pointless. We moved to discussing life as jananas and what had changed for jananas in the last decade.

In a different setting an interview was conducted with a janana who was associated with the non-profit. Unlike Imrana and Anuradha, Harita had a smart phone, was more stable financially and was associated with a more modern lifestyle which included using a smart phone and finding partners using apps and social media sites like Facebook and PlanetRomeo.

1. Ila: Aapne 377 ke baare me suna hai?   I: have you heard about 377
2. Harish: Jee   H: yes
3. Ila: Kya khayal hai aapka uske   I: what do you think about it
   baare me?
4. Kya us ghatna ke baad,   after that incident
5. December 2013 ke baad   after December 2013[7]
6. kuch farak pada hai jeewan me?   Has anything changed about your life
7. Kuch dikha kuch suna   have you seen or heard anything
8. jis se lage ki are ye kya ho raha hai? that made you feel what is happening?
9. Harish: Ma'am humlog ke jeewan me   H: Ma'am in our lives
10. to koi farak nahi pada hai   nothing has changed
11. kyunki hum log pehle bhi   because we even before this
12. chup-chup kar hi karte the   we used to do this secretively
13. Hum log utna khul ke nahi aaye hain   we have not opened up that much
14. saamne kyunki nahi aa sakte hain   we cannot do that
15. Ki humara pariwaar humara   our family our

16. samaaj humko izzazat nahi deta hai	community does not give us respect
17. agar hum apne hi baare me sochenge	if we just think about ourselves
18. to jin ne hume paida kiya hai,	then those who gave birth to us
19. jin se kuch ummeedein hain humari	who expect something from us
20. wo humare baare me kya sochenge?	What will they think about us?
21. Humare sapne toot jayenge	our dreams will shatter
22. Ye hai to.	That is the thing
23. jahan tak meri baat hai,	As far as I am concerned
24. mai to abhi khul ke aa nahi sakta hoon	I cannot be come out openly
25. to jo 377 hai, matlab mere	so this 377
26. Agar khud ke liye kahoon to	if I talk about my self
27. mere usme koi prabhaav nahi pada hai	it does not affect me at all
28. kyunki mai pehle bhi kahin	because even before this
29. idhar-udhar nahi jata tha	I did not go here and there
30. Na park me, na kahin na kuch	not to the park, not anywhere else
31. Mai kuch bhi karta tha,	whatever I did
32. kahin mere ghar me ho	it was either in my home
33. ya kisi ke wahan chala gaya	or in someone else's home
34. tab mera hota tha	that is when I did it
35. to us se mujhe	so with this
36. koi farak nahi pada hai	it does not matter to me at all
37. Par haan, humare kaam ko	but yes, our work
38. us se bahut farak pada hai	that has been affected
39. Pehle hi police pareshan karti thi	earlier police used to bother us
40. abhi bhi karti hai	it does so now too
41. Ab ye hai abhi saamne	now this is
42. open ho gaya hai	it is all open
43. To aur jyada pareshan karegi	police will bother us even more
44. Ila: Sahi baat hai	Ila: that right
45. kabhi police ne pareshan kiya hai?	has the police ever bothered you
46. Keerti: Nahi, mujhe nahi pareshan kiya hai	Keerti: no, they have ever bother me
47. Kabhi-kabhi to police wale	sometimes police men
48. road pe hi mil jaate hain.	I see them on the road
49. Kehte baith jaao, baitho chalo	they say sit, sit, let's go
50. Police wale khud hi	the policemen themselves
51. kehte hain baitho chalo, zabardasti	they say sit, forcebly
52. Ek baar mere saath	Once, it happened with me

53. zabardasti ho bhi chuki hai	I have been raped
54. Charbaug me	At Charbagh
55. Ek Policewala zabardasti baithan	One policeman forced me to sit
56. laag ki chalo	he said lets go
57. chalo na to tumko band kar denge	go with me or I will put you in jail
58. yeh hai	that is the thing
59. Hum baithe hi the uski gaadi pe	I had just sat in his car
60. Ye yehi log niyam banate hain,	these people make rules
61. khud hi todte hain	and they break rules themselves

Harita's interaction with technology was very different from Namrita's, Imrana's or Anuradha's. Harita knew that technology could make some aspects of her life more interesting. These aspects, however, did not mean that her invisibility had decreased in any way. She was still invisible – she was just invisible with a smart phone. In lines 23–36, Harita discusses the details of the effects of Section 377 on her life. She says, for her, the section has not mattered, she never had sex outside closed doors and did not solicit sex in parks and other spaces. For Harita, Section 377 did not and does not interfere with everyday experiences of finding and being with partners. The digital space, while available, is not of interest to her outside of its practical application of finding someone. Digital spaces have a role and it is not of seeking rights, it is of finding partners. In lines 37–42 Harita mentions police interference. But she says police interference happened before the law was upheld and is still happening. The law has had no tangible influence on the way the police interact with jananas and jananas interact with police. Keerti, another janana, joined us in the room during my interview with Harita. Keerti was a familiar face to me, worked for the non-profit and fit Harita's profile in terms of socio-economic status. Since she had joined the conversation and Harita and Keerti were friends, I asked Keerti about the police. Her response was that the police were interested in sex with jananas and sometimes forced jananas into accompanying them. Keerti also knew about Section 377 but did not speak about its implications or its effect on her lived experience.

I want to contrast janana stories with a cover from *India Today*, an English language news magazine. The cover shows Vikram Seth, an author who writes in Indian English and has won several awards for his fiction. Seth, as a gay man, is criminalised by Section 377 and the cover of *India Today* highlights the criminality of an award-winning author of international repute.

Figure 5.1 Vikram Seth on the cover of *India Today*, 20 December 2013

Vikram Seth's image holding a board saying, 'To not be able to love the one you love is to have your life wrenched away.' This powerful image and the message it came with became an iconic reminder of the regressive nature of Section 377. Yet the image, Vikram Seth, the message, the medium, the language and all that is associated with these is lost on the janana. Granted, jananas are not the audience for this magazine which has a circulation of less than two million but the janana are implied in this image. The janana is also denied the right that Seth speaks of without her interpretation of her rights actually being heard.

As we see from Keerti above, not only is activism absent from janana lives for the most part, the material experiences of denial of rights are also not points of discontent. I do not mean to imply that jananas are apolitical and disinterested in rights. What I suggest is that digital spaces might not be for jananas for purposes of protest and activism. Their protest comes in their dealings with injustices in a personal and group setting and in managing the experiences of their lives and their sexuality. Within the socio-cultural realities of the lived experience of economically impoverished jananas, the presence of a phone or access to the internet did not come with visibility for matters of protest, rights to be or rights to live. It just meant having a phone in the most practical sense. The right to love, to be and to protest were already denied them in their own worlds and gaining those rights with technology was neither of interest nor emancipating for janana communities who lived on or close to the streets.

Janana subalterns

Since the international coverage of Section 377 and the claims of the regressive nature of laws and their realisations hit the minds of the people, India's dealings with her LGBTQ population has been in the spotlight. Whether this spotlight is on the hardships faced by urban gay men and lesbian women, the production of videos that speak to the legitimisation of gay marriage or the various gay rights parades in cosmopolitan Indian cities, the critique of the decision has been loud in India and internationally (also see Dasgupta and Gokulsing 2014). This spotlight, though absolutely necessary, misses the men who have sex with men in the ranks of people with uneven or no incomes. These men – variously recognised as koti, janana, dhurani – are never in the front pages and many of them do not want to be, and while some speak of rights from the government, what these rights would be is unclear to them. I claim that janana invisibility and visibility is a factor of their desire to be invisible. Visibility would mean confrontation with family, with friends, with the social realities of being janana. Many jananas with uneven incomes do not want this. They want fulfilment of desire when necessary and normatively and contextually defined relationships with a family. Visibility of their person is not their goal – availability of jobs, of opportunities to feed their families, is felt as a pressing need.

Appeals to citizenship rights based in legal or religious institutions are unavailable to jananas. They don't know Section 377 and religious language frames their bodies as a sin. Jananas are a disenfranchised community who rely on informal economies and their relationship with the state is mediated through violence. Rights-based discourse is not accessible to jananas. It is in this sense that the janana is a subaltern. The jananas are rendered invisible not just because of their sexuality and desire. Class position frames the janana as a subaltern figure, whose subjectivity is untouched by moblisations against Section 377. Many of the Janana's interviewed during the course of my multi-year fieldwork mentioned to me how they are invisible to hijra communities, because they are either a threat or a bystander until they join the hijra households. They are invisible in the educated gay circles since articulating a 'gay' identity requires certain kinds of English education and class privilege. To articulate oneself as gay or lesbian requires some understanding of the transnational gay and lesbian rights politics (Cohen 2005; Hall 2003) and access to gay spaces in major city centers (Dasgupta 2017). The jananan communities involved in informal sectors of Lucknow do not hail from the English-speaking middle class, rather their class position is related to the precarious informal sector of the Indian economy. Some of them relied upon HIV prevention NGOs started by middle-class gay men with the help of international donor agencies. However, most of my respondents revealed that they were underpaid, or treated as 'not equals' in the NGO. Since the 2007/8 collapse of the world markets and the non-availability of easy funds for HIV/AIDS activism in South Asia, many jananas are invisible in these circles as well. What does this invisibility mean for the janana? Do they want to become visible? A janana I met had a Facebook profile and said his parents live in America. He did not know about Section 377. Similarly, another janana friend of mine reported that her access to Facebook on her phone is limited, since she cannot pay for high-speed internet. She feels satisfied in showing off her smart phone, but does not reveal to people that she cannot access many of its 'smart things'. In this chapter, I claim that jananas are rendered invisible in the post-Section 377 debate about rights-bearing citizenship. If, however, we look at social media outlets for the last five years, we will find that the social media space is full of ideas for protesting and tangible ways to look at the scope of those protests – photographs of the people protesting, banners, people giving speeches and people attending events. One could claim that janana are in fact not invisible and the protests and the idea that protests are meaningful ways of affecting change are reaching a wider audience. I put forward two points that refute such an argument: (1) access to organised protest that celebrates the right to love does not touch the subject formation of jananas; (2) protest is a luxury that many jananas cannot afford. It is a luxury because it involves time that could be used otherwise, and because it carries the inherent risk of being seen with other jananas and as janana by family and friends. While jananas have been rendered invisible for the most part from ideas of protest and agitation, cell phones have revolutionised their lives and friendships. At one point, parks were where communities were formed and jananas learned to be janana. Now, sex happens through phone transactions and friendships, while desirable, are not the focus of many janana lives.

Throughout this chapter I have argued that jananas are rendered invisible in the current debates about rights-bearing citizenship. Ideas about the right to love are situated within ideas about person-hood and constitutional equality. However, the subject formation of jananas remain untouched by such online and offline mobilisations. Janana subjectivity is situated in ideas about desire and sin. Janana's creatively navigate religious customs and rituals while narrating stories about their bodies and pleasure. Jananas want to live life within the local cultural norms that are bound by ideals of masculinity and family values. Many jananas feel that their desire might clash with the ideals of the heteronormative family, and the partaking of sexual activities with other men is a kind of sin. However, they creatively reinterpret religious myths which form the architecture of their being. Janana desire is at times tacit and at times hidden, since many of them are married men. Visibility for the jananas signifies joining hijra households, since hijra households occupy an organised way of living throughout the different regions of India. However, living with the responsibilities of being a married householder while practising sex with other men comes to signify being a janana. In this sense, invisibility is a central aspect of being a janana.

As we look at interactions between desire, class, social media and sexuality, people like Anuradha and Namrita are left behind. One can argue that maybe they are not left behind, they never were with the movement, so leaving them behind is not possible. On the one hand social media has definitely made access easier. It has made protest and keeping abreast with broader cross-cultural ideas about sexuality easier. On the other hand, the assumption that social media has in any way affected or surpassed rigid boundaries created by class is dangerous. Even if owning a cell phone costs little money in India, it still costs money to access the 3G high-speed internet. Namrita, Harita, Imrana and Anuradha are among the many jananas who are outside of the reach of digital activism. This does not imply that the protests are not reaching a larger audience but rather, as I have argued for in this chapter, that janana subject formation relies on invisibility. Digital LGBTQ activism geared towards the visibility of the rights-bearing sexual subject stands in contravention to janana subjectivity. Linguistic, regional and class differences need to be understood as limits to the celebratory dimension of digital queer activism in India. It is possible that not only the activist and her ideas are invisible to the janana, the janana also wishes to remain invisible to the activist – in any space, digital or otherwise.

Notes

1. http://www.ndtv.com/india-news/tharoor-gives-up-after-his-bill-to-decriminalise-homosexuality-is-defeated-1286245?pfrom=home-lateststories (accessed 11 March 2016).
2. http://www.nytimes.com/2016/03/21/opinion/dreaming-of-gay-rights-in-delhi.html?_r=0 (accessed 20 March 2016).
3. Janana and janani are used interchangeably by members of the community. Janani has the -i morpheme which implies additional femininity in the word when it is used in context.
4. http://www.forbes.com/sites/afontevecchia/2014/07/07/indias-massive-e-commerce-opportunity-and-the-explosion-of-mobile/#4fe987535c23 (accessed 12 December 2016).
5. http://www.thehindu.com/news/cities/mumbai/business/with-220mn-users-india-is-now-worlds-secondbiggest-smartphone-market/article8186543.ece (accessed 24 September 2016).
6. All names have been changed.
7. When Section 377 was upheld by the Supreme Court of India.

References

Baset, Zaid. A. (2012) 'Section 377 and the Myth of Heterosexuality', *Jindal Global Law Review*, 4 (1): 89–109.
Cohen, Lawrence (1995) 'The Pleasures of Castration: The Postoperative Status of Hijras, Jankhas and Academics', in Paul R. Abramson and Steven D. Pinkerton (eds), *Sexual Nature, Sexual Culture*. Chicago: University of Chicago Press, pp. 276–304.
Cohen, Lawrence (2005) 'The Kothi Wars: AIDS Cosmopolitanism and the Morality of Classification', in Vincanne Adams and Stacy Leigh Pigg (eds), *Sex in Development: Science, Sexuality, and Morality in Global Perspective*. Durham, NC and London: Duke University Press, pp. 269–303.
Dasgupta, R. K. (2017) *Digital Queer Cultures in India: Politics, Intimacies and Belonging*. London: Routledge.

Dasgupta, Rohit K. and Gokulsing, Moti (2014) 'Introduction: Perceptions of Masculinity and Challenges to the Indian Male', in Rohit K. Das-Gupta and K. Moti Gokulsingh (eds), *Masculinity and Its Challenges in India: Essays on Changing Perceptions*. Jefferson, NC: McFarland.

Dutta, Aniruddha (2012) 'An Epistemology of Collusion: Hijras/*Koti*s and the Historical (Dis)continuity of Gender/Sexual Identities in Eastern India', *Gender and History: Special Issue Gender History Across Epistemologies*, 24 (3): 825–49.

Dutta, Aniruddha (2013) 'Legible Identities and Legitimate Citizens: The Globalization of Transgender and Subjects of HIV–AIDS Prevention in Eastern India', *International Feminist Journal of Politics*, 15 (4): 494–514.

Hall, Kira (1995a) 'Hijra/Hijrin: Language and Gender Identity'. Unpublished PhD Dissertation, University of California, Berkeley.

Hall, Kira (1995b) 'Lip Service on the Fantasy Lines', in Kira Hall and Mary Bucholtz (eds), *Gender Articulated: Language and the Socially Constructed Self*. New York: Routledge, pp. 183–216.

Hall, Kira (1997) '"Go Suck Your Husband's Sugarcane!" Hijras and the Use of Sexual Insult', in Anna Livia and Kira Hall (eds), *Queerly Phrased Language, Gender and Sexuality*. New York: Oxford University Press, pp. 430–60.

Hall, Kira (2000) 'Performativity', *Journal of Linguistic Anthropology*, 9 (1–2): 184–7.

Hall, Kira (2003) 'Exceptional Speakers: Contested and Problematized Gender Identities', Miriam Meyerhoff and Janet Holmes (eds), *Handbook of Language and Gender*. Oxford: Basil Blackwell, pp. 352–80.

Hall, Kira (2005) 'Intertextual Sexuality: Parodies of Class, Identity, and Desire in Liminal Delhi', *Journal of Linguistic Anthropology*, 15 (1): 125–44.

Hall, Kira and O'Donovan, Veronica (1996) 'Shifting Gender Positions Among Hindi-speaking Hijras', in Victoria Bergvall, Janet Bing and Alice Freed (eds), *Rethinking Language and Gender Research: Theory and Practice*. London: Longman.

Misra, Geetanjali (2009) 'Decriminalizing Homosexuality in India', *Reproductive Health Matters*, 17 (34): 20–8.

Nagar, Ila and DasGupta, Debanuj (2016) 'Private Koti Public Love: Section 377, Religion, Perversity, and Lived Desire', *Contemporary South Asia*, 23: 4.

Reddy, Gayatri (2005) 'Geographies of Contagion: *Hijras, Koti*s, and the Politics of Sexual Marginality in Hyderabad', *Anthropology and Medicine*, 12 (3): 255–70.

Sircar, Oishik and Jain, Dipika (2012) 'New Intimacies/Old Desires: Law, Culture and Queer Politics in NeoLiberal Times', *Jindal Global Law Review*, 4 (1): 1–16.

Chapter 6

Digital Outreach and Sexual Health Advocacy: SAATHII as a Response[1]

Rohit K. Dasgupta

Introduction

Increasing HIV infections among gay men, other men that have sex with men (MSM) and trans communities coupled with the low impact of traditional HIV prevention and capacity-building approaches in enabling access to health services are a serious problem in India. This chapter reports on how an HIV capacity-building charity, Solidarity and Action Against the HIV Infection in India (SAATHII), used digital media and the internet to transform HIV prevention across India. Borrowing the concept of social capital as defined by Bourdieu (1986), this chapter attempts to understand how expertise is created and maintained in digital spaces. Beginning from Kolkata, India, I describe how SAATHII uses digital and social media for peer outreach and sexual health sensitisation. The project illustrates how through digital media and the internet, SAATHII was able to widen access, advocacy and information dissemination among multiple audiences to complement traditional community mobilisation HIV prevention approaches. To conclude I reflect on SAATHI's work with digital media and the internet with a set of key lessons that have emerged from my ethnography. I provide my reflections based on the notion of credibility and how credibility (Mowlabocus et al. 2015) is created that allow for mobilisation and advocacy in Kolkata to disrupt dominant approaches to HIV prevention in India so as to better meet the challenges of developing AIDS-resilient communities.

Gay men, other men who have sex with men (MSM) and trans individuals in India are at higher risk of new HIV infections than other men (NACO 2014). Due to the broader disempowering national, social

112

and legal frameworks that criminalise and 'regulate' their behaviours, they face robust hostility from mainstream health providers (Dasgupta 2012; Khan 2004; World Bank 2009). The availability of Voluntary Confidential Counselling and Testing (VCCT) services does not appear to have alleviated apprehension among gay men, other MSM and trans communities in accessing health services. The biggest challenge for HIV prevention and capacity-building approaches is the lack of tailored healthcare provision specifically designed to meet their needs. This situation is made worse due to the structural violence experienced by gay men, MSM and trans people, and the lack of understanding of the complexities of their sexual practices among healthcare providers (Chakrapani et al. 2008). Solidarity and Action Against the HIV Infection in India (SAATHII) is at the forefront of challenging and tackling social stigma, discrimination and violence towards gay men, other MSM and trans people in India through its innovative use of digital media and the internet.

HIV Discrimination, Prevention and Digital Media in India

Despite the decline in adult HIV prevalence in India, which has seen HIV prevalence among adults drop from 0.41 per cent in 2001 to 0.26 per cent in 2014–15 according to the National Integrated Biological and Behavioural surveillance conducted by NACO, new HIV infections among MSM and trans populations hasn't shown as steady of a decline (NACO 2009, 2014). National surveillance data from the National AIDS Control Organisation provides evidence that the MSM populations have a high HIV prevalence rate of 4.3 per cent (NACO 2014), which is more than twenty times that of the general population (NACP IV 2011). West Bengal, along with Jharkhand and Odisha, accounts for a prevalence of 6.70 per cent (NACO 2014). Globally, it has been reported that despite the scale-up of targeted HIV prevention to gay men, other MSM and trans people, entrenched stigma and discrimination impede prevention efforts resulting in proportionately higher HIV incidence among these vulnerable groups. Although 5–10 per cent of HIV infection worldwide is attributed to MSM, only 1.2 per cent of the entire funding for HIV prevention is geared towards this group (MSMGF 2010), making it one of the most underfunded groups among populations at risk.

Violence, stigma and discrimination make it difficult not only to estimate HIV sero prevalence accurately, but also create challenges for effective HIV education and prevention among gay men, other MSM and trans people in India (Chakrapani et al. 2008). Internationally, evidence of human rights violations against sexual minorities and HIV and AIDS peer outreach workers in community and healthcare contexts continues to exist (Gutierrez et al. 2010). Research further suggests that despite the continued mobilisation of marginalised communities to challenge stigma and discrimination, changing the wider social context requires building more effective and targeted structural change approaches to reduce HIV infections among MSM and trans communities (Campbell and Cornish 2010; MSMGF 2010). In addition, as Dhall and Boyce (2015) have argued more recently, economic exclusion remains a major contributing factor to HIV vulnerability. They argue:

> The issue of economic inclusion for people with non-normative genders and sexualities is therefore complex and embedded with myriad challenges, relating for example to socioeconomic precarity relating to sexual and gender non-conformity, poor health-care conditions and difficult legislative environment. (Dhall and Boyce 2015: 16)

Gay men and other men who have sex with men and trans people who do not necessarily identify as 'gay' or 'MSM' remain hidden to HIV prevention and outreach programmes (Boyce 2007; Deb et al. 2009). Married men who have sex with men also remain 'hidden', often not receiving sexual health and HIV prevention information. As my observation and working with the National AIDS Control Program (NACP) in India has shown, the section of MSM that remains most left out are male sexual partners of *kothis*.[2] These groups frequently remain outside targeted HIV prevention because it is hard to reach them (Ramakrishnan 2007). Despite the targeted interventions provided for visible gay men, other MSM and trans communities (NACO 2014) certain groups, due their invisibility, remain at higher risk for HIV infection.

It is also important to note that I view the continued use of the normative categories of 'MSM' and 'gay' as problematic when the individuals being referred to can find these terms irrelevant. While I use them in this chapter, my experience suggests it is hard to believe in a singular 'MSM' or 'trans' category with a homogenised experience. Thus I use these terms only because they are the dominant tropes, recognising they are specific subjectivities indexed by the fields of power of HIV and international development research and policy (Gosine 2009). In this chapter, I draw on the contextual backdrop presented above to consider how the use of digital media and the internet can reach out to multiple audiences and particular groups of gay men, men who have sex with men and trans people who remain 'hidden' or invisible.

A key challenge to the impact of existing HIV prevention approaches has been the widespread impact of the internet on gay men, other MSM and trans communities. This is especially true in India with its ubiquitous access to the internet at home and in public internet cafes. Many MSM in Kolkata and across India access the internet as a major resource in helping them acknowledge and 'gather more information about their sexuality' (Sahani 2008). Popular websites such as PlanetRomeo and Grindr work to shape sexual expectations, norms and practices of gay men, other MSM and trans people (Silveira 2010). These popular sites are used for socialising and 'hooking up' and provide anonymity for users who do not want to disclose their sexuality.

Shaw (1997) points out that while heterosexual people have access to participate in conversations outside the chatroom, for example the bar or a store, to find a potential sex partner, not as many opportunities and options exist for homosexual or *queer* people. The chatroom, and by extension the internet, provides the means for queer people to meet and socialise instantaneously. Following Shaw's line of enquiry Mowlabocus (2010) points out that this relationship between the online world created by new media technologies and the offline world of an existing gay male subculture complicates the questions concerning the character of online communities and identities. He says that 'the digital is not separate from other spheres of gay life, but in fact grows out of while remaining rooted in local, national and international gay male subculture' (p. 7).

Mowlabocus's statement about the digital being rooted in local gay male subcultures is important in understanding queer cyberspace. While anti-discrimination laws exist on a national level in the United Kingdom, in some countries in Europe, and parts of the United States of America, sodomy laws still exist in many parts of the world especially in South Asia as a remnant of the colonisers.[3] Prior research in India has shown how digital spaces have evolved and changed perceptions of cruising, anonymity and safe sex (Dasgupta 2014, 2015, 2017). In recent years, internet social networking and dating sites have begun to take sexual health information and awareness seriously (Clift 2010; Mowlabocus 2010; Mowlabocus et al. 2014, 2016). As Figure 6.1 below shows, PlanetRomeo regularly hosts discussions on sexual health issues including HIV prevention. Both PlanetRomeo and Gaydar have started making sexual health information prominently available on their website (also see Dasgupta and Dhall, forthcoming). PlanetRomeo announced in 2009 that they would only offer porn films for download which depict safe sex and have explicitly stated they will not endorse or host bareback porn films for their users.

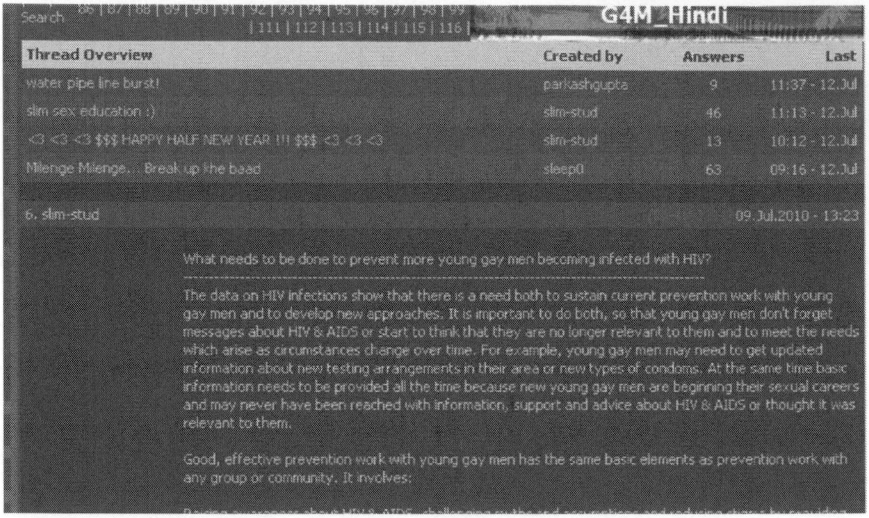

Figure 6.1 PlanetRomeo India discussion forum

Little critical analysis exists in the research literature to develop the evidence on the use and impact of these informal digital HIV prevention approaches or the extent to which they prevent/do not prevent new infections. To date, there has not been a serious effort to link these types of intervention with large-scale public health and face-to-face community mobilisation efforts in India. Furthermore, these commercial websites (such as PlanetRomeo and Grindr) lack a sustainable commitment to fighting stigma and discrimination and do not make available critical online educational opportunities. This suggests a need for context-specific community-based and led HIV prevention and education approaches (within the context specifically of India) using digital media and the internet to develop theoretically informed structural change approaches for community strengthening towards HIV prevention (Singh and Walsh 2012).

Another significant aspect of queer lives in India is their stratified existence based on class dynamics (Dasgupta 2014; Gupta 2005). Gupta (2005) explains the frustration faced by many *kothis* in mainstream society, where money and the ability to speak English dictate social boundaries. This makes it difficult for gay, MSM and trans men who cannot speak English to interact with others in many online spaces. From my observations of and participation in Facebook conversations, it's true that some Facebook spaces are exclusionary on linguistic lines; however, there are also other groups which target specific non-metropolitan vernacular/non-English-speaking populace. Facebook and WhatsApp are becoming better with regard to Indian scripts. So there are increasing online interactions in Bengali or Hindi in Kolkata as well as other districts of West Bengal. So in that sense online spaces no longer need be bound by the diktats of English.

This is where I believe digital media and the internet can meet the challenges of HIV prevention for these invisible populations. I believe there is a critical need to address the intersection of HIV prevention with the lived experiences of violence, stigma and discrimination against visible and invisible gay men, other MSM and trans communities (see also Boyce and Dasgupta 2017; Dasgupta and Dhall forthcoming). This is particularly paramount in the light of increasing internet ubiquity across the country. In what follows, I present SAATHII – a pioneer in using digital media and the Internet – to improve access to HIV prevention and capacity-building approaches in Kolkata. My intention is to highlight SAATHII's innovative use of technologies in the hope that other community-based and led organisations can design similar HIV and AIDS education and prevention programmes and contextualise them for the diverse needs of gay men, other MSM and trans communities they serve.

Digital Media and Sexual Health

Virtual spaces have the potential for greater deterritorialisation and the performance of productive identities (Wakeford 1997; Campbell 2004; Mowlabocus 2008, 2010). Wakeford (1997), citing Kira Hall and Judith Butler, sees identity as fluid and performative and the cyberspace as a place 'where you can be whoever you want to be' (25). Butler (1999), writing about this performativity says, 'practices in both homosexual and heterosexual contexts . . . open surfaces and orifices to erotic signification or close down others [and] effectively reinscribe the boundaries of the body along new cultural lines' (169).

In addition, Mclelland (2002) and Mowlabocus (2010) argue that virtual spaces can break down social and cultural boundaries. As such, virtual spaces can provide a safe space for performance of identities to make new practical knowledge and sensitivity about HIV risk. These approaches have been tried with MSM and transgenders in Thailand (Walsh 2008; Walsh, Lasky and Morrish 2011). This prior research has potential for use in India, as it implies that digital HIV prevention and education can affect and respect agency, while situated in the sexual and social practices of gay men, other MSM and trans people, in ways that traditional decontextualised approaches such as workshops may not.

SAATHII is not alone in developing digital forms of community outreach aimed at targeting MSM. There is a small but growing body of literature that reports on similar attempts to respond to recent shifts in gay male sexual cultures. While some (Welfare and Lighton 2011) urge caution in pursuing online forms of community outreach, others have identified significant benefits in utilising digital platforms for work with MSM communities. Rosser et al. (2011) have proven that digitally mediated methods of outreach increase the speed, depth and honesty of service user disclosure, compared to offline forms of engagement. This is particularly true in relation to the disclosure of sensitive or stigmatised issues such as unprotected sexual contact, risk-taking behaviours (including drug use during sex) and partner concordance.

Meanwhile, Landers et al. (2011) contend that building solidarity networks with the gay men's health movement on a global scale is key to addressing the challenges that currently face sexual health promotion workers. They contend that most of the health outreach in the US has been focused on HIV/AIDS; however, it needs to be recognised that using the discourse of HIV/AIDS to target health advocacy is not always successful as gay MSM and trans women's health goes beyond the HIV/AIDS narrative, further arguing that such policies are often enmeshed within funding and government strategies which often limit the levels within which outreach can take place. They argue that such solidarity networking requires deeper engagement with digital forms of communication, which moves activists and workers outside of the local silos in which they work and connects them up to a broader population of peer mentors. Supporting this claim, Pedrana et al. (2013) found that an intervention model built around online videos hosted on the social media platform YouTube, was accessed by men from across the world, including both the UK and Saudia Arabia. Interviews with MSM who engaged with the intervention revealed that the location of the videos (on a social media platform) provided men with an added impetus to discuss sexual health issues.

Digitally enabled networks and sites of communication and sharing are vital to the development of youth advocates and community sexual health 'champions' according to Young and Jaganathan (2014). Their claims are based on a feasibility study involving fifty-five MSM recruited to a 'secret' Facebook group in which eight peer leaders sought to facilitate and support user engagement. Of particular note is their finding that the Latino population (accounting for 60 per cent of the cohort) accounted for 82 per cent of the activity in the forum whereas the African-American population (making up almost 40 per cent of the cohort) accounted for only 25.5 per cent of the user engagement. These findings serve to underscore the need to consider each target demographic on their own terms, and demands that health promotion agencies recognise that a 'one-size-fits-all' model of community outreach simply does not work. Of particular relevance here, is the finding that only 21 per cent of the Facebook conversations that took place during the research period focused directly on sexual health. Personal conversations about user identity and sexual orientation featured more regularly. Furthermore, participants only initiated 37 per cent of conversations that took place in the group, identifying the need for peer outreach workers to be online and engaged regularly, initiating and sustaining 'relevant' conversations with the group members.

A similar conversation-based approach was also undertaken by Rhodes et al. (2008) who have reported on a chatroom-based intervention programme on two digital sites populated by MSM. Their results identify the potential success of such programmes, while also identifying the fact that those who are at the highest risk of HIV exposure failed to engage with the intervention. In short, some, but by no means all, MSM engaged with this online intervention. Meanwhile, Macmaster et al. (2003) report on a six-month pilot project based in San Jose, California, and which provided an outreach service to MSM via chat rooms dedicated to MSM. The study identified the key role that timing plays in such intervention work, with the highest success rate for user engagement being during lunch hours and between 12:00 and 17:00 on weekends. The study identified the challenges that the outreach team faced when trying to engage users during the evening when, it is assumed, the target population were more interested in using the chatrooms for their primary purpose – to arrange real-time physical hook-ups.

Collectively, the results of these studies demonstrate the feasibility and potential utility of using social networking technologies for health education and promotion. At the same time, these studies report on community outreach programmes that develop specific platforms, spaces or services in which to place the intervention. As such, they all operate 'outside' of MSM-dedicated spaces. This is a departure from the ethos of conventional community outreach and as such the opportunities for sustainability and further recruitment remain somewhat limited.

SAATHII as a response

Solidarity and Action Against the HIV Infection in India (SAATHII) was founded in 2000 during the International AIDS conference in

Durban. A registered charity in India and the USA, SAATHII primarily addresses the sexual health needs of gay men, other MSM and trans communities in India. SAATHII envisions a concerted response to the HIV/AIDS epidemic in India and strengthening the capacity of organisations working against the HIV/AIDS epidemic in India.

SAATHII was among the first non-profit organisations based in India to use digital media and the Internet in HIV and AIDS interventions (Ramakrishnan n.d). They have been working to bridge information, networking and other capacity gaps through various digital channels including: a website, a listserv, a virtual mobile library and an interactive online interface and through films and music videos. To address the problems of HIV prevention, capacity building and advocacy specifically targeted towards hidden gay, other MSM and trans communities, SAATHI strongly believed that it needed to leverage popular digital media and the internet to be as effective as possible. This was both because of the extent of the penetration of the internet into the lives of its service users, the numerous difficulties they faced in meeting publicly and their reluctance to meet up physically for fear of disclosure and stigma. Moreover, SAATHII also realised that this work needed to stretch beyond the Eastern region of India, and decided that widening access with digital media and the internet would allow for national and global knowledge sharing and collaborative learning on the ongoing problems of HIV prevention among diverse MSM and trans communities across the country.

SAATHII has its own website: www.SAATHII.org. The website serves as an online resource centre and repository of its reports, research and educational resources for vulnerable populations. It contains an event list which notifies the general public about events related to HIV and sexual health, educational programmes and training workshops. The website also works as a human resources facility, advertising the latest job postings, conferences and funding initiatives from around the world. The website boasts a comprehensive directory with information about drop-in centres and testing and counselling services within different regions of the country. The directory maintains a constantly updated report on those areas of the sector where urgent intervention is required. Thus it acts as a global communicating tool in getting together various funding and social policy bodies with service providers. The directory also has a print version used by almost 1,200 organisations including NGOs, government agencies, hospitals and educational institutions. Also integrated into the resource centre is a virtual library providing users the opportunity to browse through recent research and case studies on HIV and related topics.

SAATHII also makes use of a yahoo listserv saathii@yahoogroups. com to keep members up to date with information related to news about HIV treatments, funding initiatives and training programmes. Staff constantly post news on current research activities on HIV and sexual health initiatives around the world. This listserv provides MSM and trans activists and educators access to advocacy and research initiatives. It also enables community-based organisations to join in various discussions and networks, and acts as a site for e-conferencing between various stakeholders. Some of the recent discussions on the listserv have been about funding and consultancy invitations, and scientific and social updates on HIV relevant to MSM and trans communities.

SATHII uses Facebook to keep in touch with all their service users and the larger gay, other MSM and transgender community in India. Through the innovative Santi Seva Development Project, SAATHII worked with the transgender population in Bhadrak, Orissa to document their histories, share their struggles, write their own stories and share them on Facebook. This empowerment project culminated in a visual collection documenting their lives which was showcased as a poster in the 2008 International AIDS conference. For the first time, this transgender community decided to leverage the power of the internet to share their stories. SAATHI supported them by setting up an online exhibition on their Facebook group. By using Facebook, the impact and visibility of the project was further expanded. Such capacity-building activities have been effective in raising awareness, increasing solidarity, mobilising social capital and strengthening clout in a stigmatising context to reduce vulnerability to HIV and AIDS.

Most SAATHII staff members who are involved in the design and implementation of these initiatives and collating the information together identify as MSM or trans, thus bringing to the work a reflexive awareness of their own lived realities and social positions.

Mediated Expertise

During the course of this project formal and informal focus groups and discussion sessions were conducted with peer outreach workers as well as service users. One of the main themes that came up from these conversations was the role of the 'expert'.

Rajdeep, an 18-year-old gay man living in South Kolkata, said:

I am not out to my parents yet and as you know our schools are pretty appalling about providing any kind of information about sex education, let alone for homos like us. I have to thus look up websites and social media for information. A few months ago I thought I had some kind of a problem and ended up asking a completely random stranger on PR (PlanetRomeo) abut where one could get help. This was not useful at all. I wish there was a more streamlined Kolkata focused website or groups which have the expertise to help boys like me.

What counts as expertise remains quite contested and many of the gay men I spoke to believed it did not have to necessarily be a health or medical practitioner but rather, as Sameer put it, 'Someone from the community, who understands our language . . . stigma.' Expertise in such circumstances was not measured by how much one knew about the subject but rather in what ways service users like Rajdeep and Sameer felt comfortable sharing information with. Elsewhere Mowlabocus et al. (2015) have argued that expertise is situated within the embodied experience of users that is socially contextualised to the place. What Mowlabocus et al. means here is that expertise gets produced in a variety of ways and digital outreach requires a great deal of effort and ongoing labour for it to be effective and is directly related to the place within which outreach is being carried out. At the moment while SAATHII is already present on social media spaces such as Facebook continually hosting discussion and spreading awareness, it also needs to join the 'new spaces' where gay men are cruising and where chances of sexual risk might be harder. SATHII already has a certain amount of social capital within the gay, MSM and trans communities being one of the more well known charities in the sector. It commands respect as well as social currency for being visible in queer pride parades, hosting the annual Siddharth Gautam Film Festival which showcases queer films, and finally their physical sexual health outreach work. Social capital as Bourdieu defines it, is 'the sum of the resources, actual or virtual, that accrue to an individual or a group by virtue of possessing a durable network of more or less institutionalized relationships of mutual acquaintance and recognition' (Bourdieu and Wacquant 1992: 119). Social capital is important to expertise, as Ranjan, a trans woman, notes:

> Look I will believe that some one knows about sexual health and specifically about trans specifics if I see which organisation they are from. If it is a known organisation or I know that my friends recommend it, then I will also listen to what they have to say. Sometimes I just ask my friends online 'ei eta ki hote pare re' (What can this be). If there is someone available online all the time it will be helpful.

My own research (Dasgupta 2014, 2015, 2017) argues that digital platforms provide a useful way for queer men to connect with each other and establish communities of support. This is, however, predicated among other things on class, caste and linguistic ability as well as platform literacy. This is an area that also needs to be considered within online outreach.

Language barriers

One of the main limitations of using digital media and the internet in HIV and AIDS projects has been the language barrier. Because most existing resources available online are in English, significant numbers of gay, other MSM and transgender communities still do not have access to these resources. As one respondent Ratul puts it:

> Everyone thinks that everyone who uses the internet knows and understands English. Well I don't and never have. So how will I understand what all this is. I think organisations working for sexual health within our communities (MSM) need to understand this and translate material into Bengali and Hindi. I know they are currently doing this when they hand out fliers but this also needs to happen on the internet. (Translated)

Other queer and social equality organisations such as Sappho have understood this need and have been consistently producing their newsletter *Swakanthey* (*In Her Voice*) bilingually (in both Bengali and English). This approach has helped them to reach out to individuals in the community who do not speak English. While SAATHII has begun to translate, publish and disseminate information online in regional languages in addition to English and especially in their 'offline' outreach advocacy programmes this is yet to be implemented with their digital resource tools. More work needs to be done to better understand how to sustain the impact of online HIV prevention, advocacy and capacity-building by addressing language barriers.

Addressing Privacy and Ethical Issues

Another emerging problem is the issue of privacy and ethics. Although projects are visually documented for impact analysis and dissemination, many of the MSM and transgender participants I spoke to have felt that visibility threatens both their status and their sexual orientation. Swapan explained:

> I am worried about using digital media because I fear people might know I am gay. Especially if I join one of these groups on Facebook, it might open the door to further speculation about my orientation.

While the efficacy of the internet for communication and outreach is unparalleled, there is a particular need for vigilance around the protection of sensitive personal information stored online (Boyce and Hajra 2011). To address this issue, SAATHII makes sure that any visual material that is recorded during an event is only used for official purposes and is only available to the public with the consent of the individual who has been photographed or recorded. There is always a need to be careful about representing people in an MSM or transgender context. Boyce and Hajra, who worked on a photographic project with the MSM and transgender community in West Bengal, articulate their concern: 'We were concerned that people may not wish to be portrayed in a photographic project as a man who has sex with men or as a person of transgender' (2011: 8).

Building Digital Literacies and Capacities

While SATHII's initial efforts have allowed MSM and transgender communities to increase their access to information, future work needs to build their digital literacies and skills to transition from content consumers to meaningful participants. It is still true that much of India is untouched by the digital revolution and the internet has only reached a select few in the urban cities and fringes. Ila Nagar (this volume) has explained that this is particularly true for the kothis and jenanas who remain 'digitally untouched'. Even in cases where the internet has reached rural areas, people may not know how to use a computer. Thus there is an immediate need to implement complementary programmes towards reducing this digital divide.

The limited access to the internet by gay men, other MSM and trans people in rural or semi urban areas where there is little or no access to computers can mean that many potential service users do not benefit from perceived advantages in widening access via these digital means. In such cases, print dissemination is the only way. However, of late, mobile phones have made an incursion into rural India for e-health and e-learning use, and opportunities exist for SAATHII to leverage these developments in line with its current suite of programmes. Yet, frontline workers, educators and HIV prevention activists who teach about sexual health and human rights face tensions and dilemmas in handling controversial topics about culture and sexuality. Messages in curriculum and media that emphasise family values and heavily check sexuality through stigma and 'hetero-nationalist' rhetoric (Gosine 2009) condemn and reframe sexual behaviour and practices in the name of rational behaviour change. Such denial of desire, pleasure and intimacy is unhelpful for young people and marginalised communities struggling with sexuality and gender identity issues.

Strategic Networks

Sustaining strategic networks through e-forums moderated by facilitators for sharing knowledge and for advocacy has allowed SAATHII to leverage their limited resources to benefit large sections of the MSM and transgender communities across India. Through the sharing of experiences in online spaces, a culture of collaborative learning has emerged that overcomes historical regional separations.

As a result, new and better practices have been identified, collaboratively developed and implemented. The enhanced strategic support from mentors and experts in the e-forums for testing and trying out new ideas has increased the confidence of HIV prevention educators and activists. This approach also implies an opportunity to rethink prevention, advocacy and capacity-building to focus on the added value of strategic networking to tackle specific problems in practice, rather than locating such efforts in reified static notions of 'communities' that NGOs can 'intervene' in.

The Role of Key Individuals

What I have also observed in this project is the important role of key individuals in building and sustaining a network with digital media and the internet. The tools and resources we created and implemented were not simply 'put out there' but needed to become naturalised as part of service users' daily practices if they were to have any impact. Over time, these key individuals instigated crucial processes to ensure the success of our project. They created a 'one-stop' legitimate portal for gathering and disseminating valued information on sexual health, prevention, treatment, care and support to disrupt the negative and incorrect information on a variety of websites. They provided opinions and advice to make sharing tacit knowledge in online spaces a valued resource for service users in remote areas lacking information. As these key individuals built trust and resilience, over time, the network began to transition from merely downloading to uploading and exchanging resources with one another. These experiences challenge the traditional 'training-of-trainer' approaches that dominate HIV prevention today. Instead, it suggests a need to understand and design more effective digitally mediated educational approaches to mobilise HIV prevention activists and educators in ways that facilitate their capacities as boundary crossers, knowledge mediators and network sherpas with digital media and the internet among gay, other MSM and transgender communities.

Conclusion

In this chapter I have described SAATHII and shown how its use of digital media and the internet can make a positive contribution to HIV prevention, advocacy and capacity-building approaches among gay, other MSM and transgender communities. I have argued why it is important for community-based and led organisations like SAATHII to leverage multiple platforms to redesign conventional and dominant approaches to HIV prevention in a digital world. To date, the potential for the emerging Indian digital queer culture to disrupt regulatory habits and choices to improve the impact of normative HIV prevention and education has not yet been explored.

The call now is to build AIDS-resilient and AIDS-competent communities to fight HIV and reduce vulnerability. This has led to researchers calling for structural interventions that consider the cultural, legal and economic aspects of health and human rights (Auerbach et al. 2010), and the critical use of networking and digital technologies for community-based and led HIV prevention and education (Walsh and Singh 2012).

I suggest that how Indian gay, other MSM and trans communities can adequately meet this challenge and address these recommendations is by an analysis of the ways in which the complexities of masculinity and sexuality are being performed by Indian gay, other MSM and trans people in digital spaces. The potential for true growth lies in navigating and confronting the many difficult tensions of sex and sexuality head on, whether in digital spaces or in society. Benchmarking the best sexual health and community development practices of international donors and NGOs working in HIV prevention interventions will involve bringing in postcolonial and multicultural forms of inquiry that disrupt technical-rational thinking and programming about norms of targets, indicators and outcomes, and idealised abstractions of behaviour change, solidarity and 'empowerment' for those labelled as 'vulnerable communities'. These approaches will open up practices and spaces to widen creativity and imagination in the negotiation of non-colonising sexual identities to align with the spirit of 'redesigning the AIDS response' (Larson et al. 2011; Gosine 2009).

It appears that international agencies, national actors and civil society organisations are serious about fighting HIV in gay, other MSM and transgender communities in India. To move forward, we will now have to decide which taboos on gender, sexuality and masculinity have to be rearticulated with the dynamic use of digital media and the internet for diffusing power and contesting hetero-normativity in policy and programming practices targeted at gay, other MSM and transgender communities in order to recraft the as yet unrealised nirvana of universal access to health and human rights.

I conclude that if HIV and AIDS stakeholders want to work critically with gay men, other MSM and trans communities in social and legal environments that continue to deny human rights and equitable access to healthcare, it is time to deal with the changed sexual behaviours of gay men, other MSM and trans people precipitated by the use of digital media and the internet. The kind of interventions SAATHI has kicked-off in India, based on working with communities to leverage digital media and the internet in ways that are useful and valuable in expanding access and fighting stigma and discrimination, are productive in rethinking existing HIV prevention, advocacy and capacity-building approaches. Ultimately, solving the problems of community-based and led HIV prevention with digital media and the internet by working with the lived realities and multiple identities of gay men, other MSM and trans people is more empowering than idealised abstractions of solidarity and 'empowerment'.

Note

1. Some sections of this chapter and ideas originally appeared in an early form as: Rohit K. Dasgupta (2012) 'Digital Media and the Internet for HIV Prevention, Capacity Building and Advocacy Among Gay, Other Men Who Have Sex with Men (MSM), and Transgender (TG): Perspectives from Kolkata, India', *Digital Culture and Education*, 4 (2). The present chapter while utilising a similar methodological approach, is based on six months of digital ethnography and focus group interviews in Kolkata, India from May 2016 to October 2016. This research was funded by a Wellcome Trust Humanities and Social Sciences Small Grant Award (Award reference: 201329/Z/16/Z). Some sections will also appear as a co-authored report with Mr Pawan Dhall (Bloomsbury, forthcoming). I would like to thank Dr Paul Boyce and Mr Pawan Dhall for their help and support on this project.
2. Narrain (2004: 2–3) explains that '*Kothi* is a feminised male identity which is adopted by some people in the Indian subcontinent and

is marked by gender non-conformity. *Kothis*, though biologically male, adopt feminine modes of dressing, speech and behaviour and would look for a male partner who has masculine modes of behaviour.' The male partners of kothis are called *panthis*. Interestingly, *kothis* are grouped under MSM by NACO (National Aids Control Organisation).

3. Homosexuality is currently illegal in Afghanistan, Bangladesh, Bhutan, Pakistan and Sri Lanka in South Asia, with only Nepal legalising homosexuality in 2007. India legalised homosexuality in 2009 following a judgement by the Delhi High Court, only to recriminalise it in 2013 by the Supreme Court. In addition, seven countries (which include Iran, Saudi Arabia, UAE, Nigeria, Mauritania, Sudan and Yemen) punish homosexuality with the death penalty.

References

Auerbach, J. S., Parkhurst, J., Caceres, C. and Keller, K. (2010) *Addressing Social Drivers of HIV/AIDS: Some Conceptual, Methodological, and Evidentiary Considerations*, AIDS 2031 Working Paper 24, pp. 1–27.

Bourdieu, P. (1986) 'The Forms of Capital', in J. Richardson (ed.), *Handbook of Theory and Research for the Sociology of Education*. New York: Greenwood, pp. 241–58.

Bourdieu, Pierre and Wacquant, Loic J. D. (1992) *An Invitation to Reflexive Sociology*. Chicago: University of Chicago Press.

Boyce, P. (2007) 'Moral Ambivalence and Irregular Practices: Contextualising Male to Male Sexualities in Calcutta/India', *Feminist Review*, 83: 79–98

Boyce, P. and Dasgupta, R. K. (2017) 'Utopia or Elsewhere: Queer Modernities in Small Town West Bengal', in T. Kuldova and M. Varghese (eds), *Urban Utopias: Excess and Expulsion in Neoliberal South Asia*. Basingstoke: Palgrave Macmillan.

Boyce, P. and Hajra, A. (2011) 'Do You Feel Somewhere in Light That Your Body Has No Existence? Photographic Research with Men Who Have Sex with Men and People of Transgender in West Bengal', *Visual Communication*, 10 (1): 3–24.

Butler, J. (1999) *Gender Trouble: Feminism and Subversion of Identity*. London: Routledge.

Campbell, C. and Cornish, F. (2010) 'Towards a Fourth Generation of Approaches to HIV and AIDS Management: Creating Contexts for Effective Community Mobilisation', *AIDS Care*, 22 (1): 1569–79.

Campbell, J. E. (2004) *Getting It on Online: Cyberspace, Gay Male Sexuality and Embodied Identity*. New York: Harrington Park Press.

Chakrapani, V., Newman, P. and Shunmugam, M. (2008) 'Secondary HIV prevention among Kothi identified MSM in Chennai, India', *Culture, Health and Sexuality*, 10 (4): 313–27.

Clift, J. (2010) 'Health Information, STDs, and the Internet: Implications for Gay Men', in C. Pullen and M. Cooper (eds), *LGBT Identity and Online New Media*. London and New York: Routledge, pp. 258–70.

Dasgupta, R. K. (2012) Digital Media and the Internet for HIV Prevention, Capacity Building and Advocacy Among Gay, Other Men who have Sex with Men (MSM) and Transgenders: Perspectives from Kolkata, India', *Digital Culture and Education*, 4 (1): 88–109.

Dasgupta, R. K. (2014) 'Parties, Advocacy and Activism: Interrogating Community and Class in Digital Queer India', in C. Pullen (ed.), *Queer Youth and Media*. Basingstoke: Palgrave Macmillan, pp. 265–77.

Dasgupta, R. K. (2015) 'Dissident Citizenship: Articulating Belonging, Dissidence and Queerness on Cyberspace', *South Asian Review*, 35 (3): 203–23.

Dasgupta, R. K. (2017) *Digital Queer Cultures in India: Politics, Intimacies and Belonging*. London: Routledge.

Dasgupta, R. K. and Dhall, P. (forthcoming) *Social Media, Sexuality and Sexual Health Advocacy in Kolkata, India: A Working Report*. New Delhi: Bloomsbury.

Dhall, P. and Boyce, P. (2015) *Livelihood, Exclusion and Opportunity: Socioeconomic Welfare Among Gender and Sexuality Non-normative People in India*, IDS Evidence Report 106. Sussex: Institute of Development Studies.

Gosine, A. (2009) 'Monster, Womb, MSM: The Work of Sex in International Development', *Development*, 52 (1): 25–33.

Gupta, A. (2005) Englishpur ki Kothi: Class Dynamics in the Queer movement in India', in A. Narrain and G. Bhan (eds), *Because I Have a Voice: Queer Politics in India*. Delhi: Yoda Press, pp. 123–42.

Gutierrez, J., McPherson, S., Fakoya, A., Matheou, A. and Bertozzi, S. (2010) 'Community-based Prevention Leads to an Increase in Condom Use and a Reduction in Sexually Transmitted Infections (STIs) Among Men Who Have Sex with Men (MSM) and Female Sex Workers (FSW): The Frontiers Prevention Project (FPP) Evaluation Results', *BMC Public Health*, 10 (497): 1–12.

Khan, S. (2004) *MSM and HIV and AIDS in India*. Lucknow: Naz Foundation International.

Landers, S., Pickett, J., Rennie, L. and Wakefield, S. (2011) 'Community Perspectives on Developing a Sexual Health Agenda for Gay and Bisexual Men', *AIDS and Behavior*,15 (1) Supplement: 101–6.

Larson, H., Bertozzi, S. and Piot, P. (2011) 'Redesigning the AIDS Response for Long-term Impact', *Bulletin of the World Health Organisation*. Online at: http://www.who.int/bulletin/online_first/11-087114.pdf (accessed 12 March 2012).

Mclelland, M. (2002) 'Virtual Ethnography: Using the Internet to Study Gay Culture in Japan', *Sexualities*, 5 (4): 387–406.

Macmaster, S., Aquino, R. and Vail, K. (2003) 'Providing HIV Education and Outreach via Internet Chat Rooms to Men who Have Sex with Men, *Journal of Human Behavior in the Social Environment*, 8 (2–3): 145–51.

Mowlabocus, S. (2008) 'Revisiting Old Haunts Through New Technologies: Public (Homo)sexual Cultures in Cyberspace', *International Journal of Cultural Studies*, 11 (4): 419–39.

Mowlabocus, S. (2010) *Gaydar Culture: Gay Men, Technology and Embodiment in the Digital Age*. Farnham and Burlington, VT: Ashgate.

Mowlabocus, S., Haslop, C. and Dasgupta, R. K. (2016) 'From Scene to Screen: The Challenges and Opportunities of Commercial Digital Platforms for HIV Community Outreach', *Social Media and Society*, 2 (4): 1–8.

Mowlabocus, S., Harbottle, J., Dasgupta, R. K. and Haslop, C. (2014) 'Reaching Out Online: Digital Literacy and the Uses of Social Media in Health Promotion', *Working Papers of the Communities and Culture Network+*, Vol. 3 (April). Leeds: University of Leeds.

Mowlabocus, S., Harbottle, J., Tooke, B., Haslop, C. and Dasgupta R. K. (2015) 'Because Even the Placement of a Comma Might Be Important: Expertise, Embodiment and Social Capital in Online Sexual Health Promotion', *Convergence: The International Journal of Research into New Media Technologies*, 21 (3): 375–87.

MSMGF Report (2010) Available at: http://www.msmgf.org/files/msmgf/About_Us/MSMGF_Quarterly_Report_10_June_2010.pdf (accessed 14 June 2016).

NACO (2009) *NACO Report*. New Delhi: Department of AIDS Control, Ministry of Health and Family Welfare, Government of India.

NACO (2014) *NACO Report*. New Delhi: Department of AIDS Control, Ministry of Health and Family Welfare, Government of India.

NACP IV (2011) *National Aids Control Program IV: Strategic Approach to Targeted Intervention Among Men Who Have Sex With Men*. New Delhi: Department of AIDS Control, Ministry of Health and Family Welfare, Government of India.

Pedrana, A. et al. (2013) 'Queer as F**k: Reaching and Engaging Gay Men in Sexual Health Promotion through Social Networking Sites', *Journal of Medical Internet Research*, 15 (2). Available at http://www.jmir.org/2013/2/e25/.

Ramakrishnan, L. (2007) Putting the B Back in LGBT: Bisexuality, Queer Politics and HIV AND AIDS Discourse', in B. Bose and S. Bhattacharya (eds), *The Phobic and the Erotic*. Kolkata: Seagull, pp. 291–300.

Ramakrishnan, L. (n.d.) 'ICTs and the Fight Against HIV AND AIDS in India', *Oneworld.Net*. Available at: http://uk.oneworld.net/article/view/108250/1/1912 (accessed 14 June 2016)

Rhodes, S. D., Hergenrather, K. C., Yee, L. J. and Ramsey, B. (2008) 'Comparing MSM in the Southeastern United States Who Participated in an HIV Prevention Chat Room-based Outreach Intervention and Those Who Did Not: How Different Are the Baseline HIV-risk profiles?', *Health Education Research*, 23 (1): 180–90.

Rosser, B. R. et al. 'The Future of Internet-Based HIV Prevention: A Report on Key Findings from the Men's INTernet (MINTS-I, II) Sex Studies', *AIDS and Behavior*, 15 (1) Supplement: 91–100.

Sahani, P. (2008) *Gay Bombay: Globalisation, Love and (Be) Longing in Contemporary India*. New Delhi: Sage.

Shaw, D. (1997) 'Gay Men and Computer Communication', in S. Jones (ed.), *Virtual Culture: Identity and Communication in Cybersociety.* New Delhi, Thousand Oaks, CA and London: Sage, pp. 133–45.

Silveira, A. (2010) 'Giving a Queer Account of the Self and Culture', *Canon.* Available at: http://www.canonmagazine.org/spring10/silveira.html (accessed 14 June 2016).

Singh, G. and Walsh, C. (2012) 'Prevention Is a Solution: Building the HIVe', *Digital Culture and Education*, 4 (1): 5–16.

Wakeford, N. (1997) 'Cyberqueer', in A. Medhurst and S. Munt (eds). *Lesbian and Gay Studies: A Critical Introduction.* London: Cassell, pp. 20–38.

Walsh, C. S. (2008) 'Producing Animations to Educate MSM and MSW to Fashion Safe Sex Practices and Address Low Perceptions of Personal Risk', in *IADIS Multi Conference on Computer Science and Information Systems*, 22–24 July, Amsterdam, The Netherlands.

Walsh, C. S. and Singh, G. (2012). Building the HIVe: Disrupting biomedical HIV/AIDS research with gay men, other MSM and transgenders. *AERA 2012 Conference.*

Walsh, C. S., Lasky, B. and Morrish, W. (2011) 'Building Local Capacity to Protect Public Health and Promote Social Justice Through Online Peer Education', in *IADIS International Conference e-Democracy, Equity and Social Justice*, 2011, part of the IADIS Multi Conference on Computer Science and Information Systems 2011, 20–22 July 2011, Rome, Italy.

Welfare, W. S and Lighton, L. (2011) 'Mapping of Sexual Health Promotion in North West England, 2008', *PubFERNANDESlic Health*, 125: 101–5.

World Bank (2009) *AIDS in South Asia: Understanding and Reporting.* Available at http://siteresources.worldbank.org/SOUTHASIAEXT/Resources/Publications/448813-1155152122224/southasia_aids.pdf (accessed14 June 2016).

Young, S. D. and Jaganathan, D. (2014) 'Feasibility of Using Social Networking Technologies for Health Research Among Men Who Have Sex with Men: A Mixed Methods Study', *American Journal of Men's Health*, 8 (1): 6–14.

Chapter 7

The TV9 Sting Operation on PlanetRomeo: Absent Subjects, Digital Privacy and LGBTQ Activism

Pawan Singh

In February 2011, TV9, a Hyderabad-based Telugu news channel, aired a sting operation conducted by an undercover journalist on the nationally popular online gay dating service PlanetRomeo. The news anchor's sensationalist overtones of moral panic were accompanied by the breach of the service users' privacy whose profile content including pictures were exposed in the story. While such an egregious publication of user information in digital spaces marked a continuity with other local news reporting practices on sex scandals, the incident assumed a particular gravity given that privacy related to same-sex conduct among consenting adults was a legally recognised right under the 2009 Delhi High Court Naz ruling that decriminalised homosexuality. The Naz ruling had defined privacy as relating to the personal autonomy of the individual surpassing what Indian LGBTQ activists considered the narrower logic of spatial/zonal privacy. This essay argues, however, that the TV9 sting foregrounds the zonal logic of privacy as more urgent given that the violation occurred in online media spaces that are only ambiguously private. Further, privacy, as it pertains to the Naz judgement, is shaped by a number of critical absences of particular subjects that reconfigure privacy as secrecy, as silence and by implication as a form of safety. The paper draws upon media studies, critical studies of law, new media studies and the scholarship on the globalisation of sexuality to highlight the stakes in public identification as gay or lesbian in the Indian context within the Naz framework of rights and visibility. The essay also critiques the implicit relationship between homosexuality and privacy as having a pre-eminent status globally towards the recognition of homo-sexuality in the law.

Context

The widely celebrated Delhi High Court judgement of 2009 *in Naz Foundation v. Union of NCT of Delhi*[1] represents an apotheo-sis of the struggle for LGBT rights in India. For one, the judge-ment expressly dealt with the colonial legacy of Section 377 of the Indian Penal Code, codified in British India in 1861, with a view to punish what at the time was deemed as innate native perversity of sexual conduct (Bhaskaran 2002). In the colonial period, the law was employed as a legal instrument for the control of certain itinerant populations like *hijras* and certain tribes who were seen as ontologically criminal (Arondekar 2009). In the postcolonial period, the law was largely used to prosecute incidents of non-consensual conduct (Narrain 2003). The 2009 Naz judgment marked a culmination of a two-decade long public struggle to decriminal-ise homosexuality around which the Indian LBGT movement has organised itself. While the primary rationale in the reading down of Section 377 of the Indian Penal Code was the law's damaging nexus with the public health crisis of HIV/AIDS, the 105-page long Naz judgement framed the matter of decriminalisation in terms of an LGBT community and other iterations of a sexual minority that were understood to be vulnerable to the burden of undue criminal-ity under the aegis of the colonial era sodomy law. It is instruc-tive to recall here that the public health rationale employed by the Naz Foundation concerned the rising rates of HIV among the high-risk health demographic of men-who-have-sex-with-men (MSM), a group that, according to the NGO, was unable to freely access healthcare owing to fear of persecution and legal criminalisation of their sexual conduct. According to the late Shivananda Khan, the founder of Naz Foundation International (NFI), MSM signifies a complex behavioural category at the intersection of gender identifi-cation, sexual conduct and other local, cultural experiences of class and caste and is marked by absence in the public health outreach efforts for HIV/AIDS prevention (Parker et al. 1998).

Yet in its well-rehearsed construction of the rights to privacy, dignity, equality and non-discrimination, supported by various international sources and comparative judicial contexts, the Naz judgement fails to reflect the complexities of sexual taxonomies and the key distinction between sexual conduct and sexual identity. The distinction between sexual acts and sexual identities has animated much critical historical inquiry into the social and cultural histories of sexuality (Chauncey 1994; Halperin 1998). Anthropologists of South Asia have been similarly piqued by the discourse of acts vis-à-vis identity (Cohen 1995; Seabrook 1999), a heuristic that remains at the analytical centre of rich accounts of non-western, regional vocabularies, registers and modalities of sexuality. These few scholarly references to the distinction between acts and identity function here, not so much as a form of summons to the law and judicial decision-making to account for sexual specificity. Rather, it is intended to introduce another analytic that has generally been disfavoured to advance the political project of sexuality's visibility and presence in the interstices of texts, practices and cultural spaces as a radical body politics (Vanita 2002; Bose and Bhattacharya 2007). While acknowledging both the indispensability of this theoretical intervention and the opening up of a rich interpretive space within which it is possible to imagine a history of same-sex desire in India, this chapter proposes 'absence' as an analytic to re-contextualise the LGBT rights struggle for legitimacy, visibility and presence with respect to the specific notion of the right to privacy and public representation.

The chapter mobilises the discourse of absence, first through an examination of what the essay calls the 'optics of privacy' written into the law by the Naz judgement through the right to privacy for consensual same-sex conduct among adults. It is important to note here that the right to privacy has global purchase insofar as the recognition of homosexuality in the law is concerned. Following this analysis, the essay demonstrates how absence and the refusal to seek representation through identification as gay can complicate the function of privacy as an empowering right, which forms the material core around which generally abstract principles of equality and dignity of identity coalesce. Privacy, the essay contends, is at once the most materially urgent and tenuous of rights insofar as same-sex conduct and LGBT identity are concerned in postcolonial India, given the fraught boundaries between the public and the private in terms of class, bodily autonomy and sexual expression.

In the next section, the chapter offers a brief review of the Naz judgement, honing in on the judicial construction of the right to privacy as well as the critiques of privacy as offered by legal scholars and other commentators, including lawyers and journalists in India. This review demonstrates the formulation of privacy as a liberal right undergirding the desire for sexual citizenship and a public claim to assertive presence that is aligned with the western model of pride, visibility and coming out. Insofar as accomplishing the provisional decriminalisation of homosexuality in India is concerned, this approach has proved to be successful and has been widely acknowledged as marking a watershed in the struggle for sexuality rights. However, the 2009 Naz judgement, despite its significance as an extensive legal treatise on human rights, remains structured by certain absences and abstractions which this chapter aims to posit as the underside of the liberal formulation of privacy that elicits public visibility of the subject.

This is where the second part of the essay makes an intervention in the vaunted discourse of privacy to not only mark its limitations in the postcolonial Indian context but also illustrate an alternative discourse in which the registers of secrecy, non-disclosure and invisibility may hold sway. Through a critical reading of a nationally prominent incident of moral policing of queer subjects[2] in 2011, the chapter mobilises its central argument around absence as resisting the standard narrative of empowerment that hinges on the implicit coupling of sexuality and privacy as a legal right and the public visibility of the violated subject. The incident of moral policing occurred in February 2011, almost two years after the Naz judgement, an intermittent period marked by ascendant public discourse on homosexuality and a sense of triumphalism following the verdict (Narrain 2009). In a sting operation conducted on a gay dating service called PlanetRomeo by the Hyderabad-based regional TV news channel, TV9, the journalists exposed online profiles of users, including photos and content, on primetime news. Reporting in salacious overtones of moral panic and media sensationalism, the anchors decried the 'outbreak' of gay culture in the otherwise traditional city of Hyderabad. Immediately following the broadcast of the story 'Gay Culture Rampant in Hyderabad', legal action initiated by LGBT activists and lawyers resulted in the news channel having to issue an apology as well as pay a fine to the National Broadcasting Standards Authority (NBSA) of India. Evidently, such a course of action became possible owing to the decriminalisation of homosexuality in 2009 augmented by the language of human rights. Yet what was made clear by the TV9 sting operation was not only the tenuous foundations of privacy as the legal basis for decriminalisation but also that the legal mobilisation of claims to privacy only call forth the further visibility of the violated subject. The cost of empowerment by exercising a claim to privacy in the postcolonial context usually entails further exposure of one's sexual identity and personhood in a predominantly heteronormative culture, or what this chapter characterises as empowerment at the intersection of 'visibility with potential vulnerability'. But the key question this section asks and strives to address is: who is being represented through rights and for whom is this empowerment sought? In what follows, I stake out an often overlooked dynamic in the well-rehearsed narrative unfolding of privacy violation – legal representation-exercise of privacy rights-empowerment. The chapter demonstrates how at the centre of the contest between the media as moral police and the lawyers and advocates as guardians of human rights is the absent subject who does not emerge from the shadows of the online world of gay hook-ups and dating. This absence then also foregrounds another form of the exercise of privacy, that is through recourse to invisibility and a refusal to be represented.

The Naz Right to Privacy: Judicial Abstractions

In this section, the essay maps some key judicial logics in the Delhi High Court's formulation of the right to privacy in the 2009 Naz judgement. A close reading of these logics unpacks the various abstractions through which privacy is constructed as an empowering right for the Indian LGBT individuals and ostensibly for the men-who-have-sex-with-men (MSM) on whose behalf the right to privacy is sought in part. It is noteworthy that MSM groups were conspicuous by their absence in the court given that MSM is a behavioural category, and further the Naz Foundation case for the reading down of Section 377 was a Public Interest Litigation (PIL) to address the public health crisis of HIV/AIDS in India. Their absence accentuates the optics of representation through which the judges define privacy in the favour of self-identified LGBT individuals at the forefront of LGBT activism and the politics of human rights. This definition then is implicitly one that recognises the classed structure of spatial privacy, available usually to those who belong to an upper- and upper-middle-class socio-economic stataus.

The Naz Court assembled a range of of international sources and cases from comparative foreign jurisdictions such as the American jurisprudence on bodily privacy – cases on abortion such as *Roe v. Wade* (1973), contraception such as *Griswold v. Connecticut* (1965) and homosexuality in *Bowers v. Hardwick* (1986) – and the 1998 South African decision of decriminalisation. A critical move on the part of the judges was to couch sexual conduct in the language of intimacy, dignity and nurturing human relationships in order to construct the positivistic category of sexual orientation, which is further translated into a legally protected category. For instance, two important sources that inform this definition are the Yogyakarta Principles 2007 and the writings of the South African justice Edwin Cameron. These sources interpret sexual orientation as an innate capacity of a person for emotional and sexual relations with another person of a different or same gender. The privileging of sexual orientation as an unchanging interior core or an immutable aspect of a person's capacity to cultivate human relations gestures to an essentialist notion of sexuality that forecloses any possibility for a consideration of the social constructedness of sexual experience as may be understood from the behavioral construction of MSM (Seidman 2003). The positivistic underpinnings of establishing sexual orientation opens the pathway to sexual citizenship, a modern figuration that in the western context has been linked to the concept of sexual rights. Diane Richardson's (2000) analytic schema is useful in considering the linkages between sexual citizenship and sexuality rights where gay and lesbian groups in the UK have advanced legal rights claims on the basis of sexual conduct, sexual identity and the demand for public recognition of same-sex relationships. Regardless of the foundation for such claims, the underlying implication in each case entails a public recognition of homosexuality as a legitimate social identity category to be adjudicated by the law. The Naz judgement certainly articulates an iteration of such claims, sometimes explicitly. However, ultimately and perhaps unwittingly, its framing of sexual orientation foregrounds a class-oriented logic marked by a certain eagerness to confer rights-based recognition upon the visible LGBT representatives, without reflecting on the complexities of the everyday experiences through which sexuality also seeks to mask itself. The argument here may appear to be rather simple but it does warrant an interrogation of the frictionless juxtaposition of the MSM (absent, without real material privacy) and the self-identified LGBT groups (upper, upper-middle-class, often safely visible) through which the right to privacy proceeds to decriminalise homosexuality.

When this argument is taken further, it shows us that it may recapitulate the vital distinction between sexual acts and identities that troubles the judicial conflation of MSM and self-identified LGBT. While it is absolutely necessary to attend to this distinction, it must not be mistaken to be a binary relation in which identities ultimately vanquish the fleeting and risk-ridden discourse of acts, i.e. MSM. Rather, the chapter's deployment of this distinction provides analytical specificity through which the MSM absence in the courtroom in fact quietly exposes the classed nature of the privacy argument. A few more points are worth considering before this chapter pivots the lens onto an elucidation of the often-overlooked structuring of privacy by absence, especially when the exercise of the right to privacy is concerned.

At stake in raising the issue of MSM absence in the court is the important question of the legitimacy of injury inflicted upon sexual identity. Even in the Supreme Court of India, when the public health rationale of HIV/AIDS with respect to the MSM groups was brought up, the judges repeatedly asked if the data on them was accurate or if they were present in the court. In the Naz court, the MSM absence was glossed over in favour of substantiating privacy through an extensive interpretation of national, international and comparative sources. The Supreme Court judges, however, asked for the MSM to step forward and speak for themselves. The failure to adduce accurate data on the MSM or produce them in court then constituted a pivotal absence that underscored the meaning of privacy as a recourse to an invisibility of sorts.

Jason Keith Fernandes astutely points out this problematic with respect to other sexual subalterns such as sex workers and *hijras*. He contends that the harassment of subaltern men and sex workers soliciting MSM at the hands of the police will continue despite the provisional reading down of Section 377 and the right to privacy, primarily due to the public nature of their presence. Sex in public is clearly precluded under the right to privacy despite the Delhi High Court's formulation of privacy in broader terms of decisional autonomy, a concept that supposedly transcends the narrower scope of the zonal or spatial privacy (Fernandes 2009). By contrast, Saptarshi Mandal, a legal scholar, has reviewed privacy and consent in the context of heterosexual marriage in a manner that offers a comparison with the rights granted under the Naz verdict. Mandal argues that where public sex remains subject to prosecution under the sodomy law as well as public obscenity laws, the legitimacy of sex in private is configured by heterosexual marital norms that precludes sex workers and other public identities like *hijras*, often subsumed within the Indian LGBTQ movement. Sex work is criminalised under the Immoral Traffic (Prevention) Act 1956, while *hijras*, who earn a living by performing at public ceremonies and begging, are routinely arrested and harassed by police (Mandal 2009).

The import of these arguments, on the one hand, elucidates the classed nature of the LGBT movement and the demand for decriminalisation through a right to privacy. On the other hand, it points to the vulnerability of those whose sexuality and sexual lives unfold unambiguously in public contexts without the protective awning of the Naz right to privacy. Here, it must also be recalled that Naz formulated a transcendent version of privacy that linked privacy to persons and not places. Intended to liberate privacy from the putatively narrower conception of the zonal or the spatial, attaching privacy to persons – that is the individual exercise of decisional autonomy to make a claim to privacy – would entail the individual to identify themselves as gay or lesbian in order for their privacy claim to be meaningful. Although this judicial logic of unfettered privacy sought to expand the sphere of privacy and elevate its meaning to the privacy of personhood, it in fact abstracts privacy from the intricacies of public relationality and conduct and further presupposes and mandates the sexual personhood that would come into visibility in the same moment when privacy as decisional autonomy of the individual is mobilised. This abstraction of privacy by relegating the spatial/zonal in favour of the decisional autonomy reaches its limit when we consider the TV9 sting operation on PlanetRomeo, a nationally prominent case of moral policing of 'proliferating gay culture' in which the violation of privacy of online profile users was redressed broadly within the Naz framework of rights. Yet the absence of the violated figures, who never once came forward in public to seek justice, not unlike their MSM counterparts, circumscribed privacy within the sphere of zonal/spatial while erasing the primacy of decisional autonomy via sexual personhood to effectively refute the mandate of legal representation and public visibility. The essay now turns to an analysis of the TV9 sting operation on PlanetRomeo as an illustration of absence as an empty centre around which rights claims are organised for sexual privacy violation in postcolonial India.

The TV9 Sting Operation: Absent Subjects, Spatial Privacy

In February 2011, a regional Indian TV news channel, TV9, telecast a story titled, 'Gay Culture Rampant in Hyderabad' in Telugu[3] on prime-time news in Hyderabad. Through a sting operation conducted on the users of a gay dating service called planetromeo.com, an undercover TV9 reporter contacted profile users on the website and engaged them in conversation, with the enticement of a sexual hook-up. In what the Indian LGBT activists called a flagrant invasion of privacy of the service users as well as a violation of media ethics and the code of conduct set forth by the News Broadcasters Association of India (NBA), the story replayed the recorded conversations and exposed the profile pictures of Hyderabad users on prime-time news in sensationalising overtones of moral panic.

As the story caused national outrage, especially among LGBT groups in India, the subsequent events culminated in the imposition of a fine of $2,000 and a further issuance of an apology by the channel as ordered by the News Broadcasters Standards Authority (NBSA), an entity that governs the media code of ethics and broadcasting standards in India. Lawyers argue that this course of action became possible in the wake of the decriminalisation of homosexuality in India in 2009 through the Delhi High Court judgment in *Naz Foundation v. the Union of India* that read down Section 377 of the Indian Penal Code (Sheikh 2011). The sting operation by TV9 on online gay networking and the legal framework within which the new channel's 'investigative' practice became punishable seems to suggest a disjuncture between the global discourse of sexuality rights and the local cultures of vernacular media reporting (Appadurai 1996).

TV9 is a 24-hours news channel launched in the South Indian city of Hyderabad in 2004 by the Associated Broadcasting Company Private Limited (ABCL) that describes its mission as 'building a better society' through 'free-spirited journalism'.[4] Planetromeo.com, a gay networking service that started in Berlin, by its very name suggests a global presence.[5] The networking site went global in 2007 by adopting a sexuality rights approach and offered PLUS subscriptions[6] to its users in countries where homosexuality is illegal. The proliferation of planetromeo.com as an online space to regions like Asia where it has created a community of users is yet another iteration of the global flows of information that facilitate local articulations of sexual experiences and identities through processes such as transnationalism (Grewal and Kaplan 2001), cultural transmission (Offord 2003) and dubbing culture (Boellstorff 2003). The Indian LGBT activist movement emerged through similar processes, albeit drawing upon pre-internet media forms and rapidly expanding through online discussion groups connecting diasporic and national communities as well as gay individuals in remote parts of the country (Roy 2003). Even as spatial metaphors of proliferation, interconnection and expansion seem to characterise global flows as seamless, local mediations often disrupt this process towards varying outcomes. Where new identities and practices emerge, concomitant modes of policing them arise in response.

The TV9 sting operation on planetromeo.com exemplifies how the affordances offered by the visibility of urban gay cultures as an instantiation of global flows of information are translated into a language of moral panic through a local address to Hyderabad's supposedly middle-class, heteronormative audiences.[7] The news story opens with a female reporter expressing shock at the drastically proliferating gay culture in Hyderabad. She says, 'A boy trying to pursue girls is common but boys pursuing boys has become a fashion.' She further reports that all the gay men in the city go to pubs and clubs and drink and dance with whomever they want. The visuals cut to the inside footage of a club. The alarming tone of the news reporter and the visuals of men dancing and drinking in a club mark the urban space of the pub/club as a form of modern excess ushered in by Western/global lifestyles.

The reporter then describes the dancers to be 'software employees, rich kids and students' who are all drunk. Further sensationalising the matter, she describes the party as 'special' because all the men seen in the video are claimed to be 'gay'. She continues:

> Having got to know about the gay parties the TV 9 team went to 'investigate' and found the truth. Meeting, drinking and partying like this on weekends has become a ritual to the gay men in this city. Taking private party permission as an excuse, all the gay men unite and party. It might sound astonishing to hear but this is the reality.

The figure of the 'software employee' as a deviant, westernised subject functions to signal a global modernity ushered in by the development of the IT industry and a service economy in the city. The sensationalist narrative of corrupting modernity continues through the mobilisation of this figure as a global influence on local culture as the focus of the news story gradually shifts to planetromeo.com and its users.

Describing planetromeo.com as the most popular among the gay websites on the internet, the reporter provides user statistics from the website to substantiate her claims of an 'outbreak' of homosexuality in Hyderabad. The number of users in the state of Andhra Pradesh is 6,500, she reports, out of which '4,604 are from Hyderabad alone'. At any given time, 200 users are always logged in from the city. The language of outbreak confounds the meanings of the global and the local when she reports that software employees form the majority of the users 'who fall prey to this gay culture'. The language of reportage traffics in global metaphors and local idioms in its bid to 'investigate' an online space that is both global and local as much as it is reality and fantasy at the same time.

As the story continues, the reporter contradicts her previous statement where the gay man who falls prey to this culture is now described as a sexual predator:

> Sexy pictures, fashionable clothes, thrilling behavior and being able to communicate properly are the weapons used by a gay man to attract another gay man.

Here, the global modes of publicity and visibility offered by the website to enable users to communicate and connect with others are re-publicised to expose a local sexual subculture that originates in online spaces. As the visuals show explicit pictures from user profiles to make this 'investigation' more urgent yet salacious, the next segment plays a conversation between an undercover journalist and a planetromeo.com profile user. There are two conversations that are replayed. The second one is analysed here.

The second conversation takes place between the undercover journalist and a software engineer Sunil[8] who is described as 'working for a well-known company, with a good salary' and who 'loves going to gay parties'. As the visual cuts to Sunil's picture, the undercover journalist asks him questions about his age, address and sexual preferences. The journalist inquires about specific details such as where Sunil is at the time of the phone conversation, whether he has place to host and his sexual interests. As the conversation ends abruptly, the female reporter takes over and her interpretation reinforces the link between the global service economy and homosexuality as lifestyle when she says:

> A lot of employees in higher service positions, white collared workers, and highly qualified students are becoming slaves to this lifestyle which is against the natural way.

As the story visuals continue to show pictures uploaded by the users on their profiles, the last segment focuses on another kind of related predatory practice, blackmailing. The visual cuts to the picture of a man named Feroze[9] who is described as a part-time employee at a software firm whose actual business is 'blackmailing'. The reporter then goes into details of how he blackmails gay men by 'getting sexual pleasures from them', 'taking pictures and videos of them' and 'snatching money from the same people from those pictures and videos'. Towards the end, the story suggests reasons such as the lure of money, new pleasures and bad company for the susceptibility of men in Hyderabad to an 'anti-society lifestyle'. The story's conclusion that shifts the blame on the business of blackmailing for victimising the city's gay men renders visible another local space of morally corrupt practice enabled by access to a globalising culture.

The chapter now turns to the activist legal response to TV9's sting operation in the conclusion to briefly reflect on how the basis of legal action, too, reconfigured the global–local relationship through a logic of visibility reliant upon the global language of human rights.

Specifically, the implications for the right to privacy as the basis of legal decriminalisation of homosexuality are crucial to understand insofar as the privileging of privacy as decisional autonomy over its spatial/zonal meaning is concerned.

Conclusion

The Naz judgement's promise of privacy stood both affirmed and belied in two important cases of moral policing through sting operations following the provisional decriminalisation of homosexuality. The nationally prominent case of the Aligarh Muslim University professor, Dr Ramchandra Siras, who was exposed by local media and his university colleagues in the privacy of his bedroom space albeit within the confines of his on-campus home in 2010 was another incident when policing of homosexuality and denial of privacy was addressed through the Delhi High Court judgement. In this case again, spatial privacy was the first order of violation even though it did not matter at all to those who conducted the sting operation. The TV9 sting operation on the other hand poses the conundrum of privacy in online spaces that are ambiguously public. This is especially true of online dating websites where the expectation of anonymity and privacy is a contentious issue. With the promise of empowerment through access to information technologies, for instance being able to hook up with other gay men through a user profile, comes the risk of surveillance by different institutions.

In their study of 4,000 Carnegie Mellon University students' use of a social networking site catering for colleges, Ralph Gross and Alessandro Acquisti observe that despite different measures to control user identifiability, most dating and social networking sites encourage the publication of personal and identifiable photos. They further note the ambiguous nature of information that may range from semi-public content such as interests and hobbies but also other private information such as sexual orientation and drug use. Importantly, however, they find that the ease of joining such networks and lack of security measures makes the breach of privacy through access to user data without the collaboration of the website rather easy (2005). Their study highlights the link between the spatial nature of privacy and information about real-life individuals that defines their social reputation to a certain extent. Legal scholar Daniel J. Solove has traced a number of cases pertaining to online privacy violation and the role of gossip and rumour in shaping individual reputation on the internet.

Solove's proposal suggests a greater role for the law to protect people's privacy, specifically allowing victims of privacy violation to keep their name from entering the public record when they seek legal redress for their injury (2007). He further acknowledges the difficulties of recognising privacy in public admitting that the binary view of privacy – something that is hidden from public view – is virtuous but outmoded with the advent of new technologies.

These ideas are relevant to the Delhi High Court's formulation of the right to privacy for India's sexual minorities in the Naz decision, a formulation in which privacy was linked to 'persons' and not places (Raghavan 2009). The News Broadcasting Standards Authority (NBSA) of India determined that TV9 had violated its code of ethics and broadcasting standards on counts of privacy, sex and nudity, and sting operations. Even as privacy violation became the rallying point of initiating legal action against the news channel by the Indian LGBT activists, the profile users whose privacy was violated through their portrayal as sexual predators and slaves to a depraved lifestyle as well as further exposure through the broadcast of their profile pictures are mostly rendered invisible in this account. Their identities become flashpoints first in the TV9 story on local degeneration through its emphasis on the global figure of the software engineer as both prey and predator, and then again through the LGBT activist response that elevates the figure of the local same-sex desiring man in Hyderabad to the status of a global sexual subject that deserves a right to privacy. Nowhere in this scene of subjection and redemption do these men speak for themselves but their identities remain amenable to the news channel's agenda of boosting its TRPs and the activist mission of resurrecting a sexual subject through a narrative of global human rights. Jon Binnie (2004) has noted that the strategic essentialism implicit within the assumption of a common gay identity across the globe may be a necessity for the recognition of sexual citizenship by the state. Despite the understandable silence of the profile users for possible reasons of fear of further persecution, social backlash and ridicule, the legal action against the TV channel and the subsequent retraction of the story and issuance of apology on its part remains an important accomplishment of LGBT advocacy in India.

In their bid to promote investigative journalism, the new channel's politics of outing must be understood in terms of the news values that motivated the sting operation on private individuals made public through the language of moral panic. Larry Gross's (1993) work on the politics of outing offers a way to distinguish between exposing public figures and politicians who pursue an anti-gay public agenda despite being gay themselves and the indiscriminate outing of individuals who are not public figures. Observing the difference between privacy and hypocrisy, Gross situates the politicians and ordinary individuals on two extremes of a continuum where the act of outing and the meaning ascribed to it shifts based on the goal of such an act. Addressing the real tension inherent in this question, he states:

> The real issue is not to decide whether outing is, by one view, always a violation of journalistic and human ethics or, by the opposing view, a necessary political weapon of an oppressed minority whose pervasive invisibility fuels their oppression . . . the real question is, where in the middle one draws the line, and who has the right to decide on which side of the line any particular instance falls. (Gross 1993: 3)

Gross's examination of the media ethics involved in the outing of public figures like actors and politicians in America situates the journalistic practices of publicity and exposure within the Western LGBT politics of liberation and visibility that was politically necessary in the face of LGBT marginalisation in the context of the AIDS crisis. The response of the Indian LGBT movement engaged in the crucial activist work of generating visibility and empowerment for India's sexual minorities to the sting operation rightly identified the ethical issue of privacy invasion. To point out the absence of the voice of the violated subject here is not to undermine the important task of LGBT activism and advocacy undertaken in India, which remains absolutely paramount. Rather, through the chapter's analysis of the TV9 sting operation and the ensuing legal, activist course of action against the news channel's unethical practice, the chapter has demonstrated the tenuousness and contingency of attaching privacy to the decisional autonomy of an individual. The individual must come out and claim privacy violation in order for justice to be delivered. The absence of the PlanetRomeo profile users in the legal course of action marks the limits of LGBT activism in India profoundly. Not unlike the absent figures of the MSM groups in both the Delhi High Court and the Supreme Court, the PR users' public absence after their privacy violation directs attention to the shadow meanings of privacy, which imply safety in invisibility and non-disclosure. The politics of visibility, however important, in advancing the sexuality rights cause in India must confront such an absence, which perhaps tells us that privacy rights may be more empowering in theory but they do not make the violated subject a private entity again. Absence, in a very modest sense, is a legitimate exercise of privacy as any other.

Notes

1. *Naz Foundation v. Govt. of NCT of Delhi*, 160 Delhi Law Times 277 (Delhi High Court 2009).
2. The term 'queer' here functions to signal a range of sexual subjectivities including acts and identities that span the spectrum of non-normative sexuality. See, for example, Warner (2002).
3. Telugu is a regional South Indian language spoken in the state of Andhra Pradesh where Hyderabad is located.
4. http://www.tv9.net/mission.html. As a vernacular channel that broadcasts news in the regional language of Andhra Pradesh, Telugu, TV9 caters primarily to a middle-class, family-oriented demographic. Its 24-hour coverage and breaking news format through 'bold and fearless journalism' ostensibly represents the global values in news reporting.
5. http://www.planetromeo.com/. The predecessor of the online dating service was gayromeo.com that started in Berlin in 2002 became global as the company set up offices in Amsterdam in 2007 to launch different language versions of its websites. By 2009, the company had a million members. The current website is part of the Planet Romeo Foundation, a queer rights advocacy organisation.
6. A PLUS subscription enables greater security for users in countries where homosexuality is illegal.
7. Hyderabad is a South Indian city located in the south-eastern state of Andhra Pradesh. The city is home to Telugu-speaking Hindus as well as Urdu-speaking Muslims. Hyderabad is known for its history and traditional Islamist cultures as well as an information-technology (IT) hub for the corporate and educational sector. As an emergent cosmopolitan space, Hyderabad continues to be seen as a city with a predominant traditional culture with a rapidly developing IT and industrial sector.
8. Name has been changed.
9. Name has been changed.

References

Appadurai, Arjun (1996) *Modernity at Large: Cultural Dimensions of Globalization*. Minneapolis: University of Minnesota Press.

Arondekar, Anjali (2009) *For the Record: On Sexuality and the Colonial Archive in India*. Durham, NC and London: Duke University Press.

Bhaskaran, Suparna (2002) 'The Politics of Penetration: Section 377 of the Indian Penal Code', in Ruth Vanita (ed.), *Queering India: Same-sex Love and Eroticism in Indian Culture and Society*. New York: Routledge.

Binnie, Jon (2004) *The Globalization of Sexuality*. London: Sage.

Boellstorff, Tom (2003) 'Dubbing Culture: Indonesian Gay and Lesbi Subjectivities and Ethnography in an Already Globalized World', *American Ethnologist*, 30 (2): 225–42.

Bose, Brinda and Bhattacharya, S. (eds) (2007) *The Phobic and the Erotic: The Politics of Sexualities in Contemporary India*. Calcutta: Seagull.

Chauncey, George (1994) *Gay New York: Gender, Urban Culture, and the Making of the gay Male World, 1890–1940*. New York: Basic Books.

Cohen, Lawrence (1995) 'Holi in Banaras and the Mahaland of Modernity' *GLQ: A Journal of Lesbian and Gay Studies*, 2 (4): 399–424.

Fernandes, Jason K. (2009) 'The Dilemma After the Decision: Stray Thoughts after Gay Liberation', *Tehelka*. Available at: http://www. tehelka.com/story _main42.asp?filename=Ws220809The_Dilemma.asp.

Grewal, Inderpal and Kaplan, Caren (2001) 'Global Identities: Theorizing Transnational Studies of Sexuality', *GLQ: A Journal of Lesbian and Gay Studies*, 7 (4): 663-79.

Gross, Larry (1993), *Contested Closets: The Politics and Ethics of Outing*. Minneapolis: University of Minnesota Press.

Gross, Ralph and Acquisti, Alessandro (2005) 'Information Revelation and Privacy in Online Social Networks', *Proceedings of the 2005 ACM Workshop on Privacy in the Electronic Society*. New York: ACM Publishers.

Halperin, David (2000) 'How to Do the History of Male Homosexuality', *GLQ: A Journal of Lesbian and Gay Studies*, 6 (1): 87–123.

Mandal, Saptarishi (2009) 'Right to Privacy in *Naz* Foundation: A Counter-Heteronormative Critique', *NUJS Law Review*, 2 (3): 525–40.

Narrain, Arvind (2003) *Queer: 'Despised Sexuality,' Law and Social Change*. Bangalore: Books for Change.

Narrain, Arvind (2009) *The Right that Dares to Speak Its Name: Decriminalizing Sexual Orientation and Gender Identity in India*. Bangalore: Alternative Law Forum.

Offord, Baden (2003) 'Singaporean Queering of the Internet: Toward a New Form of Cultural Transmission of Rights Discourse', in Chris Berry et al. (eds), *Mobile Cultures: New Media in Queer Asia*. Durham, NC and London: Duke University Press, pp. 133–57.

Parker, Richard, Khan, Shivananda and Aggleton, Peter (1998) 'Conspicuous by Their Absence: Men Who Have Sex with Men (MSM) in Developing Countries', *Critical Public Health*, 8 (4): 329–46.

Raghavan, Vikram (2009) 'Navigating the Noteworthy and Nebulous in Naz Foundation', *NUJS Law Review*, 2 (3): 397–417.

Richardson, Diane (2000) 'Constructing Sexual Citizenship: Theorizing Sexual Rights', *Critical Social Policy*, 20 (1): 105–35.

Roy, Sandip (2003) 'From Khush List to Gay Bombay: Virtual Webs of Real People', in Chris Berry et al. (eds), *Mobile Cultures: New Media in Queer Asia*. Durham, NC and London: Duke University Press, pp. 180–96.

Seabrook, Jeremy (1999) *Love in a Different Climate: Men who have Sex with Men in India*. London: Verso.

Seidman, Steven (2003) *The Social Construction of Sexuality*. New York: Norton.

Sheikh, Danish (2011) 'Privacy and Sexual Minorities', *Centre for Internet and Society*. Online at http://cis-india.org/internet-governance/front-page/privacy-sexual-minorities (accessed 1 April 2016).

Solove, Daniel (2007) *The Future of Reputation: Gossip, Rumor and Privacy on the Internet*. New Haven, CT: Yale University Press.

Vanita, Ruth (ed.) (2002) *Queering India: Same-Sex Love and Eroticism in Indian Culture and Society*. New York: Routledge.

Warner, Michael (2002) *Public and Counterpublics*. New York: Zone Books.

III Digital Intimacies

Chapter 8

'Bitch, don't be a lesbian': Selfies and Same-Sex Desire

Sneha Krishnan

Self-representation on social networking websites such as Facebook and Twitter is increasingly important to young people's conception of themselves as well as of a sociality to which they belong. As scholars like Boellstorff (2008) and, much earlier, Appadurai (1996) have shown, the media have significantly widened the options for the lives people live, allowing the making of new mediated selves that might not have been possible before. In this essay, I examine practices through which young women pose for, take and upload selfies, as well as their engagement with raunchy YouTube videos as sites where forms of same-sex play come to materialise. In the literature on young men, a substantial scholarship now conceptualises such desires in the idiom of *masti* or play among friends: an idiom that is revealing of the ways in which the sexual is circulated in this context (Cohen 1995; Katyal 2013). Indeed, this literature shows that these idioms of playfulness significantly disturb universalist Western notions of LGBT identification and rather open up a field where sexual practice is more multivalent and less tethered to identity.

This remains, however, a literature predominantly about men and located in 'men's spaces': public areas where men might meet, and in the context of male homosociality. As Dave (2012) shows, same-sex desiring women not only remain an under-studied community, the practices of sexual play among women are also located in more private places – within all-female hostels, in beauty parlours and massage therapy rooms. In her analysis of Deepa Mehta's controversial film about same-sex desire, *Fire*, Gayatri Gopinath (1998) similarly shows the importance of studying practices of same-sex desire that exceed registers of public visibility under the LGBT rubric. She positions such studies as corrective to a developmentalist narrative where desire between women carries value only where it is publicly visible

151

and coalesces under the label of 'lesbian'. A reading of young women's social media use does the same thing: it offers narratives of same-sex desire that exceed and run a different course to modern 'LGBTQ' desires and readings of sexuality.

This essay unpacks gendered forms of playfulness through which middle-class women in the city of Chennai in India engage in practices of eroticism with each other. Playfulness, in Ruby Lal's historical work on girlhood (2015), is central to women's adolescence, straddling as it does worlds and practices adult and childish, as well as social and sexual. In playing, young women make sense of their changing bodies and desires, as well as the increasingly less neat division of their 'child' worlds from the 'adult' concerns of sex, reputation and class. This essay draws on ethnographic research conducted among college-going middle-class students in Chennai in 2012 and 2013. Selfies are, in this context, powerful, and increasingly practices of taking selfies together as well as the life of the selfie online are both imbricated in the ways in which homosocialities and homosexualities collide in the lives of young women. Situated in a context where 'lesbian' is increasingly both a 'modern' and 'global' category of iteration, as well as a site of anxieties about gender and nationhood, this essay will in particular consider the ways in which this word, as a term of identification as well as an accusation, structures these practices of playfulness. As such, this essay attempts to unpack, through a study of the practices surrounding the selfie, the ways in which digital cultures mediate desire, friendship and subjectivity.

The young women I interviewed and spent time with were roughly between eighteen and twenty-two years of age; all belonged to the wide and diverse bracket of the middle classes in India and were all students of women's colleges in the city of Chennai. In caste terms, the vast majority belonged to the wide bracket of the Other Backward Castes (middle and lower castes), with a small number belonging to the elite Forward Castes and an equally small number identified as Dalit and Muslim.

Technology, particularly the internet and social media, play large roles in the lives of these young women. Almost everyone possesses a mobile phone, and a significant number among them possess mobile phones or laptop computers with the capacity to connect to the internet. The most common way in which laptops are connected to the internet is through the use of USB internet sticks that most popular service providers now offer. While colleges typically ban the use of mobile phones on campus, students nevertheless use them extensively, and are often Tweeting and Facebooking from class using their phones. The main reason why colleges ban these devices is telling:

the fear that young women are using these devices to engage in conversations with 'inappropriate' men. While walls and curfews were once enough to prevent such contact, the internet and social media appear to transcend such boundaries, allowing women access to a world which they are physically restrained from entering during certain times. All the young women I met owned and meticulously hid away their mobile phones in college and in the hostel. *Youth*, one young woman memorably told me, could not be imagined in the absence of this technology.

In the following sections of this essay, I begin with a short introduction to how young women use social media and the Internet more broadly to explore and express transgressive forms of desire, before then going on in the subsequent two sections to focus respectively on dancing to Bollywood 'item numbers' and taking selfies. Through this, I make primarily two arguments. Scholars of embodiment and technology suggest that the notion of the 'body' itself has been altered by technology in the mid and late twentieth centuries. Donna Haraway (2013) has argued that we are all chimeras – none of us is wholly human alone, rather our experience of embodiment is significantly mediated by technology. She has gone on to argue that the notion of the 'human' itself has been reshaped by the emergence of cyborg subjectivities: where machines share, shape and make available to us experiences of ourselves that are embodied. In exploring virtual embodiment (Hayes 1999), it has been argued that the idea of artificial intelligence suggests reimagined connections to a Cartesian separation of mind and body: where the mind is imagined to be downloadable to a computerised 'self' even as the body might die, or be regarded dispensable. Liberal notions of selfhood as located 'in the mind' somehow then continue to persist. In this essay, I draw on Donna Haraway's early imagination of humans as chimeras and embodied experience as mediated by technology to suggest that embodiment as experienced in the use of social media and the internet suggests a reconfiguration of the capacities of the body, where the 'body' itself is imagined as encompassing a sensory realm of virtual experience.

Given that this essay focuses particularly on iterations of same-sex desire on the internet, this essay will also draw on Boellstorff's notion of 'dubbing' (2003) to then examine how same-sex desire comes to feature in these internet imaginations of self and subjectivity. Focusing particularly on 'lesbian' and other same-sex desiring subjectivities among women, in this essay I demonstrate that there is a tension between, on the one hand, 'lesbo' or 'lesbian' within global discourses as both a derisive accusation and a form of identification, and anxieties about same-sex explorations that exceed 'LGBT' configurations to suggest forms of same-sex play that many now regard 'backward' or 'childish'.

Social Media, Desire and Youth

In the time of 6 p.m. curfews and a barrage of other rules that govern the lives of college girls in Indian cities, the internet is often the only way of communicating with a friend who lives elsewhere, or even a boyfriend. The internet and its social networking websites are also attractive because they are perceived as uniquely 'youth space' where 'adults' are not expected to have a presence. Young people use texting language: 'u' instead of 'you' and 'z' where 's' normally occurs (for instance 'kidz' or 'teenz' suggesting, I learned, an extra onomatopoeic element of speed and fun) and write in short sentences that code switch between Tamil or Malayalam and English.

Men and women talk to each other in comments on photographs and playful mocking is often the code for flirtation here. A young man would rarely compliment outright a young woman he was interested in: rather there would be a short bantering exchange in which he might mock some aspect of her clothing, for instance implying that she is too traditional, or too well made-up. These are really veiled compliments and the woman responds by mocking him back. Mimicking the rough banter through which flirtation occurs in bus stops and other public places where youth meet (Osella and Osella 1998), this practice brings this banter to the more sanitised – and in the minds of many also safer – space of Facebook. With the physical distance assured by the fact that both parties are usually furiously typing into phones, aided by friends in a single-sex hostel who might have witty remarks to offer, these bantering sessions are sites of both heterosexual flirtation and same-sex friendship and bonding.

The public-ness of Friending on Facebook further has also altered some understandings of friendship and intimacy. To begin with, one is not really a friend, I found, until one has been Friended on Facebook. To be added on a blackberry messenger list or Whatsapp list – friend lists on chatting applications for mobile phones – indicated a closer ring of intimacy even than Facebook Friending. However, the publicness of Friending also means that everyone else on one's list knows whom one is friends with. One young woman who had been trying to keep her budding relationship with her friend's ex-boyfriend secret found this publicness frustrating. Her friend noticed as the two became Facebook Friends, and demanded to know what was going on when she also noticed that her ex now 'liked' many of her friend's posts on the social networking website. On the other hand, another young woman who was puzzling about an ambiguous interaction she had had with a boy she had met at a concert was immediately satisfied that he had some affections for her when she found that he had not only added her on Facebook, but also immediately 'liked' her profile picture. The romance then proceeded first on Facebook messenger for several weeks before the couple went out on their first physical date.

Same-sex desire is somewhat trickier on social media. Unlike anonymous forums on the internet, websites like Facebook and Twitter are not regarded 'safe' places for the expression of same-sex love. The exception to this was the new phenomenon of 'Confession Pages' moderated by members of different colleges in Chennai Facebook. Written to sound a bit like the gossip vignettes on the popular American sitcom *Gossip Girl*, these pages offer a link to a Google form, which allows users to post anonymously. An anonymous editor then reads these posts and puts them up, accompanied by her comments.

For instance, one confession reads: 'I kissed a girl and repeatedly have been kissing her and its awesome . . . im so lesbo.' Another one, at a different college, inched closer to confirming a rumour that I heard many times while spending time there: '. . . dammit how come nothing happens when I go to the bathroom. Probably cause it's on the first three floors. And all the hot shit seems to be happening in the 4th or the 5th floor.' Here, the much emphasised anonymity of virtual spaces plays a big role in eliciting 'confessions' about transgressive sexual practices. These 'confessions' often stand to confirm long-held rumours about certain places in the college being hook-up spots for people of the same sex, thus creating geographies of sexual transgression that young women have a lot of fun imagining, whether these are real or not. If nothing else, then, these virtual spaces and the stories told on them serve as sites for energetic imaginations of possible same-sex sexual activity. What is particularly thrilling here is that these acts are not located away from 'mainstream' life, in a bar or within a community known to be transgressive, but that they are in the college, under the gaze of the many mechanisms of surveillance that watch young women everyday.

Among the many hundred young women I met during fieldwork, only one identified as queer: Satya, then in her final undergraduate year. Satya used the internet to explore her emerging awareness of her sexuality extensively. She found me on a forum for queer women and got in touch with me while I was doing fieldwork. When we met, I realised she had done extensive research on me: something that she told me makes her feel safer when she meets people. Satya posted articles from the media supporting various LGBT-related issues on Facebook and Twitter but never actually explored her own desires on these media. Instead, she was registered under a pseudonym on the queer dating website, Pink Sofa. Satya used Pink Sofa for a lot more than dating: indeed it was more a place for her to make friends with other queer woman and build something of a community.

The heterosexual women I met did not register on dating websites to do their online flirting, seeing this as being a too overt expression of their desire for sex or romance. The internet, they often said, parroting the pamphlets on Internet safety that colleges tended to distribute, was a misleading place and 'chat room romances' – once popular in the early 2000s and late 1990s – were now considered the provenance of those who couldn't find romance in 'the real world'. Only 'despos' – desperate people – they often said would get on dating websites.

Satya, on the other hand, saw things differently. For her, the internet – where she rarely went by her own name and felt more comfortably anonymous and unaware of her usual insecurities regarding her body and appearance – was a place of freedom, and dating websites were, as she often said, a place where you could at least be sure if someone was queer. Though she never actively dated any of the women she met while I was in the city, much of what Satya enjoyed was simply being present on the website she used, and browsing the profiles of other women who might also be looking at her. She would 'send a smile' – a function the website offered as a way of expressing attraction without having to speak to each other, much as one might do if one met someone offline – and be excited if they smiled back. She would spend hours perusing pictures others had posted – somehow comforted in the knowledge that these women intended other women to look at them and express desire in response to these images of themselves. To Satya this dating website offered her the possibility of a public where she might flirt, look at and allow herself to feel attracted to women without wondering if they were straight, and might not just reject her, but feel offended by her desire for them.

It has been suggested in the literature on lesbian space, that 'dyke scenes' in films – scenes showing female same sex love or indeed the lives of queer women in some form – are moments of film watching that give same-sex oriented women the permission to stare (see Munt 2005). We might think here of everyday lesbian gatherings to watch popular television dramas centring on the lives of queer women, such as *The L Word* (2004–9) or the sheer joy that was expressed among queer-identified women in India at the idea of the famously beautiful

Madhuri Dixit playing a woman with same-sex desires in the 2014 film *Dedh Ishqiya* (*One and a Half Loves*). Satya, during the time I spent in Chennai, used the wifi connection in her hostel to download lesbian romantic comedies like *I Can't Think Straight* (2008) – popular among queer women and girls in India because it stars Lisa Ray, a Canadian-Indian actress. After, she'd call me to discuss which of the two women we'd each prefer and which one she identified with: much like others might discuss the men in films, reviewing them one by one – as my roommates at Teresa often did. For Satya, these films were sites much like the bus stop or Facebook: where she could look at and allow herself to feel and express attraction without self-censorship.

This experience of dating websites and watching films also suggests forms of embodiment that pay attention to the virtual as a site for the location of affect. As extensions of the real, virtual bodies are sites of fantasy and erotic play: removed from the physical realities of her body in the hostel, desk between herself and the next woman, Satya could, in her forays online, flirt, orient herself towards other women with desire, and stare with desire. The online networks of queer women that Satya participated in are an incitement to fantasy: through them, young women learn to desire and imagine worlds of possibility in which these desires are livable. The intangibility of these worlds, was, however, simultaneously made starkly obvious in the tragic abyss that Satya experienced when her online friend passed away. Unable to reach out to a community of friends with whom to express her mourning, it seemed as if Satya's virtual world of unrestrained lesbian exploration threatened suddenly to impinge upon her straighter real world. The collision of these two worlds of embodiment posed both risk and potential: on the one hand, Satya feared that in mourning as a physical person in her 'college world' she would be 'outing' herself in a place where 'lesbo' remained an accusation and a derisive label rather than a marker of identity. On the other hand, there was the possibility that in the collision of these worlds she might find others similarly experiencing emotions in their virtual realities that threatened to spill into their physical lives.

Two different registers of same-sex sexual experience also emerge from this: on the one hand, 'lesbian' and 'gay' subjectivities are increasingly accessible within middle-class worlds in India. Given the growing public visibility of LGBT identified people as a social movement, and as a rights-demanding group within civil society, middle-class college-going students have access to this vocabulary. At the same time, much as LGBT rights are increasingly discussed, so have terms like 'lesbo' and 'fag' entered the popular vocabulary as terms of insult and mocking, sometimes with a lot of affection. For instance, one young woman had a card on her desk signed by a friend 'Love you lesbo'. She told me that it was a running joke between them that they loved each other so much they could practically be lesbians. At other times 'lesbo' is an accusation, suggesting an 'improper' form of homosocial touch or interaction.

What this has done in some ways is to produce a median space between publicly visible queer identities and selves that might fall under global identifiers, and rubrics of same-sex desire rooted in forms of play as well as identification that are local and unrelated to these global discourses. As the following sections show, these processes are significantly shaped by the ways in which young women engage with social media, enabling forms of embodiment that allow them to explore desire in multivalent ways.

'Items' and Dancing: Fantasising Sexuality

Ranjana saunters into the room one evening and asks the others if they want to see something scandalous. The answer to that is never in the negative; so my roommates at Teresa hostel gather behind her as she opens her laptop up and connects it to the internet. The Hindi film *Aiyyaa* (2012) was soon to be released and that day, someone had told Ranjana about a particularly raunchy song from this film called 'Dreamum Wakeupum'. Literally 'Dream, Wake Up', the words in the song have the suffix 'um' to mimic the sounds of Tamil. The film itself is an interesting commentary on desire, caste and ethnicity. It revolves around a Maharashtrian Brahmin woman played by the popular Rani Mukherji, who fantasises about a dark-skinned, brawny Tamil man, played by Southern heart-throb Prithviraj. My roommates, who typically watched only Tamil and Malayalam films, had been drawn to this film only because it starred a Southern film star.

'Dreamum, Wakeupum', which we then watched together that day, to much sighing oohing and ahing, is a dream sequence song, picturing the two leading stars of the film. Mukherji's character fantasises that she is a raunchy Tamil 'item number' dancer. 'Item number' is the popular name given to erotic song and dance sequences that are increasingly popular across genres and linguistic traditions in Indian cinema. In this one, the young woman has fantasies of herself singing, dancing and simulating sex with her brawny, dark-skinned lover. By the end of the song, my roommates were speechless.

The two ways in which they reacted to this as the evening wore on are significant. On the one hand, many avowed that they had lost respect for both Rani Mukherji and Prithviraj. Both had been 'respectable' and 'lovable' so far, Ranjana said. In this song they had both 'acted like prostitutes'. Many were also offended by the song's implication that Southern Indians are somehow more sexually driven or uncontrolled. This is not an unfair interpretation of the song, and indeed the fantasy of the less modern 'Madrasi' very much forms the 'other' to the refined Bombay-based protagonist of many Bollywood films. My roommates ultimately decided that they would not watch the film when it was released: it might be too embarrassing to sit in a cinema with boys and older people in the vicinity. In this, this film acquired the status of pornography: something too dirty to be watched in public and which the girls would only watch in the privacy of the hostel room.

The other thing that occurred that day was that the young women soon began to imitate the dance moves and simulations of sex in the song, playing and replaying that and other explicitly erotic songs as they danced to them. In doing this, they would touch each other erotically, grind against each other and touch each other's waists and breasts as the actors in the song do. Imitating song-and-dance sequences, particularly item numbers, was often the pretext and context for much same-sex touching and play. During one such imitation of this very song, Ranjana went up to a first-year student in the room whom she often played these games with and began to touch her waist suggestively. 'So gay', another roommate said, laughing. Ranjana gasped exaggeratedly and said, as the others laughed, 'I'm not gay. I'm a lesbo.' Then playing 'the lesbo', she proceeded to touch the junior student even more aggressively, as she ground up against her. Others cheered on as she moved on to another roommate, pushing her down on one of the beds in the room and sitting on her as she touched her. During another occasion, the group all gathered as one of them used her phone to take selfies as they danced, many of them pouting and pretending to kiss each other, others touching each other's waists suggestively. They would not upload these pictures to Facebook, they told me. These were 'just for fun': to remember the good times in the hostel. Arti, the only woman in the room with a steady boyfriend, said she might, however, send it to her boyfriend. Others giggled at the lascivious implication.

The homosocial interactions spilling into the sexual that characterise the forms of sexual play that Gopinath (1998), as well as scholars like Katyal (2013) address, have a place within the ways in which college girls make sense of 'lesbo' and 'gay' or 'fag' identities.

At the same time, they also create distance, marking the impropriety of being 'LGBT'. Drawing on and complicating Boellstorff's notion of dubbing (2013), it might be possible to argue here then that 'lesbo' and 'fag' vocabularies appropriate, and reshape notions of same-sex desire in dialogue with, and mediated by global discourses, though in excess of the global discourse that is cited here. For Boellstorff, dubbing occurs when LGBT discourses that are Western identified are translated to local contexts in ways that reimagine these discourses. In linguistic and identity terms this is much like the arguments made about piracy and counterfeit cultures: where cultural objects produced in one place are made to make different meanings in other places, drawing on local cultural signifiers that imbue them with meaning.

Complicating this a bit, we might argue that in this context, dubbing also involves situating 'lesbo' in an incommensurate field where same-sex desire is embedded in playful horseplay between young women and has no real place outside of that. In 'dubbing' LGBT identities to these forms of desire, young women explore the possible margins of their playful explorations and the identities that they might coalesce into. At the same time, they distance themselves from them, marking themselves, in effect, as 'not lesbo'.

In this context, 'lesbo' is a charge that is enabled and given a playful life in the dreamworld created by the item number. The sociality of dancing to item numbers is enhanced by social media: the fact that young women often dance to a song posted by a friend on their Facebook Wall, as well as the fact that there are pictures taken of the dancing, and whether all the pictures are posted on a social media website or not, the photos create the sense of being out in public. Given the regime of the curfews these young women live under, this, they sometimes said, was their club. Indeed, the figure of the acceptable 'lesbo' is created under the gaze of social media: posing together in positions that they might never take otherwise, young women strive to present themselves as sexually adventurous. 'Lesbo' here suggests something of a kink, marking the woman performing it as modern, global and 'cool', rather than really same-sex desiring.

College Selfies

It's a sunny July morning and I sit in the canteen at one of the colleges, sipping on a small, brightly coloured cup of filter coffee. Around me, five young women, all first-year students in the college, appear to be staring intently into space with their hands moving mysteriously in their bags. It's texting time in a college where phones are banned and a hundred and twenty cameras are watching constantly. It is almost noon, and as boredom begins to kick in, Tara wonders out loud if skipping class was a bad idea after all, 'At least I'd be listening to that woman's droning voice by now.' Hansini makes a clicking noise of disapproval. Opposite her, Azra is resting her head on her twin sister, Zain's shoulder, eyes closed. Hansini leans over and shakes Zain, 'Come, let's take lesbian pictures. Then we can send some to Adil and Tariq.' I perk up and listen. Adil is Hansini's boyfriend – 'he's perfect, and I'm going to convert to Islam for him' was how I was introduced to his photograph on Facebook – and I haven't heard of Tariq before but I am later told Zain is dating him.

'What is this?' I ask, and Hansini giggles, and tells me that she and Zain often like to tell their boyfriends about a fantasy parallel world, where they are lesbians. 'That might mean you wouldn't be dating Adil and Tariq?' I ask, but Hansini shakes her head again, a bit impatiently, and tells me they wouldn't be 'that kind' of lesbians. So in this parallel universe, Hansini would be occasionally having sex with Zain, and Tara and Angie, a reluctant fourth in this game, would be together. They would also be with their boyfriends – who would enjoy hearing about their lesbian exploits. Not so different from real life then, I say, and am quickly corrected. In real life they would never sleep with each other. What about Azra? I wonder aloud, and Hansini laughs as there is uncomfortable silence.

In the five or ten minutes that follow Hansini pulls out a camera and poses with Zain, their bodies close, and their lips almost touching, but carefully a few centimetres apart. They hold each other's hips provocatively, and touch each other's hair, but look into the camera pouting, away from each other. Azra swings between looking uncomfortable and looking admiringly at Hansini as she watches the selfie session. Finally, she asks to pose with Hansini. Rolling her eyes at me, Hansini deigns to pose. As they draw close for a nearly-kiss, Hansini pushes Azra away, 'OK, bitch, don't be a lesbian OK? That's too gay.' The photo-session is over and the texting resumes. Later Hansini tells me she thinks Azra might have a crush on her. She is, she says, embarrassed by it, and a bit sorry for Azra. She needs to grow up, she clicks her tongue impatiently. Zain already has a boyfriend, and doesn't Azra want all that too?

The selfie sessions go on everyday like clockwork during break time. Only some of these selfies are uploaded on Facebook, after a liberal Photoshop touch up. They are the 'cool chicks' Zain tells me, and they would never want to look less than perfect. Selfies are an increasingly important aspect of young women's lives in South Asian cities. While selfie sticks have been slower to catch on, the sight of girls gathering to smile, or more often pout, into a phone camera one of their friends is holding is extremely common in youth hang-out spots, ranging from colleges, malls and cafes to the bars and clubs that students increasingly frequent. Selfies are sent back and forth between friends and lovers, and are touched up, corrected for colour and edited to make their subjects look thinner, fairer of skin and clearer of complexion before they are uploaded on social networking websites such as Facebook and Twitter.

For Azra, it seems to me, these selfie sessions are moments of nervous opportunity: on the one hand, she sometimes gets to 'play lesbian' with Hansini. On the other hand, there is the nerve wracking anxiety of crossing the line with her 'play'. Azra herself tells me resolutely that she is not 'a lesbo': something that could be entirely true. Selfie-taking, however, becomes a moment of acid testing in this case: its location within a global world of 'dating' where 'lesbo' is an accusation rather than the unsaid radar under which much same-sex exploration often slips, foreclosing any opportunities to 'cross the line' while 'playing lesbian'. Same-sex desire, for Hansini and her friends, is something of a sexual fetish: it is permitted in their worlds within a heterosexual pornographic framework. Writing about media worlds Mani (2013) comments that the sexually self determining woman is the defining female subject in neoliberal India. This self-determination is of course shaped by mediated fantasies about desirability. In 'playing lesbian' to take photos for their boyfriends, Hansini and Azra make of themselves sexually independent women who nonetheless explore their sexualities as a matter of titillation for boyfriends whom they assure me they want to marry. In some form then, same-sex exploration does continue to flourish, to paraphrase Foucault, under the nose of patriarchal control: however, in doing so, it is subsumed within neoliberal frameworks of sexual liberty, reshaping the field of playfulness away from the horseplay that the item song dancers of the previous section engaged in.

The practice of taking and posting selfies on social media also reshapes the forms of embodiment that young people experience. As discussed in a previous section, social media entail a sensory experience: young women flirt, smile and giggle all through the medium of the internet. As an experience of the body mediated by technology this is nevertheless very real for these young women: posting a selfie on Facebook is a very deliberate act, not unlike posturing at a bus stop, hoping to get a young man to flirt with. It is an invitation to a game of desire. The fact that the game occurs virtually often emboldens young women, eliminating much of the risk of flirting in a physical space where escape is not easy if the situation should get difficult. Young women often deleted, blocked and un-friended young men who they felt had 'crossed the line' with them.

Conclusions: The Internet, Bodies and Selves

The internet has, in many ways, substantially changed how people relate to themselves, their bodies and the worlds. In this article I have made two arguments about how young women's lives are mediated by selfie culture and social media. I have argued that on the one hand, their experience of embodiment is shaped by their online interactions as much as their physical experiences. In this, they are able to 'smile', flirt and otherwise conduct themselves as embodied beings in a space that is otherwise constructed as 'dis-embodied'. If, as scholars have argued, the notion of the cyborg (Haraway 2013) is complicated by imaginations of virtual reality where body and brain are completely separate and the brain is downloadable onto a machine (Hayes 1999), this suggests a somewhat more complex connection: the experience of the body, it would appear, is extended, and shaped by a sensory experience with computer and smartphone screens.

In this, I have demonstrated, young women engage with desire in a range of different ways that demonstrate tensions with modernity and global 'LGBT' identities. On the one hand, 'lesbian' and 'gay' are widely circulated identities and registers of speech among the English-speaking middle classes in India. On the other, I draw on Boellstorff's concept of 'dubbing' (2003) to suggest that they are not quite what they mean in the West alone. Instead they exceed such a citation and occupy a misty realm between accusation and the anxieties of falling into 'backward' pre-LGBT practices of same-sex sexuality that are widely decried as 'childish'.

In making these arguments, this essay has squarely situated the internet in the midst of young people's self-making struggles. Selfhood and subjectivity are subjects of increasing interest to scholars, particularly in the context of digital interventions in these realms. *Selfies* arguably herald a realm in which the self is of increasing visual and sensory interest as a site of meaning making: taking and posting selfies is a way of entering a world of importance and individuality, a global realm shared equally by roommates and classmates, and by celebrities like Kim Kardashian.

References

Boellstorff, T. (2003) 'Dubbing Culture: Indonesian Gay and Lesbi Subjectivities and Ethnography in an Already Globalized World', *American Ethnologist*, 30 (2): 225–42.

Boellstorff, T. (2008) *Coming of Age in Second Life: An Anthropologist Explores the Virtually Human*. Princeton: Princeton University Press.

Cohen, L. (1995) 'Holi in Banaras and the Mahaland of Modernity', *GLQ: A Journal of Lesbian and Gay Studies*, 2 (4): 399–424.

Dave, N. (2012) *Queer Activisim in India: A Story in the Anthropology of Ethics*. Durham, NC: Duke University Press.

Gopinath, G. (1998) 'On Fire', *GLQ: A Journal of Lesbian and Gay Studies*, 4 (4): 631–6.

Haraway, D. J. (2013) *Simians, Cyborgs, and Women: The Reinvention of Nature*. London: Routledge.

Hayes, N. K. (1999) *How We Became Posthuman: Virtual Bodies in Cybernetics*. Chicago: University of Chicago Press.

Katyal, A. (2015) 'Laundebaazi: Habits and Politics in North India', *Interventions*, 15 (4): 474–93.

Lal, R. (2013) *Coming of Age in Nineteenth-Century India: The Girl-Child and the Art of Playfulness*. Cambridge: Cambridge University Press.

Mani, L. (2013) *The Integral Nature of Things: Critical Reflections on the Present*. London: Routledge.

Munt, S. (2005) *Shame, Hate and Envy in Institutional Cultures*, in Lesbian Lives International Conference, 11–13th February 2005, University College Dublin, Ireland.

Osella, C. and Osella, F. (1998) 'On Flirting and Friendship: Micro-politics in a Hierarchical Society', *Journal of the Royal Anthropological Institute*, (4) 2: 189–206.

Chapter 9

Disciplining the 'Delinquent': Situating Virtual Intimacies, Bodies and Pleasures Among Friendship Networks of Young Men in Kolkata, India

Debanuj DasGupta

Bodies of runaway boys and working-class young men are marked as delinquent and incommensurate within the project of Indian neo-liberal democracy. In recent times media reports related to the brutal rape of Jyoti Singh in New Delhi and Suzette Jordan in Kolkata situate the young men as barbaric, pathological and improperly gendered. The face of the six young men who raped Jyoti Singh circulate on multiple memes on Facebook (FB) and has come to signal 'India's excess man problem'. The Indian population has an imbalanced sex/gender ratio. This imbalance is rooted in the violent killing of girl children, sex-selection and female foeticide. India's 'excess man problem' marks young men's sexuality as dangerous, since they are more likely to enact violent crimes against women. The violent capacities of the young men are attributed to the lack of marriageable young women in India. In this chapter, I will first situate demographic studies that construct the figure of the young working-class man or the runaway boy as dangerous and delinquent. I will then engage with the work of PDS, a non-governmental organisation located in Kolkata and working with runaway boys and young men in eighteen districts within West Bengal, India. PDS operates as an NGO that seeks to reform the young men from unruly bodies into productive subjects by undertaking gender-sensitivity and job readiness trainings. Utilising the annual reports of PDS and media coverage of recent sensational rape incidents in India, I argue the young men and runaway boys are marked as incommensurate with India's neoliberal modernity. Bodies of the young men and runaway boys (from peri-urban locations) have come to represent a failed masculine subject position that is in need of reformation.

The final section of this chapter displaces narratives of failure, criminalisation and reform by journeying into the digital spaces mobilised by young men involved with PDS. Intimacies forged through digital spaces such as FB among staff and volunteers of PDS allow for the creation of virtual intimacies that hold potentials for cutting through the discipline and regulation of the young men's bodies. The young men's bodies take on multiple meanings through the poetic memes, emojis that they post on FB messenger and WhatsApp chats. I argue the intimacies forged on FB and WhatsApp chats by the young men suggest another way of thinking about their bodies. An analysis of their meme's and poems shared on FB reveals their sense of belonging with each other, longing for the return of their lost lovers, and desire to communicate through music and theatre. I suggest that the young men and runaway boys involved with PDS refuse to be incorporated into India's neoliberal temporality. Rather, their intimacies hang in digital space, much like their fates, and create a queer time and space.

India's Excess Man Problem

In their 2005 book, *Bare Branches: The Security Implications of Asia's Excess Male Populations*, Valerie M. Hudson and Andrea M. den Boer argued that countries such as China and India have some of the highest imbalances in the male/female ratio, especially in the age group of 15–34. In China, these young men are called 'bare branches' (Hudson and den Boer 2005: 4), suggesting they are unattached, unable to produce offshoots. Hudson and Boer argue that having bare branches in countries like China and India is quite dangerous, since an excess of disenchanted young men could lead them to joining terrorist groups. The excess(ive) young male population is contributing to crimes against women, since there is a scarcity of marriageable young women in India and China. Further, the scarcity is related to heightened social competition among young men and women for success, creating rife conditions for social insecurity. The authors draw upon recent demographic trends and point to patriarchal practices of sex selection in most Asian countries. However, central to their argument is a 'scarcity' argument that construct the young men in 15–34 age group as insecure, pathologically driven toward violent crimes and ultimately toward terroristic activities. These demographic studies fail to take into account the political potentials of friendships between the young men and how young men articulate their bodies and pleasures. Following Michel Foucault's ideas about biopower,[1] I call these kinds of demographic studies as an apparatus of biopolitical power that massify the bodies of young men (especially working-class men and migrant young men) into dangerous population categories. Bodies of migrant young men and runaway boys come to be marked as a pathological problem and are subjected to regulation and discipline. The idea that young men who are available in excess are 'bare branches' and do not have enough marriageable young women not only bestow compulsory hetero-sexuality upon the young men, but also construct them as excessive figures whose bodies need to be contained through reform measures. The death sentence for the five men charged with the raping of Jyoti Puri (the sixth young boy was declared a juvenile and sent for refor-mation to a juvenile home for delinquent boys) comes to represent the dangerous capacities of these bare branches. A meme with the faces of the five young men with a noose on top of them circulated throughout the internet. This meme circulated virally through mul-tiple digital platforms and comes to represent both a literal as well as a slow death that lie ahead for working-class young men. Young working-class men migrating from rural to urban areas or living in peri-urban areas are marked as failed subjects as compared to the modern, cosmopolitan, entrepreneurial Indian citizen-subject.

Modernity in the postcolonial Indian context is to be rational, secular and metropolitan (Srivastava 1998; Chakrabarty 2002). Sanjay Srivastava's study of Doon School, an elite boys school in Northern India, reveals the inculcation of the boys into a kind of educated masculinity which comes to represent rational, proper gender behaviour as the code of conduct for modernity (Srivastava, 1998). Sarada Balagopalan argues ideas about children's rights within emerging democracies such as India was developed based upon notions of bourgeois childhood from the West. In her study of a street children programme in railway platforms of Kolkata, Balago-palan argues juvenile care programmes developed by NGOs serve to create children and young people who are not 'human', fram-ing poor children as backward and the middle classes as modern. The other to the postcolonial modern remains poor, barbaric, uneducated and improperly gendered (men). A series of sensational rape incidents in India has led to media as well as academic inquiry into the psyche of heterosexual men.[2] Bodies and sexual desires of men and boys marked as heterosexual have become the subject of inquiry, and considered as otherwise to the modern rights-bearing female subject. The otherwise is backward gazing, rapist, archaic and in need of proper gender training. The containment and disciplining of those considered otherwise to the modern rights-bearing gendered subjects occur in multiple sites such as jails, juvenile delinquent homes and shelters for runaway children (Appadurai 2000; Balagopalan 2002; Rajagopal 2002). The incommensurability of certain subjects with the space-time of neoliberal Indian modernity and democratic citizenship occupies an intensified indeterminate zone between life and death (Povinelli 2006, 2011). Elizabeth Povinelli argues for an inquiry into the striatiated spatial arrangements of those marked as otherwise within 'late liberalism'.[3] The demographic modelling, coupled with neoliberal ideas about success, entrepreneurial abilities and social competition, frames the bodies of young men as bare branches in need of reform and containment.

However, as the next section will suggest, the intimacies forged on digital spaces by young men such as the boys involved with PDS signify a creative expending of their excessive desires. Following George Bataille, I will argue that there exists an excess of bodily energies in all kinds of bodies (Bataille 1988: 21). The young men of PDS write about their bodily sensations on diverse digital platforms, and in this way their bodily sensations circulate, generate speed and energy in and through digital space. Unlike the scarcity suggested through demographic modelling of their bodies, the young men of PDS are creating a new social project built through digital spaces that seek to creatively expend their excessive energies. I now turn to discussing how PDS works to reform the bodies of runaway young men in Kolkata, and how the digital intimacies forged by the young men might cut through the regulation of their bodies.

Ordinary City, Sexual Modernity and Spaces of Abandonment

A city of 14 million people located on the banks of the river Ganges, Kolkata is perhaps best known as the dying city through Hollywood blockbusters like Dominque Lapieres *City of Joy* or the iconic missionary Mother Teresa. Alternately, leftist-minded activists across the world imagine Kolkata as the final hellhole of Communist intellectuals and labour organising. The Communist Party of India (Marxist) (CPI (M)) has been the ruling party in West Bengal since 1969. The CPI (M) was defeated in a landmark election by the Trinamool Congress in 2011.

Kolkata is also a concurrent space of a pre- and post-liberalised economy, in its physical structure as well as social fabric. The city's urban development is encapsulated within larger national efforts to attract capital, enhance political linkages and (re)make images in a globalising economy (Hutnyk 1996; Roy 2002). Mamata Banerjee, the Chief Minister of West Bengal, in 2011 had publicly expressed the ruling government's plans to turn Kolkata into London, into a 'world-class destination' likening the Hoogly River that runs through the city to that of the Thames. The collapsing of Kolkata's geography with that of London represents a twisted tale of postcolonial modernity, one that aspires to connect Kolkata with circuits of global capital. As a globally aspiring city, Kolkata is also a crucial node in the region. The city extends its influence beyond surrounding suburbs and villages to neighbouring states in India and countries such as Bangladesh, Bhutan and Nepal. The city is one of the nodal points in the railway network of India. The suburban railway network contributes to the morphology of the city. The suburban railway region of Kolkata covers the nine districts of South Bengal, namely Burdwan, Nadia, Hooghly, Howrah, East and West Midnapur, North and South 24 Parganas including the Kolkata district itself. The two major railway junctions are Sealdah and Howrah stations (Dey 2012). Railway stations and their peripheral areas serve as living areas for runaway children and youth (Chakraborty 2014). Reports indicate children escaping from their homes and living in railway stations are characterised as pathological, undertaking 'delinquent activities' (Chakraborty 2014). Another study reports that 30 per cent of street children surveyed in the study reported non-tobacco substance use and about 9 per cent of the street children reported sexual abuse, whereas sexually transmitted diseases were reported by 4 per cent of the street children and HIV incidence was 1 per cent (Bal et al. 2010).

PDS and Developmentalist Temporality

PDS works with runaway boys and young men within railway stations and juvenile delinquent homes. Many of the boys are involved in the informal job sector or within the drug trade industry. The website of PDS decribes their mission as 'PDS seeks to establish a gender-just and gender-equitable society where women as well as men work together to dismantle the oppression of patriarchal social structures thereby ensuring that the human rights of all people are protected against stigmatization and discrimination' (PDS website). Established in 1997, PDS is a non-governmental development organisation dedicated to preventing the abuse and exploitation of children and young people, especially those who occupy marginalised social locations in caste, class, gender and sexuality.

PDS has targeted intervention programmes for children in eleven cities and towns of West Bengal and support programmes for vulnerable children and youth in eighteen districts of the state. PDS utilises dance movement workshops and theatre as tools for mobilising homeless young and runaway boys living at railway stations. Dance and theatre creates a different relationship with the bodies of the boys and men who are escaping violence from father and elder male figures. The PDS volunteer base for campaigns to end violence on girl children and young boys draws from the men and boys who emerge as community leaders from these projects.

PDS mobilises the young men and boys to organise repatriation efforts for runaway children in their localities. Young men are recruited from within the railway stations, juvenile homes or surrounding neighbourhoods and are then sensitised about issues related to juvenile justice and the protection of street children, sexual identity and ending violence against women through gender and sexuality training institutes. Cultural tools such as theatre workshops are held regularly in order to deal with issues of surviving violence, bodily trauma and gender equity. The runaway boys are paired with young men from the areas who develop street theatre skits. In these plays the runaway boys narrate stories of abuse, instances of sexual harassment and how friends can intervene when the young men are either abusing or being sexually abused by others. In this way, PDS creates a continuum of gender (re)training in order to impart proper gender skills on the runaway boys. PDS's FB page is regularly updated with images from these workshops.

The PDS website and annual reports regularly narrate stories of success. Stories of success typically follow a linear temporality, whereby one of the boys who was interdicted at railway stations stealing railway property or engaged with drug trade have now given up drugs, alcohol or stealing. PDS claims that many of the young men have successfully been completing school and being trained in computer skills. PDS reports that FB is one of the favourite activities among the young men. Many of the runaway boys grow up and become volunteers as well as staff of PDS. In this way PDS mobilises the friendship networks of the runaway boys and young men toward their reform-related initiatives. In his letter for the 2015 annual report of PDS, the Executive Director of PDS states that many of the runaway boys are now PDS staff and volunteers. He thanks the young men for their friendship and support (PDS Annual Report, 2015).

PDS maintains a significant presence on FB. Key volunteers from PDS operate as the administrators for their FB page. They post regular updates and showcase the success stories about the runaway boys on their FB page. The FB page of PDS operates a nodal point through which many of the staff and volunteers find each other on FB. As a scholar/activist working with PDS, I am connected to the PDS FB page and many of the young men via FB and WhatsApp chat groups. In this way, many of the young men chat with me or tag me on their FB posts, allowing me to enter and participate in the intimate networks forged on these spaces. As an immigrant researcher from India living in the New England area, I feel a sense of belonging with many of the young men. Many of them look forward to my visits to Kolkata. I am aware of how my US-based location and access to income in US currency operate as icons of success for many of the young men. When I have brought this up as an issue during our chat sessions, some of them have pointed to my single status and how they worry about my health. They have mentioned the lack of a thick sociality in my life. I remain tethered to an everyday intimate sociality forged through digital spaces. We discuss PDS's organising initiatives; however, our chat sessions extend to conversations about dating, their career choices, our sexual desires and their creative projects. Across material inequalities, these digital platforms allow us/me to remain connected in each of our daily lives. I wake up to new posts from some the volunteers of PDS. Many of these posts are pictures of PDS events or pictures with their friends during major festivals. The young boys often post creative memes that are typical of digital art. These include images or collages of images, with their poems pasted on the images. These memes are different from organisational updates and images. They reflect the creative capacities of the young men, and their desire to communicate about their bodies and pleasures.

I now turn toward discussing two of the meme's posted by the young men as vignettes from our intimate exchanges.[4]

Spaces of Virtual Intimacy
Who owns the far skies?
The sky belongs to the one who has snatched it away.
Who owns the light breeze?
One who feels it owns the lights breeze.
Unrequited love wields a stick of tears
Tears form mountains.
Who belongs to the far lights?
The one who helps in seeing the light belongs to the light.
Come, let us go across the far skies.

Subesh Poddar

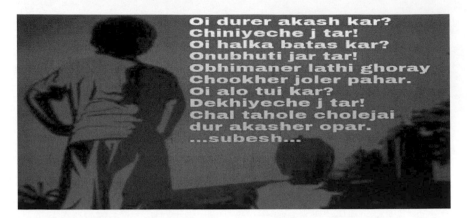

Figure 9.1 Subesh's meme

A string of words attached to an image regularly get posted by volunteers of PDS on FB. I along with PDS staff and other volunteers are tagged on these posts. Each of these posts generate comments, appearing on my news feeds, drawing my attention, since I am keen on understanding the ways the young men involved with PDS utilise FB. One meme depicts two young boys wandering into the distant skies across a blue silhouette. One of them is taller than the other, his hands are placed on the hips gesturing a kind of confidence with which he is gazing into the skies. The shorter figure is suggestively sketched as a younger boy. Both of the boys are turning their backs on the screen. They refuse to face the screen and reveal their faces. The refusal to reveal their faces suggests a kind of anonymity, which allows several users of FB to enter the visual/scape. The poetic meme is posted by one of the part-time staff members of PDS. Subesh grew up in a small town in North Bengal. He has been involved with theatre activism and was studying Geography in a college located in North Bengal. Subesh's involvement in the creative arts and local activism received objections from his family. According to Subesh, his family expects him to study sciences and find a lucrative career. However, Subesh remains interested in cultural activism, and organises theatre workshops with the runaway boys of PDS, which are then showcased at the *abhayatra* (annual cultural festivals at different sites). The meme articulates feelings of pain, unrequited love and the yearning for an imagined horizon as potential futures for intimate belongings.

The meme suggests an imagined conversation between the two boys almost drawing the reader/viewer into an imagined emotional geographic horizon, wherein the volunteer and the runaway can find a sense of belonging through mutual acknowledgement of pain.

Perhaps, together, by climbing the mountain of tears, feeling the light breeze on their skin and seeing the light the two boys can reclaim the vast sky. The vast sky suggests a utopic horizon, one that has been snatched from them. Together, they can reclaim their space. Bodily sensations and fluids overflow through the screen, and all those tagged on the meme (including the author) remain intimately entangled in virtual space. The meme also points out to the intimate bond forged between the runaway boys and the young men who are volunteers and staff of PDS. As mentioned earlier, many of the staff and volunteer of PDS are from the juvenile homes and railway shelters. The young men have grown up through PDS programmes and remain connected to each other through online and offline spaces. The meme hangs in (digital) space signifying the intimacies forged between the young men and their desires for different futures. Different perhaps from the reform- and re-education-related projects of PDS. Subesh's poem expresses his desires to collectively journey toward a different world. The journey is rife with sensations. The Bengali word *onubhuti* translates to sensation. Subesh names sensations such as sadness, unrequited desires, warmth, the feeling of a light breeze against his skin. The sensations and the silhouette assemble an affective horizon, one that exceeds the reformatory projects of PDS.

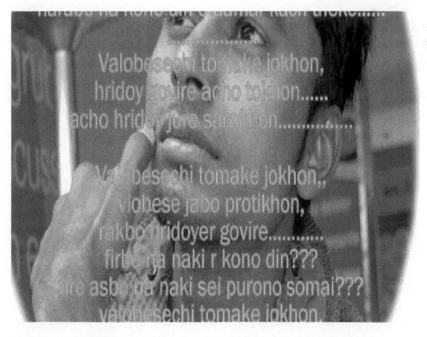

Figure 9.2 Mejbul's meme

One day you came to me and brought light in my heart
How did I lose you in the bat of an eye?
You are still here in my heart
I am holding on to your memories with care
I will never lose you.
Once I have loved you
I will love you forever
You will be throughout my heart forever
Will you ever return?
Will our past times return?
Hopefully my past shall return to me someday
I shall await your return? Always
I am here for you forever

Mejbul Haque

Another meme posted by a volunteer of Muslim origin residing near the main offices of PDS in New Alipur (bordering Khidderpur in western Kolkata, an area with large Muslim settlements) articulates feelings of love and pain from his break-up and yearning for a (lost) beloved. Mejbul studies English literature at a local college and works in the Bengali film industry as a freelance camera hand. The young man mourns the loss of his lover and awaits their return. The author is facing the screen, his eyes gazing away from the screen suggesting a yearning for the return of his beloved. The author is mourning his past while gazing towards the possible return of his beloved, suggesting a perverse sense of time within which his past and future are hanging in space, just like his meme remains perpetually hanging in virtual space. Mejbul wrote this poem as he was breaking up with his girlfriend. In our conversations, Mejbul mentioned to me that he had posted the meme with his poetry as a way of expressing his loss. The meme received several comments from his friends that allowed him to grieve (his) loss. The Bengali word he used in our FB chat is *buke byatha* (heartache). Mejbul said that he needed to let his friends know about the pain. The FB creative meme helps him to do something constructive with his pain and sadness rather than committing some harmful actions out of that pain. Mejbul's intentions are clearly not to harm his ex-girlfriend through revenge. He needed a creative avenue to express his feelings. Mejbul has found encouragement and the nurturing of his creative writing skills through PDS and he has learnt to creatively share his feelings.

Subesh and Mejbul's memes suggest a yearning for different futures, the search for love, intimacy and a sense of belonging. While Subesh articulates friendship and the search for utopic horizons,

Mejbul articulates the loss of his beloved, and hopes for the return of his past lover in the near future. Both the memes present a vision of friendship, potential futures and belongings, which are different from the reformatory projects of PDS. The boys' innermost bodily details flow across the virtual space of FB, and the exchanges follow posts through posts, images to images, rhizomatically multiplying and gesturing virtual intimate worlds. The bodies of the young men take multiple forms and meanings scripted through words, images and the many comments they generate. The intimate possibilities at best inhabit an interstitial space in the middle of these multiple posts and at worst die untimely death leaving space for new formations of words/images/posts to arise. Pain, loss, looking forward to utopic futures while yearning for the past create a rather perverse configuration of time and space. Demographic studies about India's excess man problem situate the bodies of runaway boys and young men as dangerous, marked through their propensity to commit crimes against young women. These studies frame the bodies of young men such as Subesh and Mejbul through ideas about scarcity. The scarcity of young women leads to competition, or lack of potential sexual partners. However, an analysis of the intimacies forged through digital space among the young men of PDS helps us understand their bodies differently. Georges Bataille argues that there is always an excess of energy in the universe (Bataille 1988: 27). According to Bataille there is a superabundance of bioenergy in all of the universe, including our bodies. Human beings exist not just in restricted rational economies based upon scarcity of resources, rather we also exist within an unrestricted economy based on the exuberance of energy. The three luxuries based upon this exuberance in nature are eating, death and sexual reproduction (Bataille 1988: 33). Resituating the bodies and pleasures of the young men involved with PDS allows us to see how their bodily sensations and feelings inform the formation of an unrestricted economy. The excessive desires of the young men are creatively spent through digital spaces such as FB. The memes suggest that unrequited love, their desire for intimacy, feelings of pain and sadness operate as a kind of kinetic energy that gathers speed on and through digital spaces. In this way, the use of FB, the chat sessions on FB messenger and WhatsApp create a social project that cuts through the regulation and disciplining of their bodies.

The young men involved with PDS remain marked as runaways, failed subjects in need of discipline and regulation through civil society initiatives such as PDS. Virtual intimacies affectively forged through digital spaces such as FB allow for a different meaning of the bodies of the young men, thereby deterritorialising their bodies and sensations. The young men forge friendships within material spaces such as railway stations, drop-in shelters, rallies and cultural festivals. PDS's efforts to retrain the runaway boys with job readiness skills and mobilising the young men to take up legal reforms territorialise the friendships. However, the young men forge affective bonds on virtual platforms such as FB, through a different articulation of their bodies and pleasures. The two vignettes presented in this chapter highlight their feelings of belonging, pain, mourning for lost lovers and melancholic yearning for different futures. Such affective bonds create an intimate landscape on virtual spaces which detrritorialises the friendships forged by the young men and runaway boys of PDS. Both the memes point us toward a different time and place. Subesh's meme conjures the desire for a different place, suggesting a feeling of kinship between an older and younger boy. Mejbul presents us with his yearning for a lost lover. Mejbul's longing for the (future) return of his past lover creates a non-linear time and space configuration. I have referred to this temporality as queer time and space, since both Subesh and Mejbul would like to be in a different time and place than what is available in the here and now. The here and now does not satisfy their expectations. The desire for different futures signifies a break from PDS's developmentalist linear temporality. There is no delinquent past and a reformed productive future. Rather, there is a utopic horizon of shared joys or melancholic yearning. The memes represent how the young men creatively navigate digital spaces, and offer a different way of thinking about young men's bodies. Subesh and Mejbul are not 'bare branches' who are at risk of committing crimes against women. Both of them come to signify the creative potential within young men in India. Georges Bataille argues that bodies have an excess of energy that are in need of expenditure. According to Bataille, the excess energies in our body are spent through creative outlets. I argue that the meme and FB posts of the young men are creative methods that allow for the expenditure of their excessive energies. In this way virtual intimacies forged through digital spaces have the potential to cut through the regulation of the young men's bodies. Further research in masculinity studies will need to explore the use of digital spaces by young men in India, and indeed will have to interrogate the ways in which young men are being constructed as dangerous rapists. Queer and feminist researchers need to rethink how sexuality and gender advocacy is a project of neoliberal modernity through which certain bodies are marked as delinquents and failures, and how such bodies creatively manoeuvre regulatory regimes.

Notes

1. In his lectures on the birth of biopolitics, Michel Foucault identifies the emergence of a different modality of power. Termed as biopower, this form of power emerges in the late eighteenth and early nineteenth centuries. The discovery of life-enhancing technologies and the anatomological knowledge about the human body allows for the creation of technologies that seek to govern life and liveability. According to Foucault, categories such as fertility rate, mortality rate, disease diffusion patterns and sex/gender ratios come to signify how human beings are massified into large categories. These categories connect individuals to larger social and political structures that seek to discipline and regulate their bodies in order to govern life and death. The primary purpose of biopower is to ensure quality of life and to minimise the dangers posed by diseases, delinquent bodies and biological threats to the economic circuit in society. I argue that the category of runaway boys and young men is formed through demographic studies that massify the bodies of young men. Population programmes and civil society formations work to regulate their bodies in order to minimise the risks posed (by their dangerous sexuality) to Indian society (Foucault 2003: 244–5).

2. A series of rape incidents have been reported in the national and international media, including the case of a young woman who succumbed to brutal in juries in December 2012. These cases have promulgated major media inquiries into the psychic interiorities of young boys and men who work informal sectors within large metropolitan areas. One such television show aired on NDTV was titled as *Journey into the Heart of Darkness*.

3. Elizabeth Povinelli defines late liberalism as management of difference within postcolonial nations. The management of difference arises out of complex race, class, caste, gender and sexual differences mitigated through courtroom cases. Povinelli delineates court cases regarding the rights of Aboriginal populations to recognition within the Australian constitution as ways for incorporating communities marked as impossible or failures within economies and polities marked by key concepts such as productivity, entrepreneurial citizenship and freedom of individuals from excessive state incursion. Following Michel Foucault's discussion of neoliberalism as a set of manoeuvres which seek to convert the social into the economic and the economic into the social (Foucault 2003), Povinelli argues any form of life which fails to produce market value is considered a failure, deemed not worthy of state investment. Povinelli terms those dwelling in spaces of failure as 'Otherwise' to late-liberalism and dominant neoliberal economic policies. Following, Povinelli I situate neoliberalism as an ensemble of economic-political-social manoeuvres that seek to reduce state support for welfare-type social programmes. Further, I build upon Foucault's ideas wherein he

argues that neoliberalism as a form of social rationality that seeks to engender competitive, dividend-earning subjects and generalises cost-benefit analysis into every domain of social relations. The idea that a lack of marriageable young women has created a scarcity and competition among the young men (and women) connects their bodies with economic rationalities of free market competition. In this way the runaway boys and young men come to be marked as failures, as 'Otherwise' to India's neoliberal modernity (Povinelli 2011: 118; Foucault 2004: 242).

4. I received permission from both of the young men to share the memes. I have shared this chapter with them to receive their feedback and suggestions on my analysis. The analysis is derived in conversation with both of them. Both of them have provided permission to use their names in this chapter. I have utilised both their names as a way of honouring their desire.

References

Appadurai, A. (2000) 'Spectral Housing and Urban Cleansing: Notes on Millennial Mumbai', *Public Culture*, 12 (3): 627–51.

Bal, B., Mitra, R., Mallick, A. H., Chakraborti, S. and Sarakr, K. (2010) 'Non tobacco Substance Use, Sexual Abuse, HIV, and Sexually Transmitted Infection Among Street Children in Kolkata, India', *Substance Use and Abuse*, 45 (10): 1668–82.

Balagopalan, S. (2002) 'Constructing Indigenous Childhood: Colonialism, Vocational Education and the Working Child', *Childhood*, 9: 19.

Bataille, G. (1988) *The Accursed Share: An Essay on General Economy Vol. I: Consumption*. New York: Zone Books.

Chakrabarty, D. (2002) *Habitations in Modernity: Essays in the Wake of Subaltern Studies*. Chicago: University of Chicago Press.

Chakraborty, S. (2014) *Reaching the Un-reached: Case Studies of the Learning Initiatives of the Street Children in Kolkata*. Paper presented at IFLA WLIC 2014 – Lyon – Libraries, Citizens, Societies: Confluence for Knowledge, in Session 169 Literacy and Reading. In IFLA WLIC 2014, 16–22 August 2014, Lyon, France. Available at http://library.ifla.org/884/ (accessed on 28 September 2016).

Dasgupta, R. K. and Gokulsing, K. M. (2014) *Masculinity and Its Challenges in India*. Jefferson, NC: McFarland.

Dey, T. (2012) 'Suburban Railway of Kolkata: A Geographical Appraisal', *e-Traverse: The Indian Journal of Spatial Science*, 3 (1). Online at http://indiansss.org/pdf/pdfset-8/issueset-9/Art_017.pdf (accessed on 14 October 2017).

Foucault, M. (2003) *Society Must Be Defended: Lectures at the Collège de France 1975–76*. New York: Picador.

Foucault, M. (2004) *The Birth of Biopolitics: Lectures at the Collège de France 1978–1979*. New York: Palgrave Macmillan.

Hudson, V. M. and den Boer, A. M. (2004) *Bare Branches: The Security Implications of Asia's Surplus Population*. Cambridge, MA: MIT Press.

Hutnyk, P. (1996) *The Rumour of Calcutta: Tourism, Charity, and the Poverty of Representation*. London: Zed Books.

Povinelli, E. (2006) *The Empire of Love: Toward a Theory of Intimacy, Genealogy, and Carnality*. Durham, NC: Duke University Press.

Povinelli, E. (2011) *Economies of Abandonment: Social Belonging and Endurance in Late Liberalism*. Durham, NC: Duke University Press.

Rajagopal, A. (2002) 'Violence of Commodity Aesthetics: Hawkers, Demolition, Raids and a New Regime of Consumption', *Economic and Political Weekly*, 37 (1): 35–7, 65–7 and 69–76.

Roy, A. (2002) *City Requiem, Calcutta: Gender and the Politics of Poverty*. Minneapolis: University of Minnesota Press.

Srivastava, S. (1998) *Constructing Post-Colonial India: National Character and the Doon School*. London and New York: Routledge.

Chapter 10

Kashmiri Desire and Digital Space: Queering National Identity and the Indian Citizen

Inshah Malik

Introduction

The 'invisiblising' of the Kashmiri desire for *Azadi* (Freedom) is 'queer' in response to the Indian postcolonial state's reproduction of a norma- tive 'upper caste', 'Hindu', 'heterosexual' subject. Postcolonial nation states such as India are patriarchal through the punishing of sexual difference as well as other differences such as ethnic identities, which are considered in contravention to the interests of the nation-states (or monstrous as Dasgupta and DasGupta argue in the Introduction to this volume). In this sense, experiences of queerness could be extended to the understanding of how other political identities do not conform to the 'state-approved' idea of Indian citizenship and how these bod- ies come to be cordoned for death. The state, conspicuously through modes of disciplining and punishment, engages in creating its 'accept- able' citizens. The political identity of a Kashmiri is similar to that of a queer sexual identity as both do not conform to the image of the 'ideal' Indian citizen and are constantly shaped in their relationship with the imagined Indian nation-state. The chapter foregrounds theoretical formulations of sexual citizenship, queer theory and cultural studies, which argue that bodies that resist 'self-disciplining' in an attempt to acquire favourable citizenship become an ultimate test of the limits of the sovereignty of the state. Here necropolitics becomes inevitable. The normative identity subject, whether in terms of sexuality or religious/ ethnic diversity has its 'other', and both sexuality and ethnic difference come to inhabit this space of 'otherness'.

Furthermore this chapter demonstrates how the 'Kashmiri body' signifies populations cordoned for death and an excess to the Indian nation-state. The use of the internet represents a site of 'coming out' of the Kashmiri desire for freedom. I analyse this 'coming out' of the Kashmiri desire as a desperate response to the Indian corporate media's complicit siege over happenings in Kashmir's mass uprising in 2010 (Bukhari 2010). I will then delineate how the Indian state's military operations in Kashmir are a form of queer necropolitics that seeks to erase Kashmiri desire (political or sexual). Even though 'Kashmiri desire' widely circulates through the internet, Kashmiri bodies and their politics continue to be violently regulated and killed en masse. It is important to note that all citizenship is essentially sexual, and the way a Kashmiri protestor's body resists sharing this citizenship transforms the site of citizenship into a 'queer site' of contested narratives and is subsequently cast off as non-existent.

Kashmir was in a rage after news of the death of a Kashmiri boy named Mudasir Kamran flashed up on the internet, especially on social networking sites such as Facebook, on 3 March 2013.The news was one more addition to the announcements of the deaths that have become normative to Kashmir. In the same year, the hanging of a Kashmiri man named Afzal Guru, whose remains were denied to his family, had set a sombre mood in Kashmir. Some sections of Kashmiri society on the internet were quick to react and term it 'one more death of a Kashmiri' at the hands of the brutalising Indian state. Mudasir Kamran, a student at the University of Hyderabad, had committed suicide, with the university claiming that he was a 'homosexual' and a 'mentally deranged' person and these were the reasons that forced him to take his own life. A critical analysis of these narratives unravels peculiarly interlaced appropriations of 'sexuality' and 'citizenship' by the structures of the state power, aimed at preserving the nationalist claims on bodies by terming the 'dead Kashmiri body' either 'misguided', 'deranged', 'drugged' or 'homosexual'. The widespread normalisation of death is even more visible when bodies come to be marked by their sexuality.

There is an assumed 'heterosexuality' in Kashmir's political project and in the discourses of the gender of Kashmir. I will examine this 'heterosexuality' in the face of a brutalising militarism and torture by establishing the idea of sexual citizenship and then link it to the case of a Kashmiri student Mudasir Kamran, whose death was labelled alternately by the state and the resistance as a suicide and a murder for reasons of being a Kashmiri/homosexual. Kamran's body became a site of contestation, of claiming a 'queer hero' and a 'Kashmiri martyr' on social media. Finally, I will argue, queerness as an idea is also extendable to bodies that do not ascribe to the state-approved ideas of being a dutiful Indian citizen. I will argue that digital activism opens up spaces of self-assertion and the formation of alternative political identities. I highlight how silence about the killing of Kashmiri bodies is constructed through digital spaces by shutting down websites and FB pages of Kashmiri activists. In conclusion, the chapter highlights how bodies of Kashmiri activists, and the desire for Azad Kashmir is a queer desire that finds expression through creative digital activism.

Violence in Kashmir

The former British princely state of Jammu and Kashmir has been a site of perennial conflict since the formal end of British colonial rule, resulting in the formation of the two modern nation-states of India and Pakistan. The people of Kashmir are subjected to enormous violence and are witnesses to three massive wars between India and Pakistan over Kashmiri territory. The people of Kashmir have engaged in resistance politics ever since, most recently, in a full-blown armed struggle against Indian rule in 1989. The British ruled Kashmir through foreign rulers, namely Dogras who acquired Kashmir given their good will with the British. The authoritarian Hindu monarchy of the Dogras came to be remembered for their brutal anti-Muslim

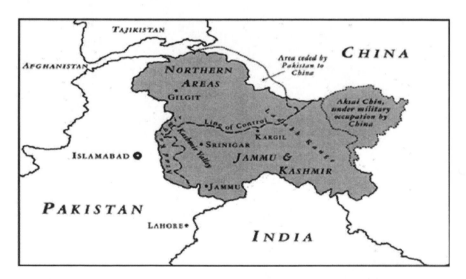

Figure 10.1 Former British princely state of Kashmir, disputed region of Kashmir, divided into three parts under Indian, Pakistani and Chinese control. The line of control (LoC) stands between the Indian and Pakistan administered regions.

Source: Perry-Castañeda Library Map Collection, University of Texas library online catalogue (2003).

policies (Rai 2004). The massive massacre of Muslims under the Dogras in Jammu in 1947 led to the displacement and creation of a refugee regime that sought to free Kashmir for Pakistan (Snedden 2012). Hence, the 'tribal invasion' necessitated the Dogra ruler Hari Singh to acquire military aid from India. The help offered was subject to the Instrument of Accession and the Indian army formally entered the state on 27 October 1947 to curtail the Muslim upheaval, resulting in the Poonch rebellion that led to the creation of Azad Kashmir in 1947. The former British princely state was divided up into two parts, Azad Kashmir and Jammu and Kashmir, with a de facto line of control (LoC), or ceasefire line, where the armies of India and Pakistan came to permanently halt aggression against each other. The United Nations assisted in the ceasefire that came into place on 1 January 1949. Ever since the formation of this LoC its nature remains impermanent, shifting and violent (Robinson 2013).

The armies of both countries are locked in an incessant stand-off weaving a saga of violence against the common people. Kashmir's recent history on the Indian side is replete with violence and bloodshed after the active insurgency against India's continued occupation of the Kashmir region with complete impunity, which makes the experiences of violence in this context singular. Over 100,000 people have been killed, 11,000 people made to disappear and an unprecedented level of sexual violence against Kashmiris by the army. There are stories of mass rapes of women, children being orphaned and thousands of unidentified mass graves that bear witness to the culture of violence in Kashmir. Mental health is declining every day, pushing young people into cultures of drug consumption and self-abuse.

Information on Kashmir in mainland India in the 1980s and 1990s was largely framed in terms of the 'army' clashing with 'terrorists' or the Indian army's heroism in protecting the local people from ruthless attacks of 'terrorists', labelled so by the media. The statist narratives continue to portray Kashmir as a problem of religious fanaticism and terrorism which must be controlled by India so as to ensure 'security' for India's 'national integrity' along its assumed borders. This holding on to Kashmir comes at a cost of the heaving militarisation of the place.

'Coming Out' of Kashmiri Desire

Kashmiri subjection and its understandings are mediated through the violence of misrepresentation. While the local media is brutally repressed, mainstream media in India uses it as an opportunity to strengthen the colonial control of the Indian nation-state over Kashmir. Such use of media, therefore, presents the perpetual perversity of a Kashmiri subject, by referencing him as a 'terrorist' or 'extremist'. Through such a controlled mediation of the representation of people, the state attempts not just to formulate the foundations of an ideal citizen but also assigns the liveability and grievability to its subjects (Butler 2010). The Indian state's sovereignty has worked towards identifying itself through having power over the relating of Kashmiri experience, by not only making Kashmiri bodies dispensable but also through controlling ways in which the experience of those bodies could be retrieved. The colonial ways in which the Indian state has maintained control over Kashmir through necropower has created a Kashmiri colony whose attempts to resist have been met with the Indian state's absolute sovereign repression.

Necropolitics attempts to expose the limits of sovereignty of a state and argues that sovereignty rests in a state's pronouncements of who should live and who should die (Mbembe 2003). The Indian state's necropolitics is even more visible in its 'counter-terror' strategies and robust militarisation of the Kashmiri space, attempting to create a psychic assault or trauma and achieve the mutilation of the manhood (humanity) of the colonised. The culture of militarism creates psychic trauma and injury and, while appearing to be accidental, is also structural at the same time (Fanon 2001). In this sense, sovereignty is not just a pronouncement of who should live and who should die, but also of who should speak for those who live. By centralising the narrative control in the idea of establishing sovereignty, it is important to understand that use of digital media in an attempt to create a vent for a muzzled voice is a further challenge to that sovereignty.

In Kashmir, Indian militarism has racist and Islamophobic dimensions as it is pitted against ethnically and religiously divergent masses of people. This militarism has crushed an indigenous struggle for freedom waged by people and has seen over 100,000 deaths, mass rapes, torture, enforced disappearances and violence unabated. It is difficult to make comparisons with the Shoah since the latter is a singular act of violence incomparable to other events: the happenings in the concentration camps can never be retrieved in a sense to make generalisations about human suffering as was argued by Mbembe. In the case of Kashmir, a prison-like situation has been created to establish India's sovereign control over the territory which means that pronouncements of life and death have taken precedence over law and human rights. Information about what it is to live a Kashmiri life is repressively subjected to the realm of state sovereignty. It is the Indian state's discursive power that can be the active representation of even the feelings of its subjects and can determine what desires of its subjects can remain and propagate.

In the year 2008, a shift in methods of resistance employed by the Kashmiri masses was observed. The Quit Kashmir Movement of 1946 started against the Dogra regime was a powerful expression of collective political struggle. Taking a cue from that, the Quit Kashmir Movement II became a response from people during the Amarnath land row, a movement that emerged as a response to the government's decision to transfer land to a Hindu religious body managing the Amarnath Yatra, and then from the year 2008 to 2010 a transformation in the methods of resistance in Kashmir took place. Using peaceful modes of protest during the Amarnath agitation a new space opened up for the 'children of conflict', referring to the generation of young Kashmiris who grew up during the mass armed resistance movement that started in 1989 against the continued political occupation of Kashmir by India. While the roads in the Kashmir Valley flooded with non-violent protesters, scores of pro-freedom organisations including the Jammu and Kashmir Liberation Front (JKLF) were instrumental in paving the way forward. In 2008, people spent days and nights on the roads raising slogans of freedom such as 'go India go back' and 'we want freedom' from the Indian rule and the performance of celebratory dances demanding the 'smashing' of the state's supremacy became a common occurrence.

Kashmir saw the worst form of economic blockade which lasted three months from neighbouring Jammu Province through which Indian goods reach Kashmir. The camaraderie was immense and villages started to distribute free grain and fruit to sustain the Srinagar city when even baby food remained unavailable for months (Jaleel 2013). The protests met with massive repression from the military and state authorities, forcing the younger generation to express their dissent in other creative ways such as art, writing and poetry. The impact of militarism has also led to methods of gendered resistance, especially after sexual violence became a tool of war against the Kashmiri people. For women, the streets are no longer safe and joining non-violent protest movements endangers the idea of 'honour' socially vested upon female bodies. The mass rape such as that in Kunan-Poshpoor that occurred on the night of 23 February 1991, when the personnel of the 4 Rajputana Rifles of the Indian Army raped the women of these villages in the north of Kashmir, is a tactic of torture that has left women alienated from street protests. Although, suffering sexual violence is seen as a contribution to the struggle, it is also posed as a question of 'women's honour' among the Kashmiri nationalist leadership. Nevertheless, mainstream media continued to block information coming out of the Valley and frequently called the protests as the 'handiwork' of Pakistan.

With the emergence of social media, an alternative space had already been constructed for various diasporic Kashmiris to connect with each other at a social and cultural level. The social media platforms such as Facebook became instrumental in creating newer groups for Kashmiris to connect with every day. However, it was in the year 2010 that these connections between Kashmiris online became political. In the year 2010, after a series of aggressive attacks on teenage children, the killing of the fifth child Tufail Ahmed Mattoo enraged online Kashmiris in the diaspora. While the violence quickly sprang further into repeated cycles and the death toll rapidly reached 147 in a period of four months, unlike in 2008, in 2010 no street protests were tolerated, and even mourners carrying the dead were killed. This tightly imprisoned valley could only send posts through social media that led to the sharing and resharing of information among diasporic Kashmiris.

This mammoth network that 'came out' into the open with the Kashmiri 'desire' for freedom soon began to challenge the statist media narratives on Kashmir, young Kashmiris adding their memoirs of repression and anecdotes on the witnessing of violence, and the myth of the perversity of Kashmiri subjects began to implode. The internet became an alternative space of repressed Kashmiri sovereignty. Several pages sprang up, mostly operated from outside of Kashmir, that attempted to collect and reproduce content that Kashmiris in the besieged valley were sharing. This quick response in the solidarity groups to the content that could be banned and removed easily by the state proved important in the long run to expose the unreason of the state sovereignty. The impunity with which the disposal of Kashmiri bodies is violently regulated by the postcolonial Indian state exposes the idea of how 'disposable', 'perverse' and 'unwanted' bodies that do not fit the ideal of normative citizenship are deemed unfit to live, hence exposing the necropolitics of the state. Out of the 147 boys killed in 2010 alone, none of them were offered any justice in the courts and the parents of many have been humiliated for insisting on the deliverance of justice. The Kashmiris become instrumental in making Indian control effective in Kashmir by negating their own experience and towing the political line of the state. This negation of own experience is manifest in how the state institutes the self-knowledge and imparts it to Kashmiris, Jawaharlal Nehru becoming a leader for freedom and Maqbool Bhat a double agent for asking for Kashmir's right to self-determination.

Kashmiri political consciousness falls outside of the terminologies of identification that India has employed to refer to it. 'Terrorist' and 'double agent' have perhaps plagued the conversation since 1947 but recently 'homosexual' and 'mentally deranged' are some other labels plastered over Kashmiri bodies to diffuse their political waywardness. While Maqbool Bhat[5] was called a double agent because he seemed neither to belong to the Indian or Pakistani state, Mudassir Kamran, a student in Hyderabad University, was called a homosexual and a mentally deranged person. This comparison is not to evade the possibility that Mudasir might have been homosexual but an attempt to reflect upon the ways in which sexuality eclipses the idea of citizenship in contemporary times. While the liberal articulations of Mudasir's sexuality attempted to equate the violence of 'Kashmiri nationalism' and 'Indian nationalism' in similar terms by creating a hero for gay politics, these articulations were plagued with Islamophobic assertions about Kashmiri society and Kashmiri political consciousness. For example questions were raised about meanings of Kashmiriness while already assuming that Kashmiriness was fundamentally compulsorily 'heterosexual' and 'patriarchal' (Vasa 2014). In the narratives that appeared online the bizarre accounts that justified Mudasir's homosexuality were his behaviour in hugging, kissing and touching his roommate. The internet immediately split into sections: on one side were Kashmiris claiming a martyr for their cause and on the other were queer individuals in India claiming a hero. This assumed 'heterosexuality' of Kashmiri nationalism, and the intent to insult by displacing desires, either Azadi seeking or sexual liberation, needs us to understand in depth the assumed violent context of the body in question.

Sexual Kashmiri Subject

A brigadier says, *the boys of Kashmir break so quickly, we make their bodies sing, on the rack, till no song is left to sing.*

Agha Shahid Ali

The gendered playful ways of children in Kashmir are representations of their subjections. Whether it is in their enactment of mock ambushes or celebrations of martyrdoms, it reflects the ways in which society is functional today. Family, which is the fundamental unit of organisation and where limits of sexuality are ascertained, are indeed transformed into sites of political war, a space where gender roles are inverted, subverted or banished in order to produce resistance or survival. Men can be seen to experience 'emasculation' or a stripping down of their traditional manhood which was designed for them to claim superiority and maintain control of the family unit. Under military colonial conditions, such manhood is assaulted and displaced. In their precarious living conditions any armed/uniformed man can pull or drag them out in the street and parade them naked or, worse still, sexually assault them. All citizenship is essentially a sexual citizenship, since it assumes its citizens live in familial ties of kinship where a man is a patriarchal controller of such a unit. It is fundamentally their sexuality that organises the citizenship (Bell and Binnie 2000). Therefore a Kashmiri political consciousness informed by traditional Muslim ideals of sexuality such as polygamy, systems of marriage and divorce and child rights already conflicts with the approved sexual practices of Hindu patriarchy. Thus an ideal Indian citizen is by definition also a good Hindu heterosexual male who conversely also is secular-heterosexual-militaristic in the majoritarian sense, and lives in a state-approved idea of monogamous marriage. In this sense, Kashmiri political consciousness too is already inclusive of 'sexual deviance' and 'homoeroticism'. In a Kashmiri Muslim society where accepted relationships between men are not just affectionate but also intimate and where sexual encounters between men are at the same time covered up and seen as 'playful' ways of youth, what could be more threatening than to observe that sexual identity movements feel no need to pick up a separate identity (that demands liberal rights from the state) but merge within the larger movement of ending Indian occupation in Kashmir.

A meme[2] which was shared widely on the internet on the Indian army's Facebook Page presents a collage of two images, one of Kashmiri teenagers masking their faces and moving with flags of the Islamic State in such a way as to provoke the Indian army, while the other depicts the Indian army marching forward violently with guns. The image text is a reproduction of a Bollywood song that reads 'Chehra Chupa ke Rakhna, Jhanda Fehra ke Rakhna, lene tujhe o Gori Ayenge tere sajna' ('Keep your face hidden and spread your flags, / To take you away, oh beautiful woman, will come your man'). Hiding your face is seen as a feminine attribute and used as an insult in this context while 'taking you' becomes an expression of utmost violence, not merely that manifest in heterosexual bonds between men and women but real, actual and ultimate death. This exposes two things. One is that militarism's power to proclaim the lives of even the most violence-endorsing Kashmiri bodies is tactically far higher because of the predisposition of necropolitics coming from the surety that they have both power and control over these lives. Second is that heterosexuality is not merely a sexual orientation but a sovereign power that resides in bodies that align the most with that power.

What are the ways in which such power also shapes the subject bodies? Sexual violence and torture against men is often sidelined as it does not help the narratives of war. The sexuality of a Kashmiri subject is termed feminine, is in need of emotional intimacy and is essentially weak. In this sense, is Kashmiri heterosexuality between men and women of Kashmir or against queer bodies truly heterosexual? Or is this assertion that Kashmiri nationalism is less accommodating of sexual difference merely premature? Many narratives of women suffering violence by the military have reported that the reason for suffering violence has often also been due to intervening in a violent incident being perpetrated upon their men.

In 2013, social networking sites became abuzz with reports about death of a boy in Hyderabad University. The moment it became obvious that he was from Kashmir, Kashmiris started to post messages about 'how one more Kashmiri life was lost'and video messages soon surfaced of young Kashmiris on the campus, shouting pro-freedom slogans and demanding justice from the university authorities. The pro-freedom parties in Kashmir were quick to term him Afzal e Saani (Second Afzal). The Mutahida Majlis e Mashwarat or joint advisory council of pro-freedom parties issued a statement claiming that it was a politically motivated murder of a Kashmiri man by the 'Hindu fanatics'. The statement went on to claim that his murder was simply due to his participation in the protests against the hanging of another Kashmiri, Afzal Guru, in 2013. The statement did not share the means through which they had acquired the information, only claiming that the Hindu teachers had an argument with him after which he was locked up and tortured. They even claimed that the body bore torture marks. As Mudasar Kamran's body arrived in Kashmir, a local doctor went on YouTube to confirm that the body bore serious signs of torture and it was a clear case of murder. Though much of this information clearly contradicts the information that emerged at the scene in Hyderabad University, this statement is a testimony to the mistrust Kashmiris have of the Indian administration and it depicts the naked politics played with Kashmiri lives.

The social media soon began to bring in news which not only contradicted the claims of the body but also obscured the way in which the issue could be politicised. Mudasir Kamran was in his mid-twenties from a village named Parigam in Pulwom district and was a doctoral student in at the English and Foreign Languages University, Hyderabad. He was found hanging in his hostel room by his colleagues. While the police in Hyderabad didn't initially comment, the police in Kashmir said they were informed by Hyderabad police that a case was registered against the proctor of the university for 'Abetment to commit suicide'.

Then the reports began to emerge that Mudasir had a 'problematic' relationship with his roommate and for this reason his roommate had complained about him to the proctor. This marked a drastic turn in the narrative as reports of him being a homosexual started to pour in. There was an immediate owning up to his identity in the LGBTQ community both on the campus and several queer groups who were discussing it on online platforms. One could easily see the former claimants slowly retracting their statements as these 'dubious' reports made their way online. Mudasir began to be idealised as a queer hero and many narratives spoke about his 'problematic sexuality coming from an extremely homophobic society of Kashmir', then having to deal with Hyderabad University administration. The later claimants became aware about the 'Kashmiriness' of Mudasir's identity and started projecting it in their narratives as homophobic 'victimhood' for someone born in Kashmir. At the same time the entanglement of his Kashmiri identity with issues of homophobia, Islamophobia and violent nationalism cannot be discounted (Vasa 2014). Samia Vasa points out that the problem with mainstream 'Indian' society is that it refuses to enter the consciousness of gay and Kashmiri subjects. However, Vasa stops short of entering those protocols herself while she fails to engage her own claims about Kashmiri nationalism and Kashmiri subjection. Thus the debate of liberal gay rights that ensued online in various forums such as *Gaylaxy* magazine itself rests on falsified and sometimes premature understanding of both Kashmiri subjection and the Indian state.

Though it did not become an oppositional identity war about Mudasir it did seem to point to the 'silence' caused by ignorance, mistrust and assumptions. The complex world of that 'silence' came to the fore when the state attempted to displace Mudasir's body and its political intent and also by the various ways through which 'sexuality' politics in India further obscured the resilience of such a body by politicising it for liberal sexual rights. This leads to the bigger problem of how states push their agendas on their subjects. Though sexual identity and queer rights movements have frequently attempted to demystify the body and its sexuality, what remains unchallenged is how postcolonial nationalisms seek to homogenise political bodily experience. The ethnic/racial, dissident/terrorist and homosexual/deviant come to inhabit the same spaces when viewed in relationship to the subjection/citizenship projects that postcolonial states push. In Mudasir's case his Kashmiriness was negated by his supposed queerness. What was the underlying effect of doing so? Was it to displace him and make him an undesirable body as a Kashmiri subject in India and as queer in Kashmir? Would it have mattered if, instead of the allegation surrounding his queerness, he was found to be a Pakistani agent? Would his body and identity then be able to claim any space in the mainstream media or from the queer communities which was projecting him as their hero?

In 2014, India's right-wing pro Hindutva party, the Bharatiya Janata Party (BJP), came into power at the centre, with Narendra Modi as India's new prime minister. With this the public discourse is increasingly about the country's politics taking an excessive right-wing shift detrimental to the civil liberties of ordinary people. This public discourse, however, has largely remained silent on India's continual record of human rights abuse and military occupation in Kashmir. For Kashmiri subjects it has hardly ever mattered which party rules at the centre in New Delhi: Kashmiris articulate their political subjection in the idiom of India's illegal and military rule in Kashmir. Kashmiri subjection remains unaffected by the polarising debates of any parties that sway Indian masses since democracy is dysfunctional here. The Supreme Court's recriminalisation of homosexuality in late 2013 was followed by the advent of the BJP and their homophobic policies thus making India's queer communities more vulnerable. However, despite claiming Mudasir's sexuality merely for a pre-set agenda of sexual rights, it also negates the way Mudasir would have wanted to engage with his sexuality. The obsession within mainstream media was around trying to determine whether Mudasir really was homosexual or not but insidiously what it did not do was use this as a point to enter into a larger debate about the loss of civil liberties and human rights. The silence that ultimately became the destiny of this debate, therefore, is not a merely 'forgetfulness' or 'fruition' or 'the end' but it is a space where sexuality takes the centre place in the agenda of citizenship. Thus neither can Kashmiri political consciousness distance itself from the questions of sexual liberation nor can the Indian state use queer sexuality to champion a better citizen. As Puar argues in the context of the United States, the oriental constructions allow the limiting of the sexual citizen project by sidelining the racially/sexually queer identities. In the case of India, too, the sexual liberation project seems to embrace Islamophobia to merely present itself as a better citizen option (Puar 2013).

Conclusion

In this essay, it becomes clear that the internet is a site of 'coming out' for repressed Kashmiri desires, and contextualises the Indian state's necropolitics vis-à-vis Kashmiri lives. Through the popular uprisings and media blackouts in 2010, it is seen that the Kashmiri body is dispensable and Kashmiri consciousness is informed by violence, of which sexuality is an essential part. The consciousness that the death of Kashmiri children created online is that Kashmiri bodies are dispensable. In Mudasir's case it can be further visibly seen that such necropolitics attempts to homogenise desire and treats sexual desire and political desire with similar patterns of repression. Even though the 'Kashmiri desire' became widely accessible on the internet, Kashmiri bodies and their politics continue to be displaced. Also, since all citizenship is essentially sexualised and a Kashmiri protestor's body, which resisted sharing this citizenship, is transformed into a 'queer' site of contesting narratives, is subsequently cast off as non-existent.

Through the incident surrounding Mudasir, the internet and social media allowed a conflation between political desire and sexual repression. However, as the media narratives surrounding this case showed the incommensurability of queer bodies as Kashmiri or Kashmiri bodies as queer hides within it the various forms of regressive queer nationalisms and misogynist/patriarchal forms of martyrdom which invisibilises queer bodies and contribution. Mudasir's sexuality was appropriated by the state, media, internet, Indian queer rights activists and such an appropriation negates his subjection/individuation or individual identity as it is transposed into the arena of collective and public debate. This incident also demonstrates the various ways through which sexuality takes centre stage in the agenda of citizenship. Neither can Kashmiri political consciousness distance itself from questions of sexual liberation nor can the Indian queer community use sexuality to champion a better citizen by distancing itself from 'terrorist'/Kashmiri bodies. The role of social media in protests and activism is well documented.

It was not the purpose of this essay to look at only how social media is being used by Kashmiri protestors but rather to talk of this particular incident as a point of departure from how the fight for Kashmiri freedom has so far been discussed and represented. It has thus allowed us for the first time to think about Kashmir through the lens of sexuality and sexual citizenship and the various conjunctures and fissures between them.

Notes

1. Maqbool Bhat was a Kashmiri nationalist leader jailed several times in Pakistan for being an Indian agent and hanged in India for being a Pakistani agent. In the mainstream consciousness he was titled a double agent but never a representation of Kashmiri consciousness.
2. This picture was widely shared on the internet on an Indian army Facebook fan page.

References

Anand, D. (2011) *China and India: Postcolonial Informal Empires in the Emerging Global Order*. London: Taylor & Francis, pp. 68–86.

Bell, D. and Binnie, J. (2000) *The Sexual Citizen*, 1st edn. Bristol: Polity.

Bose, S. (2005) *Kashmir: Roots of Conflict, Paths of Peace*. New York: Harvard University Press.

Bukhari, P. (2010) 'Kashmir 2010: The Year of Killing Youth. Retrieved from *The Nation: Kashmir 2010: The Year of Killing Youth*, 22 September.

Butler, J. (2010) *Frames of War: When Is Life Grievable*. Verso Books.

Fanon, F. (2001) *The Wretched of the Earth* (Penguin Modern Classics). London: Penguin.

Gockhami, A. J. (2007) *Politics of Plebicite* . Srinagar: Gulshan Publishers.

Jaleel, M. (2013) 'How New Delhi manages Kashmir', *Indian Express*. Available at: http://archive.indianexpress.com/news/how-new-delhi-manages-kashmir/1137356/.

Marxist Internet Archive (2015) *National Liberation Movement*, 27 April. Retrieved 1 April 2015 from Marxist Internet Archive at: https://www.marxists.org/glossary/events/n/a.htm.

Mbembe, A. (2003) 'Necropolitics', *Public Culture*, 15 (1): 11–40.

Perry-Castañeda Library Map Collection, University of Texas library online catalogue (2003, 7 June). *Kashmir Map*. Texas, USA.

Puar, J. (2013) 'Rethinking Homonationalism', *International Journal of Middle East Studies*, 45 (2): 336–9.

Rai, M. (2004) *Hindu Rulers, Muslim Subjects: Islam, Rights and History of Kashmir*. Princeton: Princeton University Press.

Robinson, C. d. (2013) *Body of Victim, Body of Warrior: Refugee Families and the Making of Kashmiri Jihadists*. Oakland, CA: University of California Press.

Snedden, C. (2012) *The Untold Story of the People of Azad Kashmir.* London: Hurst.

Vasa, S. (2014) *Heterosexuality and Sexual Violence*, Avenshi, 7 January. Retrieved from: http://www.anveshi.org.in/heterosexuality-and-sexual-violence/.

Contributors

Niharika Banerjea is Associate Professor of Sociology at Ambedkar University, New Delhi. She was previously associate professor at the University of Southern Indiana. She is co-editor of the forthcoming volume *Friendship as Social Justice Activism* (Seagull/University of Chicago).

Debanuj DasGupta is assistant professor in the Department of Geography and Women's Gender and Sexuality Studies at the University of Connecticut. He is co-editor of the forthcoming volume *Friendship as Social Justice Activism* (Seagull/University of Chicago) and a special issue of the journal *Gender, Place and Culture*.

Rohit K. Dasgupta is lecturer at the Institute for Media and Creative Industries at Loughbrough University, UK. He is co-editor of *Masculinity and Its Challenges in India* (McFarland, 2014) and *Rituparno Ghosh: Cinema, Gender and Art* (Routledge, 2015).

Aniruddha Dutta is Assistant Professor in the departments of Gender, Women's and Sexuality Studies and Asian and Slavic Languages and Literatures at the University of Iowa. Dutta also works in voluntary and advisory capacities with non-governmental and community-based organisations of LGBTIQ (especially trans, Kothi and Hijra) communities in eastern India. They have published in several journals such as *Gender and History* and the *International Journal of Feminist Politics*.

Rahul K. Gairola is the Krishna Somers Lecturer in English and Postcolonial Literature, School of the Arts, Murdoch University. Prior to this he taught at the City University of New York and the University of Maryland, Baltimore. He is the author of *Homelandings: Postcolonial Diasporas and Transatlantic Belonging* (Rowman & Littlefield, 2016) and coeditor of *Revisiting India's Partition: New Essays on Memory, Politics and Culture* (Lexington, 2016).

Radhika Gajjala is Professor of Media and Communication and American Cultural Studies at Bowling Green State University, Ohio, USA. She has published numerous books on cyberculture and gender including *South Asian Technospaces* (Peter Lang, 2008), *Cyberfeminism 2.0* (Peter Lang, 2012), *Global Media Culture and Identity* (Routledge, 2011) among others. She is also a member of Fembot Collective and FemTechnet.

Jack Harrison-Quintana is a queer Latino activist, demographer and researcher currently serving as the director of Grindr for Equality. Prior to their current position, Jack worked for the National LGBTQ Task Force, the Global Trans Research and Advocacy Project (GTRAP), the National Center for Transgender Equality and Khmera.

Kareem Khubchandani is Mellon Assistant Professor in Drama and Dance at Tufts University. Prior to this he was an Embrey Foundation Postdoctoral Fellow at the University of Texas at Austin. He has a PhD in performance studies from Northwestern University and is working on his book project *Ishtyle: Labour, Intimacy and Dance in Gay South Asian Nightlife*.

Sneha Krishnan is a Postdoctoral Research Fellow and Teaching Associate at St John's College, University of Oxford. She completed her doctoral studies in international development studies from Wolfson College, University of Oxford. She has published widely in the areas of gender, sexuality and politics.

Inshah Malik completed her PhD in International Relations with a thesis titled 'Political Struggles, Agency and Muslim Women: Study of Resistance Movement in Kashmir' from Jawaharlal Nehru University, India. She was until recently a Fox International Fellow at Yale University.

Ila Nagar is Assistant Professor in the department of Near Eastern Languages and Culture at Ohio State University. She previously served as lecturer of Linguistics and Hindi Language. Her areas of expertise include Language, Gender and Sexuality. Her recent publication includes an article in the journal *Contemporary South Asia*.

Amit S. Rai is Senior Lecturer in New Media and Communication at Queen Mary, University of London. He was previously Associate Professor at Florida State University. He is the author of *Untimely Bollywood: Globalisation and India's New Media Assemblage*

(Duke University Press, 2009) and *Rule of Sympathy* (Palgrave Macmillan, 2002).

Pawan Singh is currently a lecturer at the University of California San Diego. He has recently completed a PhD in Communication also from UCSD. His areas of expertise include health communication, bioethics and global media studies.

Index

Page numbers in *italics* refer to illustrations.